HENRY DYER

PIONEER OF ENGINEERING
EDUCATION IN JAPAN

HENRY DYER

HENRY DYER

PIONEER OF ENGINEERING
EDUCATION IN JAPAN

NOBUHIRO MIYOSHI

UNIVERSITY OF HIROSHIMA

Translated by
TAKUJI and AIKO SARADA

GLOBAL
ORIENTAL

GLOBAL ORIENTAL MONAGRAPH SERIES (JAPAN) Vol 2

HENRY DYER: PIONEER OF ENGINEERING EDUCATION IN JAPAN

First published in 2004 by

GLOBAL ORIENTAL LTD
PO Box 219
Folkestone
Kent CT20 2WP

© Global Oriental 2004

www.globaloriental.co.uk

British Cataloguing in Publication Data
A catalogue record for this book is available from
the British Library

ISBN 1-901903-66-4

Typeset in Stone Serif 9.5 on 12pt by Mark Heslington, Northallerton, North Yorkshire
Printed and bound in England by The Cromwell Press, Trowbridge, Wilts

Contents

Acknowledgements to the English Edition

Let me express my deep sense of gratitude to Sir Hugh Cortazzi, who over many years has offered inspiring suggestions to Japanese people and given his strong support for the publication of this book, and to Mr Paul Norbury, Managing Director of Global Oriental, who kindly took on the publication. This book would certainly not have seen the light of day without the good offices of Mr Kosuke Matsumura, the Japanese representative of the Anglo-Japanese Economic Institute (London). Not only did he introduce me to Sir Hugh and Mr Norbury, but he also gave me a number of helpful suggestions when necessary, for which I thank him from the bottom of my heart.

This book was translated from Japanese into English by Mr Takuji Sarada and Ms Aiko Sarada, the former having been my student at Hiroshima University, and is published with three purposes in mind. First of all, it is intended to show people in Britain what a great contribution Henry Dyer made to the modernization of Japanese industry. The second purpose is to enable me, as a Japanese, to express my gratitude to Dyer. The final purpose in writing this book is to attempt to unravel the evolution of Japan for the many researchers, including Southeast Asian students studying in Japan, who are interested in the experience of a nation that succeeded in the modernization of industry in the East.

NOBUHIRO MIYOSHI
April 2004

To mark the publication of my book in Britain, the last chapter, 'Dyer Revisited', was newly written as an addition to the original volume published in Japan in 1989.

Acknowledgements to the Original Japanese Edition

An engineer and educationalist of strict morals and integrity with hardly a blemish on his character might seem to be the last person to be the main character of a drama for entertainment purposes. In many historical dramas, however, it is such inconspicuous people who often played the most significant roles.

Dyer lapsed into oblivion for years both in Britain and Japan. I presented my first paper on him twelve years ago, and he has since grown upon me. I made every effort to locate materials concerning Dyer, a British teacher hired by the Japanese Government, and I found that this involved considerable effort in investigating many places both in my own country but also in Britain. With the support of the Kikawada Foundation (*21-Seiki Bunka Gakujutsu Zaidan*), which provided a grant for conducting research in Britain, I succeeded in making my long-cherished dream come true. Now it is my great pleasure and relief to have completed my work that has resulted in Dyer's biography.

It is 115 years since Dyer came to Japan, and it is 70 years since his death. What a surprise it is that Japan in Dyer's time and Japan as she is now look so much alike! Also, what a disappointment it is that many of the problems that Dyer tried very hard to remedy have remained unsolved! Is history so slow to evolve, or was Dyer so farsighted? Not being a celebrity in the spotlight, he must have kept cool and looked at the world of the future. Many of his statements discussed in this book strike one as relevant today.

Allow me also to express my heartfelt thanks to Dr Hiroshi Kida of the Kikawada Foundation, who was the former president of the National Institute for Educational Research, and to Sir Hugh Cortazzi, a leading figure in Japanese studies and formerly the British

Ambassador to Japan. Both of them provided generous support and encouragement for my work. Also, I am very grateful to Assistant Professor Yasushi Fujii of Matsuyama University of Commerce, who studied at the University of Birmingham and kindly offered assistance for my research in Britain. I am much obliged to Mr Michael Moss, Archivist of Glasgow University, who provided me with not only valuable data but also good suggestions. I also thank the Archives of the University of Strathclyde and the Archives of the Imperial College of Science and Technology for supporting my research.

NOBUHIRO MIYOSHI
August 1988

Prologue to the Original Study

There are three main reasons why I chose to do a study on Dyer in particular. First of all, the value of Dyer's achievements cannot be ignored in considering the relationship between industrialization and education in Japan. He was requested to come to Japan by the Department of Public Works and stayed for nine years, during which time he devoted himself to the organization of engineering education in Japan and trained a number of engineers to a high level of competence. The education at the Imperial College of Engineering was of an experimental nature and it was unparalleled in Britain or in other Western nations. Dyer's excellent work at the Imperial College of Engineering was one of the forces that made Japan's industrialization such a success. Studies on Dyer are of great importance in the analysis of the relation between industrialization and education.

Dyer was the first Westerner to undertake intensive research on Japan's industrialization and education, and he played a leading role in the national projects of industrialization and education as a foreign teacher hired by the Japanese Government. He had a unique and important role in the industrialization of Japan and in the training of the Japanese youth who would maintain it. He devoted himself to the foundation of machine industry at the Akabane Works, which was under the supervision of the Department of Public Works. He also utilized the factory for the practical training of his pupils at the Imperial College of Engineering. Teaching mechanics and civil engineering, he was also involved in the construction work by the Department of Public Works. Dyer compiles his many experiences into the theory of Japan's national evolution, which revealed that the engineers were supported by the solid educational system on the national level.

Secondly, Dyer's achievements illustrate the dynamics of Japan's educational exchange with other countries. Dyer brought the findings at the Imperial College of Engineering back to Britain and utilized them for the establishment of an engineering college in Glasgow. In other words, he was the trail-blazer of the 'boomerang phenomenon' in the history of educational exchange. Ayrton and Perry, who were Dyer's subordinates, also brought the findings at the college back to an engineering college in London.

Dyer was in the vanguard of observant studies on international relations within Japan's educational system. *Dai-Nippon*, one of Dyer's books, was published at the beginning of the twentieth century, when hundreds of Chinese students were being sent to Japan in preparation for the coming reform in China. Dyer noted in the book:

> Hundreds of Chinese students are now in Tokyo and other parts of Japan fitting themselves, in many ways, for their future work in China; so that in a sense Japan is repaying to China the debt she owed to her former civilization.

He stated that Eastern philosophies and ideas were 'streaming back' to the West, and expected Japan to play the principal role in the 'blending' of Eastern and Western cultures.

By using words such as 'repay', 'streaming back', and 'blending', Dyer was the first to express clear and accurate views on the international aspect of Japan's education.

The third reason why I chose to do a study on Dyer is that Dyer was the pioneer of studies on Japan. He published a number of books and essays covering Japan, which, unlike the records of personal experience of Japan that had been compiled as primers, was grounded upon the methodology of history and comparison.

In his writings, Dyer succeeded in unraveling the secret of Japan's evolution in terms of social science and in pinpointing Japan's mission to assume a place within the global community. By providing lessons from Japan, Dyer's studies served as an incentive to slump-ridden Britain, in addition to making Japan known to the rest of the world. Dyer's work also had a profound influence on the studies of Japan by other foreign teachers of the time.

Above all, *Dai-Nippon* (1904) and *Japan in World Politics* (1909) are Dyer's longest works, extending to nearly 500 pages each. These books show his comprehensive and positive study of Japan's past, her existing condition and her plans for the future.

Both books received good news. The back flap of *Japan in World Politics* shows eight excerpts from reviews of *Dai-Nippon*. A review from *The Times* noted:

> Since the termination of his service, Dr Dyer has closely followed the progress and history of Japan, and in his book which he describes as a study in national evolution he furnishes us with a carefully compiled description of present-day Japan.

The Glasgow Herald remarked:

> There are few men in this country better qualified than Dr Dyer to speak with authority on the processes which, in the course of comparatively few years, have evolved from a feudal state to the Japan of to-day.

The Manchester Guardian observed:

> I would be difficult to speak too highly of the merits of Principal Henry Dyer's new book on Japan. Philosophic in conception, scientific in method, minute and reliable in its information, it combines many excellences seldom united.

As I will recount later, *Nature* also carried a two-page review on the book. It would be hard to find another study on Japan that attracted so much attention.

Despite Dyer's many achievements, Dyer had been forgotten for years in Britain and in Japan. I published my first paper on Dyer entitled 'Henry Dyer as a Principal of *Kobu-Daigakko*' in the *Japanese Journal of Educational Studies* in 1976, and then went on to publish a number of other papers on Dyer.

Then, Professor Masami Kita, who specializes in social and economic history at Soka University, published *The People who Developed Japan: The Bond between Japan and Scotland* (1984). This book was a compilation of papers based on materials collected while he was studying at Glasgow University. Professor Kita's excellent methodology based on positive historical science accelerated studies on Dyer by the Japanese.

Following in both Dyer's and Professor Kita's wake, I visited Glasgow in the late spring of 1987, hoping to blend materials from Britain and Japan into a substantial study on Dyer. When I left for Glasgow, I had identified eight questions that I wanted to investigate. With these eight questions in mind, I embarked on a tour to Glasgow and London in order to search for data. The questions provided me with a viewpoint which was different from that of Professor Kita, and which was lacking in my previous work.

1. Why was Dyer appointed principal of the Imperial College of Engineering at the age of 24?

It is known that Hirobumi Ito, who was later to be the Prime Minister of Japan, visited Britain as an ambassador and asked H. M. Matheson, who had earlier accommodated Ito when he studied in Britain, to name the principal of the Imperial College of Engineering. It is also known that Dyer was appointed after Matheson's discussions with

L. D. B. Gordon, a former professor at Glasgow University, and with W. J. M. Rankine, who was then a professor at Glasgow University. However, it is not clear why Dyer was entrusted with the responsibility of the principalship while the teachers who came to Japan with Dyer were senior to him.

2. On what did Dyer model the educational plan of the Imperial College of Engineering?

In Japan, it has been argued that Dyer modelled his educational plan on the politechnicm of Zurich. My research shows, however, that he undertook a unique educational experiment based on the British people's practicality-oriented outlook on education, while also taking the educational systems of the Continent into account. It is of immense interest how a mere engineer, who was not a specialist on education, succeeded in such an unusual educational experiment.

3. How was the news about Dyer's educational experiment at the Imperial College of Engineering delivered to Britain?

People in Britain may have dismissed Dyer's educational experiment as something minor that took place in an insular country in the Far East. It is doubtful whether it occurred to them that the experiment would lead to Japan's industrialization actually threatening Britain's status as an industrially-advanced nation.

4. Why did the Institution of Civil Engineers reject Dyer's proposals?

During his stay in Japan, Dyer wrote a long letter to the Institution and insisted that Britain should initiate a reform in engineering education. I wanted to know why his proposals had been turned down.

5. Why was Dyer unsuccessful in his attempts to become a professor at Glasgow University?

Dyer left Japan for Britain in June 1882. A new post of professor of naval architecture was established at Glasgow University in the following year, and Dyer applied for that position without success. He made his second attempt in 1886, only to fail once again.

Dyer had gained the opportunity to go to Japan as the most brilliant graduate recommended by Professor Rankine, and returned with flying colours, convinced there would be an opportunity to teach at his alma mater. I wanted to find out why his two attempts had failed.

6. *What ideas from the Imperial College of Engineering were adopted for Dyer's new technical college and what effect did they have?*

Leaving Glasgow University, Dyer contributed to the establishment of a new engineering college in Glasgow. He admitted that he then applied his findings at the Imperial College of Engineering, which I call the boomerang phenomenon, and on which I have done some research. It is not absolutely clear what ideas were adopted and what effects they had.

Dyer's engineering college is now Strathclyde University and is almost as prestigious as Glasgow University. It is important to collect materials on Dyer from that university.

7. *Did Ayrton and Perry bring their experiences and findings at the Imperial College of Engineering back to Britain?*

W. H. Brock pointed out another form of boomerang phenomenon. Ayrton and Perry, who were Dyer's subordinates, worked on his educational experiment at the Imperial College of Engineering. It is thought that some of the findings at the college were brought back to Britain by Ayrton and Perry when they were appointed professors at an engineering college in London. How can this be proved?

That particular engineering college in London is now called the Imperial College of Science and Technology, which is one of the best institutions for research and education in Britain. The achievements of Ayrton and Perry at the college remain to be examined.

8. *What led Dyer to pursue studies on Japan?*

Dyer came back to Glasgow and carried on his research in industrial evolutionism and social evolutionism, and he himself became a social revolutionist.

In his later years he focused on the study of Japan. He regarded Japan as a typical example of national evolution, and maintained that the Japanese model should be given due consideration in British social reform. I wanted to find out more about his reasons for focusing his studies on Japan.

Although I was not as capable of clearing up mysteries as Sherlock Holmes, my quest was nevertheless rewarded with some interesting findings. I have left a number of points unexplored, and younger scholars may shed light on these in their research in future years. Here I compile my findings on these questions under one cover, in the hope of providing some insight into Dyer's role in the UK-Japan exchange.

List of Plates

List of Tables

Introduction

by

Sir Hugh Cortazzi

Henry Dyer (1848–1918), the first Principal of the Imperial College of Engineering in Tokyo from 1873–1882 was an outstanding engineer and educator in late nineteenth-century Japan. He was one of the most important British employees of the Meiji government and his achievements deserve to be better known. Professor Miyoshi of Hiroshima University, the author of this monograph, has delved deeply among the available archives in Japan, Britain and other countries and has produced an illuminating account of Dyer's life and achievements. He also discusses the development of engineering education in Japan, Britain and other countries and makes some interesting comparisons.

Dyer was appointed to the post of Principal when he was only 24. He was selected by Hirobumi Ito, the then Vice-Minister of Public Works, on the advice of H. M. Matheson (1821–98) of the firm of Jardine Matheson, who acted as London agents for the Japanese Department of Public Works. A total of four names were considered for the post by Professor Rankine to whom the task of selection was delegated. Dyer, who had graduated in engineering from the University of Glasgow, was known to be diligent, intelligent and upright. He was ambitious, adventurous and self-confident and attracted by the relatively generous salary offered by the Japanese government. Matheson was a Scot and the first chair of civil engineering and mechanics in a British university had been established in Glasgow in 1840. Nevertheless, despite Glasgow University's long history and involvement in the development of science, technology and industry in Scotland, it was only in 1923 that Glasgow had a full faculty of engineering and, curiously, the first Professor of Engineering at Glasgow, L. D. B. Gordon, had a difficult time in gaining recognition for engineering as a degree course.

Dyer attached importance to engineers gaining practical experience but he also considered that a qualified engineer needed a good grounding in theory. His scheme for the college, therefore, combined both academic studies with practical work. In preparing his syllabus for the college he drew not only on his experience in Scotland but also on what he had learnt of systems on the continent especially in France and Germany.

Dyer was fortunate in having some very able colleagues from Britain and some outstanding students who went on to important posts as engineers and educationists in Japan. Professor Miyoshi's book outlines the careers and achievements of some of these men. Engineering was not for women in the Meiji period at least.

Dyer was disappointed on his return to Scotland in 1882 not to be appointed to a chair at Glasgow University and he nursed a grievance against the University for many years. He was, however, able to see some of the ideas which he had promoted in Japan taken up in Scotland and his contribution to the education of engineers was finally recognized when the 'Henry Dyer Symposium on Industrial Globalization' was held in 1995 at the University of Strathclyde, organized jointly with Tokyo University. The University of Strathclyde was originally Anderson's College, founded in 1796, with which institution Dyer was closely associated.

Professor Miyoshi says that Dyer sank into oblivion in both Japan and Britain until recently. It is true that for some decades Dyer did not receive the attention he deserved, but his contribution to the development of modern Japan has been recognized in the post-war years by historians of Anglo-Japanese relations.[1]

A significant number of practising engineers, who contributed to the development of Meiji Japan, came from Britain. Probably the most important of these was the lighthouse-builder and general engineer Richard Henry Brunton, whose book Building Japan 1868–1876 was published by Japan Library in 1991. In preparing this account for publication I came across an acrimonious exchange in *The Japan Weekly Mail* in 1875 between Brunton, the practical engineer, and Henry Dyer, the educationist.[2] This arose from a review which Dyer wrote of William Thomas Thornton's book Indian Public Works and Cognate Indian topics in *The Japan Weekly Mail* for 18 September

1875. He criticized the Engineering College for attaching too much importance to theory:

> What we imagine the Japanese desire, and what will probably be of the greatest value to them is to learn how to build a bridge, how to form a railway, or how to make a harbour, and they in all likelihood desire to gain this knowledge in the shortest possible way.

This provoked an outburst from Dyer, defending the system for educating engineers which he had devised for the Imperial College of Engineering. This elicited a further riposte from Brunton who had learnt his engineering basically through practical work.

The Japanese railways in their early days were built by British railway engineers and operated initially by British staff. Edmund Morel who was closely involved in the building of the first Japanese railway line from Yokohama to Tokyo died of tuberculosis in 1871 after only one year of his five-year contract. According to Neil Pedlar[3] there were 104 foreign railway engineers employed by the Japanese. One of these was Richard Francis Trevithick (1845–1913), grandson of the famous Cornish engineer Richard Trevithick, who 'organized the building of the first steam locomotive to be made in Japan'. Francis Henry Trevithick (1850–1931), who worked in Japan for twenty years, was put 'in charge of the construction of a line through the mountains in Karuizawa in central Japan'. Another British railway engineer Edmund Holtham left an account of his experiences in Eight Years in Japan, 1873–1881 which revealed better than any other 'the achievements and frustrations of British engineers who worked in Japan during early Meiji years.'[4]

A British engineer and friend of Meiji Japan was Major General Henry Spencer Palmer (1838–93)[5] who was responsible for the construction of the Yokohama waterworks and other projects. Another outstanding British engineer involved with Japanese waterworks was W. K. Burton (1856–99).[6]

Professor Miyoshi comments on the British attitude towards engineers and suggests that the snobbish attitude of some members of the British establishment has meant that in Britain engineers have not been given the respect which they deserved. It is true that there were some people who took a supercilious attitude towards engineers on the grounds that in their work they had to get their hands dirty, but this is no longer the case. My predecessor as British Ambassador to Japan was an engineer. Engineers have risen to top managerial posts in Britain, although not so many proportionally as in Japan. In a recent poll, organized by the BBC, one of the candidates for the title of the greatest Briton was the famous and outstanding nineteenth-century British engineer Isambard Kingdom Brunel. His engineering achievements have been rightly trumpeted and he is certainly regarded as one of the greatest British engineers and industrialists of the Victorian era.

Professor Miyoshi's study should be of interest to all students of Anglo-Japanese relations and of the history of engineering education.

NOTES

1   Grace Fox in her comprehensive history *Britain and Japan 1858–1883* (Oxford 1969) devotes a chapter to 'British Influence on Japanese Science and Medicine, and gives Dyer a prominent place. Dyer also features in H. J. Jones *Live Machines: Hired Foreigners and Meiji Japan* (Paul Norbury Publications, 1980). Olive Checkland in her book *Britain's Encounter with Meiji Japan 1868–1912* (Macmillan, 1989) devotes a chapter to 'Educators for Engineers' and gives prominence to the work of Henry Dyer. She also contributed a Biographical Portrait of 'Henry Dyer at the Imperial College of Engineering, Tokyo, and afterwards in Glasgow' to volume III of *Britain and Japan; Biographical Portraits* (Japan Library, 1999). At the Japan Society Henry Dyer's contribution to relations between the two countries has been long remembered. For our book to mark the Japan Festival in the United Kingdom in 1991, *Britain and Japan 1859–1991 Themes and Personalities* (Routledge, 1991), Janet Hunter wrote an essay on 'British Training for Japanese Engineers: The Case of Kikuchi Kyozo'. Among those who worked with Henry Dyer were Josiah Conder about whom Dallas Finn wrote an essay in the same volume. W. E. Ayrton was the subject of a biographical portrait by Ian Ruxton in volume IV of *Britain and Japan: Biographical Portraits* (Japan Library, 2002). Mention should also be made of the chapter entitled 'Henry Dyer – First Principal of Tokyo's Imperial College of Engineering' in Neil Pedlar's book *The Imported Pioneers* (Japan Library, 1990). *John Milne, Father of Seismology* was the title of the book devoted to his life and career by L. K. Herbert-Gustar and P. A. Nott (Paul Norbury publications, 1980). Other works in English relevant to Professor Miyoshi's book include Andrew Cobbing's *The Satsuma Students in Britain: Japan's Early Search for the 'Essence of the West'* (Japan Library, 2000) and *Scottish Samurai, Thomas Blake Glover 1838–1911* (Canongate Press, 1993). Hayashi Tadasu who was involved in the hiring of Dyer and later became Japanese Ambassador in London was the subject of a portrait by Professor Ian Nish in *Britain and Japan 1859–1991: Themes and Personalities* (Routledge, 1991).

2   Pages 180/181

3   Neil Pedlar: *Imported Pioneeers*, Japan Library 1990, Page 98.

4   Ibid, pages 148/9.

[5] See biographical portrait by Jiro Higuchi in *Britain and Japan: Biographical Portraits*, volume IV, Japan Library, 2002.

[6] See biographical portrait by Olive Checkland under the title 'Engineer Extraordinaire' in *Britain and Japan: Biographical Portraits, Volume IV,* Japan Library, 2002.

1

The Scene is Set for the 'Britain of the East'

Dyer often referred to Emperor Meiji's Charter Oath when discussing the Meiji Restoration, finding the ideal of Japan as an emergent nation in the fifth article. In his translation, it stipulated that 'knowledge shall be sought for throughout the whole world, so that the welfare of the Empire may be promoted (or in order that its status may be raised ever higher and higher)'.[1] Formerly, he had adopted the translation by Tadasu Hayashi, which was true to the original and declared that 'knowledge and learning shall be sought after throughout the whole world, in order that the status of the Empire of Japan may be raised ever higher and higher'.[2]

Takayoshi Kido, who was about to become the leader of liberal bureaucrats, finally revised the Charter Oath, and, under his guidance, Hirobumi Ito, Shigenobu Okuma, Kaoru Inoue and others endeavoured to realize the national ideal it stipulated. Liberal bureaucrats tend to play a leading and significant part in a rising capitalist country in the pursuit of knowledge; certainly in Japan's case, Ito and others gave top priority to practical expertise in areas such as industry, economics, law and military affairs, selecting a model nation from which Japan would introduce knowledge in each field. The final decision was not solely Japan's, of course, since it was affected by the interests of the Western powers involved in the opening of Japan.

After the Meiji Restoration, the foreign powers struggled to gain leadership in Japanese industrial projects in the belief that, although such projects required considerable capital investment, they would lead to future concessions of inestimable value. So it was that the United States and Britain became locked in a cut-throat competition for the railway construction project. The US urged Japan to respect its rights of railway construction granted to Portman by the Tokugawa shogunate. Meanwhile, Sir Harry Parkes, the British Minister to Japan, tackled bureaucrats such as Okuma and Ito and obtained a signed and sealed agreement for Britain to provide financial and technical aid. And, it was this agreement that ultimately clinched Britain's leadership in Japan's developing industrialization process. Takayoshi Kido, who was about to become leader of the liberal bureaucrats, also supported the British case. The Scot, R. H. Brunton, the first British engineer to go to Japan after the Restoration to assist in the construction of lighthouses, also influenced Japan's railway-building programme and emphasized that Britain had more advanced expertise than the Americans.

☐

In March 1870, it was decided that Edward Morel would become Japan's chief railway engineer. Little is known of his early career; various accounts suggest he took part in railway construction in either Ceylon or New Zealand.

The most reliable information on his background came to my attention while I was perusing *The Engineer*. An article carried in the 1 April 1870 issue reported:

> The first section of twenty miles from Yeddo [Tokyo] to Yokohama has, we believe, already been commenced. Mr Lay has, we are pleased to find, made a judicious selection in his engineer, Mr Edward Morel. That gentleman was one of Mr Edwin Clarke's best pupils, and was ordered from Australia – where he has been working for Mr Clarke – to the scene of his new labours and responsibilities.

H. N. Lay was a British entrepreneur, who, with an introduction from Parkes, had promised Okuma and Ito to advance the necessary funds for railway construction. On his journey home on leave, he met Morel and reached an agreement for him to be hired by the Japanese Government.

In Japan, Morel made decisions that were technically important. He adopted the narrow 3.5-foot gauge, as he had already done in Australia. He also opted for wooden instead of iron sleepers, taking Japan's natural resources into account.

At the end of April 1870, at Ito's request, Morel made a recommendation that provided the keynote of Japan's industrialization. The original text has yet to be found, but a Japanese translation was referred to by Ito in his lecture to the Imperial Railway Association in 1902 and is contained in *Views on Railways in Japan: Tenth Anniversary*.

According to this translation, the recommendation, made in

response to an urgent request from the Emperor, was that Japan should set up a department or ministry of *kenchiku* (construction, although I suspect the word used was 'engineering' in the original) with schools under its control, to enable Japan to develop its own technology without Western assistance. It was said that there were such ministries in some European countries, although not in Britain. It is perhaps akin to France's *Ministère des Travaux Publics*, which in those days supervised mines, engineering schools and other similar organizations.

I imagine that Morel based the recommendation on the situation in British-ruled India, where the government early on had established a Department of Public Works. At the time when Morel was in Japan, plans were underway in India for the Royal Engineering College at Cooper's Hill, intended to train engineers who would work for the Department of Public Works. At the time, engineering magazines published in Britain, such as *The Engineer* and *Engineering*, carried many articles on the qualifications required for engineers working in the Department of Public Works and on the plans for the Royal Engineering College. India, therefore, was obviously ahead of Britain in this kind of project.

Acting on this recommendation, Ito established the Department of Public Works in a somewhat high-handed way, supported by Kido, Okuma and others. Yozo Yamao, one of Ito's comrades, took the initiative. Brushing aside opposition from conservatives such as Toshimichi Okubo, he succeeded in establishing the department in December 1870. The prospectus written at that time, and contained in the archives related to Okuma, declares that the intention was to develop industries, improve knowledge and skills, strengthen the nation and benefit the public.

Although he paved the way for Dyer's great contribution, Morel did not survive long enough to see his ideas put into practice. He died of tuberculosis aggravated by overwork and the poor medical and living conditions prevalent in Japan; his wife, who nursed him, also died of the same disease. The couple were buried in the cemetery for foreign residents at Yamanote in Yokohama. It is said that a white Japanese apricot tree the couple had treasured was planted beside the grave, bearing fruit in pairs. According to an article in the 18 October 1871 issue of the *Yokohama Mainichi Shinbun*, Japan's first daily newspaper, Morel had been admired as a most skilled and celebrated engineer. The article also stated that Japan owed much to him and that his death was a great loss to the country.

□

When the Department of Public Works was set up, Yozo Yamao and Masaru Inoue assumed the top posts. In October 1871, Hirobumi Ito took office as Vice-Minister of Public Works, which was virtually the highest position in the department at the time. Later, Ito was promoted Minister of Public Works, with Yamao as Vice-Minister until he became Minister of Home Affairs in 1878. In light of the frequent reshuffles of the government offices in those days, Yamao's eleven-year stint in the department was exceptional.

His first and greatest contribution was the establishment of the Imperial College of Engineering. In 1871, he submitted his plan for the college to the Emperor, explaining that the distribution of knowledge and its utilization for the greater public good were essential to national prosperity, especially the training of people with practical knowledge. He made a grand plan of founding preparatory schools (*Sho-Gakko*) and colleges (*Dai-Gakko*) and hiring teachers from the West: seven teachers for the former and six professors and six assistant professors for the latter.

What made Yamao so dedicated to engineering education? And what influenced his plan to found schools and colleges? Experiences in his youth offer some clues. Yamao made a secret journey to Britain in the closing days of the Tokugawa era, along with Ito, Kaoru Inoue, Masaru Inoue and Kinsuke Endo. Dyer was quite impressed by these five Choshu clansmen. The story of the young men who were able to exercise so much influence is one of the most romantic in the history of Japan, and deserves some space here.

In 1859 the shogun concluded a treaty of peace, friendship and commerce with Lord Elgin, the daimyo of Chōshū expressed a great desire to send some of his young men to England so that they might study the science and industries of the West with a view to the advancement of their country. As it was still illegal for anyone to leave Japan, he arranged that five young men should be quietly put on board a vessel belonging to Jardine, Matheson & Co., with funds for their support in Britain supplied through the same channel. On their arrival in London, Ito, Kaoru Inoue, Yamao, Masaru Inoue and Endo were placed in the care of Mr H. M. Matheson, who made arrangements for their education. Two years later, however, Ito and Kaoru Inoue asked leave to return to Japan, as they knew that significant events were taking place there and wished to be part of them. Endo's health was not good, and he also returned shortly thereafter. The two who remained, Yamao and Masaru Inoue, made good progress in the study of the principles of science and in their industrial applications. Yamao went to Napier's shipbuilding yard, and attended evening classes in Anderson's College, Glasgow.[3]

Yamao returned to Japan towards the end of the year of the Meiji Restoration. He was involved in teaching naval engineering in Chōshū until the end of the following year, 1869, when he accepted a post with the new government as the director of the Yokosuka Ironworks, which was based at the shipyard, which the Tokugawa government had founded in 1865 with French support. The yard already had a technical school under the direction of L. Verny, the chief engineer. In 1867, Verny submitted to Roches, the French Minister to Japan, a draft plan for a school like the *École Polytechnique* of Paris, in Yokosuka. He also planned to have the best graduates study at a naval academy in France so that they could become trained shipbuilding engineers. It should be noted that France founded the polytechnics and had the most advanced engineering education in the world at the time. But, given the confusion surrounding the Meiji Restoration, Verny's plan was not acted on.

After the Restoration, as the director of the Yokosuka Ironworks, Yamao might have been expected to revive Verny's plan, as the latter was still chief engineer. But, after the reconstruction of the school buildings in Yokosuka, Yamao chose to promote engineering education in cooperation with Britain. Yamao's plan for the school, submitted in 1871, was based on his studies in Britain, and was composed of 'schools' providing the first stage of education to be followed by 'colleges', most probably modelled on Anderson's College where Yamao had studied.

It so happened that both Yamao and Dyer attended evening classes at Anderson's College, although it seems they did not know each other at that time. After Dyer came to Japan and discovered this coincidence, he and Yamao became close friends. Dyer spoke highly of Yamao, saying, 'To his efforts much of the success of [the Imperial College of Engineering] was due'.[4] And yet, Dyer did not stick to Yamao's plan, but proceeded to develop his own project to found a completely new college that would be unparalleled anywhere in the world. As a friend, Yamao wholeheartedly supported Dyer's project, thereby creating an institution that was going to change the history of education in Japan.

☐

In order to explain the complicated circumstances behind Japan's employment of Dyer, we should go back to the time when the young men of the Chōshū clan left for Britain.

Chōshū, the influential clan in south-western Japan, lagged behind such strong clans as the Saga and Satsuma, who were the leaders in the modernization of armaments. The five men hoped to offset this by learning naval engineering in Britain. They asked S. J. Gower of Jardine, Matheson & Co. at Ei-ichibankan (the first British factory in Yokohama) for help. Gower's trading firm was founded in Canton in 1832, in partnership of W. Jardine and J. Matheson. Later, the firm relocated its headquarters to Hong Kong. Then, soon after Yokohama Harbour was opened in July 1859, W. Keswick of the firm had a two-storey trading house built there. That building burnt down in 1866, to be replaced by a brick structure that survived until the devastating Kanto earthquake of 1923. A monument to the first British factory stands today in front of the Silk Centre at Yamashita-cho.

Jardine, Matheson & Co. supported the Chōshū clansmen in accordance with the British Government's policy towards Japan at the time. The firm made arrangements for their journey to Britain, and asked H. M. Matheson (1821–98), its London representative, to assist them on arrival.

Matheson entrusted their education to A. W. Williamson, professor of chemistry at University College, London. According to a biography of Williamson carried in *Annals of Science*, Williamson and his family gave the clansmen private lessons on the basics of English and Science. Yamao and Masaru Inoue, who stayed longest, left for Japan in November 1868. The biography noted:

> [O]n their departure Mr Matheson wrote to Williamson saying that 'both lads are deeply sensible of what they owe to you for having so ably directed their time of study and insisted on a thorough ground work at the beginning ... I incline with you to hope much for their future in Japan'.[5]

In 1871 Yamao and Ito decided to ask Matheson to select teachers for the Imperial College of Engineering, and Ito, who was scheduled to leave Japan as a member of the embassy to Europe and America led by Iwakura, the Junior Prime Minister, took on the task. After his departure, Yamao gained official approval for the contact with Matheson. In those days, not only the Department of Public Works but also many other departments and schools sought to hire foreign teachers. Some hired foreigners already living in Japan, or people recommended by them; others worked through the official diplomatic channel, or sent a Japanese bureaucrat abroad to undertake the task, like the Department of Public Works.

The embassy's negotiations in the US took a long time, and the members only arrived in London in August 1872. Ito lost no time in getting Tadasu Hayashi, his private secretary, to visit Matheson and ask for his recommendations for teachers. Matheson later recounted this occasion in a lecture, saying:

> The story is interesting and I have very rarely told it. Several of those who are now prominent members of [the Japanese Government] had been placed under my care at an early period; and one year after their return to their own country and when the revolution occurred, which abolished the Daimyo and established a partially constitutional government, several of my friends became ministers of state and they requested me to assist them in founding an institution that would train young men for efficient service in the Public Works Department, which, for the first time, was felt to be all important in the development of the country. (*Ross Shire Journal*, 15 September 1882. Extract from speech at Dingwall by H. M. Matheson, Esq.).

Why did Ito and Yamao ask Matheson, rather than Williamson, to recommend teachers? The answer would seem to be as follows. Around 1870, Jardine, Matheson & Co. consisted of six partners, one of whom was H. M. Matheson, according to Kanji Ishii of the University of Tokyo, who compiled *Modern Japan and British Capital*, based on the research of materials relating to the firm that are held by the University of Cambridge. It is also shown that the Department of Public Works began to make remittances to this firm in 1872, when Ito arrived in London. On Ito's direction, a remittance of 10,840 dollars (Mexican) was made in April 1872, and 4,654 dollars was sent in August 1873. In February 1874, a remittance of 4,604 dollars was made to the firm on the instruction of Dyer. The account of the payments is not given, according to Ishii.

When Dyer was hired by the Japanese Government in 1873, the agreement was signed by Dyer and Matheson in his capacity as Agent for the Minister of Public Works of His Majesty the Mikado of Japan. In 1883, Matheson, as the London Agent of the Japanese Government, recommended Dyer for a position as a professor at Glasgow University. Professor Ishii wrote in his book that Jardine, Matheson & Co. acted as a merchant bank in selling accounts rather than as a broker of commodities. It is hinted, accordingly, that Ito left both the selection of teachers and the settlement of accounts to Matheson because he had been helpful to Ito and the others.

□

In order to comply with Ito's request to find prospective teachers for the Imperial College of Engineering, Matheson opted for Glasgow, rather than turning to Williamson at University College, London. Behind this decision lay complicated circumstances related to the history of education in Scotland, an overview of which is indispensable to understanding the background to Dyer's employment.

The late Shido Sumeragi, who was my teacher at Hiroshima University, recounted in his autobiography his visit to Glasgow in 1963 at the invitation of the British Government. In his speech at the graduation ceremony in 1964, he referred to Strathclyde University, formerly the engineering college that Dyer had established in Glasgow. He stated that he had been very much impressed with the Latin words inscribed at the university's main entrance, '*mente et manu*', meaning 'mind and hand', reflecting the fact that harmony of intellect and skill was its educational goal.

During my time in Glasgow, I was able to find these words inscribed on the outer wall of the Thomas Graham Building on the Strathclyde campus. As can be seen in plate 4, the head (*mente*) and the hand (*manu*) are balanced on a pair of scales. The inscription on the left side of the relief shows the year 1796, and the one on the right side 1962. It was in 1796 that Anderson's Institution was founded, while 1962 was the 50th anniversary of the receipt of its royal charter; until then the relief had been the official coat of arms of Strathclyde University.

The city already had a college that had been established in 1451, and its traditional Oxbridge curriculum was turned into a more practical one with James Watt's revolutionary invention of the steam condenser in a workshop there in 1765. That workshop had been built on the advice of Adam Smith, author of *The Wealth of Nations*, who insisted that colleges should be independent of guilds. Watt's great invention was brought about when he was working on the repair of a conventional Newcomen engine, which had been requested by physics professor James Anderson. The latter died in 1796, and left a legacy to be utilized for human welfare and scientific development. Anderson's Institution was founded in the same year.

The college's name was changed later, as is indicated in Table 1. Still, Dyer and Yamao continued to call it 'Anderson's College', which is the name also adopted in this book.

Dyer stated in his lecture in 1905:

> The total value of the property which he left was only about £1,000; but the influence which Anderson's College had in education in Glasgow, and, indeed, it may be said, on the destinies of the world, is not to be measured by that amount of money, a fact which proves

that the value of an institution depends much more on the spirit which animates those connected with it, than on the amount of its wealth or the extent of its buildings.[6]

Dr George Birkbeck, who was a professor at Anderson's College, had begun mechanics classes for artisans, and in 1823, these became the basis of an independent Mechanics Institution. Glasgow then came to be known as the centre of engineering education.

Who was it that used the phrase, '*mente et manu*'? I suspect, though I am not certain, that it was D. Hume, the Scottish philosopher. In that phrase, Bacon's axiom that knowledge is power is made stronger by taking skill or art into account, and this reflects the emphasis put on useful learning in Scotland. In fact, Scotland turned out many men of practical science, such as engineers, industrialists and bankers, who were in the forefront of the modernization of Britain. Scotland, often enough, appears to be a kind of 'frontier' district that paves the way for reform in modernization, as with the clans of Saga and Satsuma who took the lead in Japan's modernization. Industrialization in Scotland was centred on Glasgow, which had access to abundant natural resources such as iron and coal, and to great facilities for water transport that led to the establishment of steel mills and shipyards. Dyer called Glasgow 'the greatest engineering centre in the world'.[7]

□

In 1840, Glasgow University established the chair of civil engineering and mechanics, and L. D. B. Gordon became the first holder. Established by the Royal Charter, the chair was the first to offer programmes different from traditional Oxbridge ones. University College, London, had actually founded a chair of civil engineering in 1833, but its professor did not take office until 1841. Thus, Gordon was a pioneer showing the way forward for other colleges in English-speaking countries. The chair was extended to become what is today the Faculty of Engineering.

It makes one wonder why the first chair of engineering was opened in Glasgow, and not in one of the great industrial cities of England such as Birmingham or Manchester. C. A. Oakley, who published *History of Faculty* on the fifteenth anniversary of its establishment, offers the following explanation. At that time, Glasgow University had enjoyed a long history going back some four hundred years, and had observed the centenary of James Watt's birth only four years earlier, the event being brought to the attention of Queen Victoria. Sir Robert Peel, the Prime Minister of the day, strongly recommended the university – not least because its students had once played an important role in his election to office and therefore he was naturally favourably disposed towards the institution. Oakley also notes that the creation of Gordon's chair aroused strong opposition in the highly conservative world of English universities.

Gordon, who was appointed professor at the age of 25, had a glorious career. He had attended the University of Edinburgh in his home town, before going on to study at the Freiburg Mining School in Germany and at the *École Polytechnique* in Paris. He had returned home planning to establish a factory in Glasgow when he was offered the professorship. Minutes of Faculty 1839–48, in the Archives of Glasgow University, contain Gordon's letter dated 13 November 1840, in which he states:

> It being my anxious desire to commence the duties of the chair of Civil Engineering and Mechanics in the first week of December, I respectfully beg the favour of your appropriating to my purpose suitable accommodation in the College.

But soon after assuming the professorship, he found his plans frustrated by a number of obstacles. His classroom was an attic with one small window and without a blackboard. The chair of engineering was regarded as a minor one within the Faculty of Arts, and was unable to confer a bachelor's degree. He had to start his classes at seven in the morning, thus attracting few students; sometimes he had no students in an entire year. The chair was provided with a subsidy of £275 a year, arousing envy among professors of the traditional arts such as the classics, philosophy and mathematics, some of whom tried to persuade the board of trustees that the money should be used for better purposes.

Tempted to resign several times, Gordon held on out of respect for the Royal Charter. In his sixth year, W. Thomson arrived as a professor of physics. This man, who, in later years was to become Lord Kelvin, enjoyed considerable influence in Glasgow and Gordon was greatly encouraged by his generous support. Having held the chair for fifteen years, Gordon went back to business as an engineer in 1855, as he had long desired, and was succeeded by his former assistant, W. J. M. Rankine. Gordon became active in engineering-related consultancy, such as railway construction, and made a contribution to new technical developments, including the development of a wire rope.

Engineering had to overcome strong resistance within universities, before finally gaining recognition. Glasgow's chair of engineering only became a faculty in 1923, by which time Japan already had four imperial universities with departments of engineering. Among them, the Imperial College of Engineering took the lead, with Gordon playing a significant part in the selection of teachers and the organization of the programme of studies.

□

A biography of Gordon for private circulation written by his friend Constable was published in 1877, presumably printed soon after the former's death. This was discussed in a book written by Kenzo Sakamoto of Chiba University, who discovered the work during a visit to Glasgow University in 1984. It contains two important letters that prove the relationship between Matheson and Gordon and sheds light on the reasons why Dyer was selected. One letter, dated 25 January 1873, was written by Gordon to Matheson, and the other letter of 20 January 1877 was written by Matheson to Gordon's sister, Mary. Let me first discuss the latter.

This letter was written seven months after Gordon's death and discussed his great accomplishments. It reads in part as follows:

> My Dear Miss Gordon – Having had charge of some of the first students sent to this country from Japan many years ago, I was requested in 1872 by one of the number, who had become Minister of Public Works, to assist the Government to found at Yeddo a College of Civil and Mechanical Engineering. I was to select the professors, fix the scale of their salaries, arrange a programme of studies, and procure all the necessary books and materials required for an institution designed to train a large body of Japanese youths for the service of their country in connection with public works. The commission was felt by me to be a most difficult and responsible one, but as it was conveyed in the most generous terms, expressing unbounded confidence in myself, I resolved to set about its execution.

Ito commissioned Matheson to make the necessary decisions on the establishment of the college, including the programme of study and the procurement of books and materials. Matheson was the agent of the Department of Public Works in every sense. Since the department did not have any programme of study or definite plan regarding the specialities of prospective teachers, Matheson had to pick out the fields of study that would be required at the college, and had to select qualified teachers as well as a person suited to the position of principal.

Matheson was not a specialist in education, but he took on the important duty, hoping that he would accomplish it with some advice from Gordon, his friend. Matheson's letter continues:

> I knew that there was one friend to whom I could apply with the certainty that he would give me good advice, and I lost no time in driving over to Totteridge to lay the matter before your dear brother. He gave me the encouragement of which I stood in need; and as the first thing was to obtain a man who could take the position of principal, to whom the government wished to give a good deal of authority, he recommended my communicating with the late Professor Macquarn Rankine of Glasgow University, his own successor in the Chair of which he was the first occupant. That distinguished man was laid aside at the time by the illness of which he soon afterwards died, but he sent me several names, among them that of Mr Henry Dyer, a young man of twenty-four, who had passed through his college course with much distinction. When I eventually received the certificates and testimonial which were furnished by Mr Dyer, I took them at once to your brother, and will not easily forget the enthusiasm with which he gauged the character, the talent, and the attainments of the applicant, and without the slightest hesitation pronounced him the man for the post. Some doubts were at first entertained by another eminent Professor as to Mr Dyer's fitness for the [principal's post], but Lewis Gordon never wavered; the doubts also disappeared, and I am delighted to say that the appointment of Mr Dyer has been more than justified by the result.

Here we have four important points to be noted. First, Rankine mentioned several names, including Henry Dyer, for the post of principal. Secondly, Dyer submitted his certificates and testimonial of his own accord. Thirdly, some doubts about Dyer's competence were at first expressed by an eminent professor, whom we know from other sources to be Lord Kelvin. Lastly, Dyer met with Matheson's approval, and then with Gordon's wholehearted support. (These four important facts are considered in the following section.)

Matheson's letter also shows how other teachers were screened:

> [Gordon] then discussed with me the scheme of study in framing which I had also the advantage of some counsel from Sir William Thomson, and Professor Williamson of London. Some further appointments were made, and on 25 January 1873 your brother sent me some admirable notes, based upon his wide experience and thoroughly practical views, which have to a large extent been adopted and acted upon. I send you these notes to show you how heartily he went into the subject.

The notes, carried in the appendix of the *Memoir of Lewis D. B. Gordon, F. R. S. E.*, are namely Gordon's letter of 25 January 1873 addressed to Matheson, which was mentioned earlier.

In Gordon's notes, the draft for the curriculum was grounded upon his own experience of studies on the Continent. He also took Lord Kelvin's advice into consideration. Gordon's letter states:

> As to Sir William's scheme, it is excellent, and of course the College, if it be the only source of education in exact science, must have a Professor of Mathematics and another of Physics.

He then set out the programmes and hours of teaching of the three professors of civil and mechanical engineering, physics and mathematics. At this stage, Dyer was to be in charge of civil and mechanical engineering, while the names of a professor of mathematics and another of physics were not given. Probably the designation of these two professors was left to the discretion of Lord Kelvin, who insisted on the necessity of the two subjects. Gordon's letter continues:

> There is vast body of such collected experience now well recorded in books in English, French, and German, with good drawings; and as I have said, courses of lectures are regularly delivered on these subjects in Paris, Hanover, Berlin, Aix-le-Chappelle, Karlsruhr, Munich, Vienna and Zurich, in fact in all polytechnic schools. Again, a special college for engineers for Japan should have Professors of Chemistry, Theoretical and Applied; Professor of Geology and Mineralogy; teachers of Drawing.

The British teachers who came to Japan in the summer in 1873 to teach at the Imperial College of Engineering had been selected in accordance with Gordon's plan. A total of nine came from Britain: Dyer of Civil and Mechanical Engineering as Principal, W. E. Ayrton in Physics, D. H. Marshall in Mathematics, E. Divers in Chemistry, E. F. Mondy in Drawing, W. Craigie in English Language and Literature, G. Cawley, R. Clark and A. King who took charge of the practical parts of the instruction in engineering. In 1876, the post of professor of Geology and Mining that had been included in Gordon's plan was taken up by John Milne (later to become known in Japan as 'Father of Seismology'), again with help from Matheson. Though Yamao was at first thinking of hiring six teachers for preparatory education, those highly specialized teachers initiated engineering education of the collegiate level from the very beginning.

Matheson extended his sincere thanks to Gordon in his above-mentioned letter of 1877, which was addressed to Gordon's sister. The letter says:

> In conclusion, I can never cease to be grateful to your lamented brother, for the singular kindness with which, although so great an invalid, he entered with true and deep interest into my Japanese

affairs; and I have no hesitation in saying that, if the College turns out the success which it seems likely to do, much will be due to the clear decided plan which was laid down by your brother at the beginning, and the wise and invaluable counsel which he gave so readily to one so little qualified as I was to carry through an enterprise of this nature, and which gave me the confidence I could not otherwise have had in acting for a distant Government.

The matters Ito had placed in Matheson's hands and further promoted by Gordon, the first British professor of engineering, were now a fair way towards achieving success.

RANKINE – A PIONEER IN ENGINEERING

Ito's request for the selection of the principal of the Imperial College of Engineering was finally entrusted to Professor Rankine of Glasgow University, 'a pioneer in the application of scientific principles to engineering and one of the earliest university professors of engineering (D. F. Channell, *Rankine, Scotland's Culture Heritage*, University of Edinburgh, 1986)'. Rankine's career is outlined in the obituary published in the newsletter of Edinburgh Royal Society and written by Gordon, who was then his senior. In 1955, a century after he took up his professorship, a memorial lecture was held at Glasgow University; a year later, the Institution of Civil Engineers also held a lecture, which was reported in its newsletter. In 1986, D. F. Channell of the University of Texas, whose speciality was the history of science and technology, published a comprehensive biography of Rankine, as referred to above, and this provides the main source for the following overview of Rankine's career.

Rankine was born in Edinburgh in 1820, the son of a railway engineer. After graduating from the University of Edinburgh, he served a four-year apprenticeship in railway construction in Ireland. He then returned to Edinburgh, where he presented his first thesis on railway wheel axles, and continued his study into the application of scientific principles. He came to Lord Kelvin's notice and worked as an assistant at a time when the latter was obtaining his first patent relating to telegraphy. Rankine also assisted Gordon in his business in London and gave a lecture in his place at Glasgow University. When Gordon retired in 1855, Rankine succeeded him in the chair of civil engineering and mechanics.

His first step was to improve the curriculum in the hope of raising the status of his department. The goal, reflected in what we call 'the four great manuals of Rankine', was the establishment of engineering as a science and the development of a teaching approach that balanced theory and practical application. This approach was adopted in many countries up to the beginning of the twentieth century, including Japan when the Imperial College of Engineering was founded. The oldest editions of Rankine's manuals are kept at the University of Tokyo, and these are cited below in chronological order:

1 *A Manual of Applied Mechanics* (seventh edition of 1873; first published in 1858)
2 *A Manual of the Steam Engine and Other Prime Movers* (fourth edition of 1869; first published in 1859)
3 *A Manual of Civil Engineering* (seventh edition of 1871; first published in 1862)
4 *A Manual of Machinery and Millwork* (first edition of 1869)

The third work, *A Manual of Civil Engineering*, was translated into Japanese by Yukitoshi Mizuno and was the first of the manuals to be published by the Department of Education in 1880. *A Manual of Applied Mechanics* was translated into Japanese by Kyuichiro Nagai and was published by the department in 1885. According to the 1876 Catalogue of The Library of the Imperial College of Engineering, more than twenty copies of each of the four manuals were purchased for student loan. Other publications by Rankine are also in the catalogue, such as *Cyclopaedia of Machine and Hard Tools*, *Mechanical Text Book* and *Rules and Tables*.

Rankine, in cooperation with Lord Kelvin, inaugurated a programme of reform at Glasgow University with two specific results. One was the relocation of the campus from the High Street to Gilmorehill, the present location. The new buildings, which were completed in 1870 and for which Rankine designed the heating systems, attracted much attention and acclaim at the time. The other result was the institution of degrees for students majoring in engineering, which had to be approached by stages. Initially, he devised the title of 'Certificate of Proficiency in Engineering Science' in 1862, and then he got the college's approval on the conferment of a B.Sc. As Dyer later recounted: 'Twenty-one years ago, when I was a student of engineering at Glasgow University, there were no degrees available to engineers, [so] a few of us who were interested in the matter got up a petition to the Senate, asking that a Science Degree should be instituted, and this, *so far as I know*, was the beginning of the movement which led to degrees being given in Scotland in the Department of Science (italics in original).'[8] This became a reality in 1872, and Dyer was among the first students to benefit.

Rankine was very much impressed with Dyer as a student, judging from documents kept in the Archives of Glasgow University, of which the three most outstanding are mentioned below.

The first is a transcript showing the ratings that Dyer received in Civil and Mechanical Engineering, a course taught by Rankine, while attending classes from 1869 to 1871. Throughout, Dyer was given 'Excellent' in Oral Examinations, and 'Most Excellent. Marks 100 per cent' in Written Examinations. In the second year, it was remarked as follows: 'A highly distinguished student. Gained the first Walker Prize for a Written Examination. Marks 95 $^1/_2$ per cent.'

The second document is a letter of recommendation dated 3 May 1871. The name of the addressee is not known, but perhaps the letter was intended for proposing Dyer for a chair in Anderson's College. As Dyer says: 'My friend Mr Richard Cunliffe offered me the prospect of the Chair of Applied Mechanics which it was proposed to found in Anderson's College.'[9] Rankine stated in the letter:

> Mr Henry Dyer passed with most distinguished success through the course of study and examination in Engineering Science in this University, and obtained a Certificate of Proficiency ... As Mr Dyer intends pursuing his studies in order to fit himself as an Academic Teacher of Engineering, I will refrain from adding more in the meantime; but when he has completed that course I shall be most happy to give him a testimonial reviewing the whole of his career, the remainder of which I have no doubt will be as distinguished as the part of the past.

In this letter, Rankine referred to Dyer's intention to expand his studies, which presumably also included his ambition to study shipbuilding as well as civil and mechanical engineering after graduation from Glasgow University. The transcript and letter of recommendation were among the documents Dyer submitted to the Imperial College of Engineering.

The third document is a letter by Rankine himself, dated 7 December 1869 and addressed to Professor Weir, a member of the university board of trustees, in which he recommended Dyer for the Whitworth Scholarship because of his 'diligent and successful studies and good conduct'. The scholarship, established in 1868 by Whitworth, an inventor of precision machine tools, provided £100 each for 30 recipients selected every year for their excellence in the theory and practice of engineering. Dyer was the first Scottish recipient in 1870, and he remained justly proud of this distinction.

Returning to Rankine, we find him gradually establishing a national and even international reputation. He acted as president of the Institution of Engineers and Shipbuilders in Scotland and the Philosophical Society of Glasgow, and he was also well known in England as an honorary member of the Literary and Philosophical Society of Manchester and of the Historic Society of Lancashire and Cheshire. He became an honorary member of the American Academy of Arts and Sciences and of the Royal Society of Tasmania. Unfortunately, diabetes cost him his eyesight and he died on 24 December 1872 at the relatively young age of 52. It is a pity he did not live long enough to see his protégé Dyer vindicate his recommendation as Principal of the Imperial College of Engineering.

The documents submitted by Dyer in the application for this post were compiled in a booklet entitled *Selections from Testimonials*, dated February 1873 and now kept in the Archives of Glasgow University. It is not known who issued the booklet, nor for what purpose, though it seems likely that Dyer had it privately printed at Matheson's request.

The 16-page booklet consists of the lists of degrees and prizes, the Certificate of Proficiency in Engineering Science, the ratings given by Rankine in Engineering and Mechanics, the letter of recommendation written by Rankine, the letter of recommendation from the faculty of Glasgow University that included the signatures of W. Thomson, or Lord Kelvin, of Physics, H. Blackburn of Mathematics, J. Young of Natural History and T. Anderson of Chemistry, the official approval of the Whitworth Scholarship, the plan of studies submitted by Dyer, the certificates written by T. Kennedy and A. C. Kirk as Dyer's former teachers when he was an apprentice, and a letter of recommendation by R. McNab, who taught Dyer at primary school. Thus, it is an important source of information about Dyer's personal history before he left Scotland for Japan.

□

Henry Dyer was born in 1848 as the first son of an artisan in Bothwell, located near Glasgow, referred to by Dyer as 'a moorland parish of Lanarkshire'.[10] In the neighbouring town of Shotts lay the Shotts Iron Works, and Dyer attended the primary school attached to it. He was a high achiever, his teacher McNab stating:

> [He] ... exhibited uncommon perseverance and industry, which, combined with an excellent memory and natural talents of the highest order, enabled him to take the foremost place in his respective classes, and at the annual examinations carry off all the first prizes. He was taken from school to one of the offices in connection

with the Shotts Iron Works, in which he continued for some years, and where his knowledge of figures was put to a practical test, giving him an accuracy in calculation which no mere school drill could confer.

From Mr Robert McNab, F. E. I. S.,
Wilson's School, Shotts Iron Works.

Dyer's family moved to Glasgow so that the youth could take up an apprenticeship. In 1863, he was trained at the James Aitken & Co., iron works in the Cranston Hill Foundry. His teachers were A. C. Kirk, the manager, and T. Kennedy, the foreman, both of whom wrote letters of recommendation for Dyer that are included in the booklet. Kennedy's letter states: 'During [Dyer's] last year he was employed more as an assistant to me in drawing and in getting the work forward for the erectors and machine men. He was paid a higher rate of wages than the other apprentices owing to his superior intelligence and ability.' Kirk also praised Dyer: '... latterly I employed him in the Drawing Office, where by his assiduity and attention he made rapid progress'.

Oddly, the booklet does not include any letter of recommendation regarding the evening classes of Anderson's College that Dyer attended as an apprentice. In this connection it is interesting to note Dyer's lecture in 1905, in which he touched upon the college:

When I was a boy at school in a moorland parish of Lanarkshire, one of the ministers of the district gave an address on three distinguished Andersonian men – namely, Thomas Graham, David Livingstone, and James Young; and the first time I came to Glasgow I went direct to George Street to see Anderson's College, and to inspect the wonders of its museum. A few years later, when I came into town to complete my apprenticeship, I took the first opportunity of joining the evening classes. They were very different from what they are now. Professor Laing taught elementary mathematics; Professors Penny, Herschell, Buchanan, and Kennedy gave popular lectures in chemistry, natural philosophy and astronomy, physiology and botany; but practically none of the applications to engineering or industry generally were taken up in the classes.[11]

A college that attached importance to theory rather than application must indeed have been disappointing to Dyer.

Finishing his apprenticeship, he went on to Glasgow University, and Kirk was his certifier. Dyer states: 'On the completion of my apprenticeship I attended Glasgow University for five sessions, taking work in the shops or drawing offices during the summer, supplemented by an occasional evening class in Anderson's College.'[12] At that time, students of Glasgow University were supposed to attend lectures in winter and engage in practical training and other activities in summer. Thus, Dyer attended the university for five years, from the winter of 1868 to that of 1872. According to the class register, Dyer took such subjects as Civil and Mechanical Engineering by Rankine, Physics, Mathematics, Natural History and Chemistry by the aforementioned professors, along with other subjects such as Latin, Greek and Ethics.

The letter written by Rankine is dated 3 May 1871, making it much older than others in the booklet. Rankine, however, died before he could write a testimonial for the Imperial College of Engineering, so Dyer had to be content with one written for an earlier occasion. He commented:

A few days before [Rankine's] death he asked me to furnish him with an outline of my whole career in order that he might express an opinion on it, with special reference to the proposed Japanese appointment, and on Saturday he told his amanuensis to remind him of the matter on Monday; but on Sabbath he was struck with paralysis, and remained insensible up to the hour of his death, which occurred about midnight last night. Although it is a matter of regret that I have not got his opinion as to my abilities for any academic post, yet I think a very fair inference may be drawn both from my class certificates and the above testimonial, and also from the fact of his nominating me as a candidate for the Principalship of the proposed Engineering College in Japan, that I had at least fulfilled the expectations he had formed of me. I will only say that if appointed, it will be my utmost endeavour still further to realise these expectations.

Dyer even attached the amanuensis's account for the circumstances showing how keen he was to be selected to go to Japan.

Among the awards he received from Glasgow University was the Certificate of Proficiency in Engineering Science signed by the professors of such required subjects as Mathematics, Natural Philosophy, Inorganic Chemistry, Geology and Mineralogy, and Civil and Mechanical Engineering. The list of prizes consisted of two Whitworth Bursaries, the Whitworth Scholarship, Arnott Prize for Natural Philosophy, Walker Prize for Engineering and Shipbuilding, Watt Prize for Astronomy, Thomson Scholarship for Experimental Science and First Prize in Sir William Thomson's Higher Mathematical Class. After his death in 1918, his obituary in *The Glasgow Herald* stated that his name had been found as many as twelve times in the list of university prize-winners.

A manuscript of Dyer's thesis to gain the Watt Prize is kept in the

Archives of Glasgow University, the title of which is 'The Influence of the Newtonian Principles on the Progress of Science during the Eighteenth Century'. He dealt with the subject in a methodical way, putting the text on the right-hand pages and showing the references on the left. The seventy-four-page text is really a great work, and implies that Dyer was interested in history at this stage. His intellectual facility for historical analysis was going to be further developed and displayed in full in his later years.

☐

The doubts expressed by Lord Kelvin regarding Dyer's fitness for the Japanese post finally disappeared, as noted by Gordon in his letter of 25 January 1873 to Matheson:

My dear Hugh Matheson,

In reply to your letter on the subject of the Japanese Professorships, let me in the first place say, that it was quite a pleasant relief to a first disappointment in reading page 2, to read in page 3 that Sir W. Thomson's doubts about H. Dyer's fitness for the Principal's place had vanished on second thoughts. I feel greatly interested in Dyer from his account of himself which you read to me.

Both Matheson and Gordon were well aware that any objection from Lord Kelvin was a major impediment.

It is not clear why he doubted Dyer's fitness. Lord Kelvin's testimonial dated 20 December 1872, which was one of those submitted to the Imperial College of Engineering, did not say that Dyer was qualified for the position of the principal, while highly rating his scholastic ability in natural philosophy. He might have been thinking of recommending some professors for the teaching positions of the Imperial College of Engineering, and thus might have been unwilling to support Dyer, who was much younger than the candidates he had in mind. In fact, the teachers who came to the College, such as Divers of Chemistry and Ayrton of Natural Philosophy, had strong connections with Lord Kelvin. Each matched Dyer in academic background and professional career and were older than him.

However, Lord Kelvin came to the conclusion that Dyer was qualified, and so the selection was made. The agreement was finalized and entered into on 2 April 1873; it was signed by Dyer and Matheson, who served as the employer and as the Agent for the Minister of Public Works of His Majesty the Mikado of Japan. It was signed in the presence of D. F. Goldsmith of Glasgow.

The Articles of Agreement consist of the preamble and seven articles. The preamble stated that the agreement was signed by Dyer and Matheson, and stipulated Dyer's assignment as follows: 'The said Henry Dyer engages himself in the service of the said Minister of Public Works and of his successors, for and during the space of five years, to commence from his arrival in Japan on the conditions following.' Dyer's five-year period of service was longer than that normally offered foreign teachers in those days, which, in the case of those employed by the Department of Education and other organizations was three years at most.

The first article set out the broad details of the job description:

> The said Henry Dyer shall proceed to Japan direct by the mail steamer leaving England on the 10th day of April current, & immediately upon his arrival, and thenceforth during the term aforesaid, shall faithfully and diligently & to the best of his knowledge and ability employ himself in the service of the said Minister of Public Works and his successors in office for the time being, as the Principal of the College of Civil Engineering at Yedo, and as the professor of Civil & Mechanical Engineering in the said College.

It is interesting to note that the name 'College of Civil Engineering' differed from that used in the documents submitted by Dyer for application two months earlier, namely, the Imperial College of Engineering. On his arrival in Japan, Dyer adopted the latter as the official name.

Actually, the principal or *kocho* of the college was a Japanese, as was required in Japanese administrative organizations. Accordingly, Dyer's title in Japanese was *token*, which was archaic, though his English title in the Agreement was still the principal. Such a position as Dyer's in other imperial schools was referred to as *kyoto* in Japanese, which means the teacher who is next to the principal in position, as W. S. Clark was *kyoto* of Sapporo Agricultural College.

The second article went into the details of the job:

> He shall devote his whole time and attention, with zeal and energy, to the due & faithful performance of the duties of his position as aforesaid, and shall use his utmost exertions to promote the establishment and successful maintenance of the said College, in all its branches, during the whole of the aforesaid period of five years, and shall not at any time absent himself from daily and due attendance at the said College, except on Sundays, or when unavoidably prevented by illness or during the regular annual holidays, or with the previous consent of the said Minister of Public Works for the time being.

The third article stipulated that Dyer should not engage in any other capacity or in trading:

> He shall in all things be subservient to and obey the decisions & instructions of the said Minister of Public Works for the time being & shall not, during his continuance in the service, directly ore [sic] indirectly be engaged in any capacity whatsoever, other than in the service of the said Minister of Public Works as aforesaid, without the previous written authority and consent of the said Minister of Public Works, nor shall he engage in trading.

Provided that Dyer met the obligations specified in the article, Matheson as an agent promised Dyer a certain reward, which was stipulated in the next article.

The amount of reward, which was a matter of primary concern for foreign teachers to be hired, was provided in the fourth article as follows:

> That the said Minister of Public Works shall pay the said Henry Dyer the sum of two hundred and fifty pounds stg for defraying the expenses of his outfit and passage to Japan and also during the aforesaid term of five years, a salary or sum in Dollars equal at the exchange of four shillings and six pence per Dollar to one thousand five hundred pounds sterling per annum, payable monthly, to commence from the date of his arrival in Japan; and on completion and fulfilment of the service hereby agreed to be rendered by the said Henry Dyer the said Minister of Public Works for the time being will defray his expenses home to England, and if, in the course of his engagement, he should be permanently disable [sic] by sickness, regularly certified by two approved medical men as not arising from his own intemperance or misconduct, then the said Minister of Public Works for the time being will defray his expenses home to England, and further, during the period of his engagement the said Minister of Public Works for the time being will provide the said Henry Dyer with a suitable unfurnished house as a place of residence.

As is indicated in the article, the sum of 250 pounds sterling for Dyer's journey and outfit amounted to more than 1,111 dollars. His monthly salary, calculated from the annual sum of 1,500 pounds sterling, came to 555 dollars and 55 cents. The Japanese Government's documents show that Dyer's salary was raised up to 660 yen in the meantime, which was equivalent to a rise of more than 100 dollars, as one dollar was equal to one yen in those days. He got an extra allowance of 200 yen when he started his lessons at the Akabane works.

How favourable Dyer's terms of employment were can be judged by comparing his salary with the salaries proposed by Dyer himself for those professors and instructors of the technical college back in Scotland. He suggested to the Institution of Civil Engineers that the college should have three professors and two instructors, and that a professor should be paid 500 pounds or less annually and an instructor 100 pounds or less annually.[13] Dyer's entry-level salary was three times higher than that of the professor. Given the rise and additional allowance, Dyer got five times as much as a professor. As a foreign teacher hired by the Japanese Government, Dyer was entitled to such preferential treatment.

The fifth article mentioned the right of dismissal by the Minister of Public Works as follows:

> That if the said Henry Dyer shall at any time neglect or refuse, or from any cause whatsoever (other than unavoidable sickness as aforesaid), become or be unable to perform or comply with all or any of the articles of this Agreement or any of the duties required by him, or all of the decisions or instructions of Public Works for the time, shall in any manner misconduct himself, or shall enter into trading, or employ himself in any capacity whatsoever otherwise than in the sole employ and interest of the said College, without the previous written authority or consent of the said Minister of Public Works for the time being, it shall be lawful for the said Minister to declare the employment of the said Henry Dyer at an end, & immediately thereupon the salary and every other payment which the said Henry Dyer may then or might thereafter be entitled to receive, and all benefit and advantage whatsoever to be derived by him under or by virtue of this agreement, shall cease.

The sixth article stipulated the possible extension of the assignment, which read as follows:

> That in case the said Minister of Public Works for the time being shall at the expiration of the said term of five years be desirous of continuing the services of the said Henry Dyer for a further period not exceeding five years, and shall give notice to the said Henry Dyer of his desire, at least six months before the expiry of the said term of five years, and specify the extended term for which he desires such services to continue, and if the said Henry Dyer shall consent to continue in the service of the said Minister of Public Works during such extended period, all the stipulations and provisions of the present Agreement shall continue in force and be binding on the said Minister of Public Works for the time being and on his successors in office and the said Henry Dyer until the expiration of such extended term, not exceeding Ten years from the date of his arrival in Japan.

As already noted, Dyer's five-year period of service was longer and more advantageous than those of other foreign teachers. What is more, he was given a possible five-year extension of his assignment, which was quite exceptional. The provision of this article became a reality, and Dyer's engagement was renewed in 1878. He stayed in the post until 1882, thus completing nine years' service in total.

The seventh article dealt with the question of penalty for any violation:

> The said Henry Dyer hereby binds himself under penalty of one thousand pounds stg to the said Minister of Public Works and his successors in office for the time being diligently and faithfully to keep & perform the various stipulations, agreements, matters, & things contained in this agreement until the end and expiration thereof, whether by effluxion of time or otherwise howsoever.

The article was also meant as a safeguard against the frequent government reshuffles at the time.

Prior to hiring a large number of foreign teachers, the Department of Education had begun working on a standard form of agreement, and giving guidelines on this to prefectural governments. Dyer's agreement entered into greater details than the form prescribed by the Department. The guidelines also gave directions on the terms of employment for foreign teachers. For example, their period of service in Japan was to be two or three years, and the monthly salary of a principal was to be between 500 and 600 yen. Also, a teacher coming from Britain, France or Germany was entitled to 650 yen for the journey. Again, Dyer was granted more preferential treatment in each category.

Thus, the stage was now set for him to undertake the great challenge of teaching engineering in Japan.

NOTES

[1] 82, p. 48–49.
[2] 69, pp. 28, 78; 70, p. 151; 73, p. 4; 75, p. 110; 79, p. 154.
[3] 69, p. 25.
[4] 69, p. 3.

5   Harris, J. and Brock, W. H., From Giessen to Gower Street: Towards a Bibliography of Alexander William Williamson, *Annals of Science*, Vol. 31, No. 2, 1974, p. 124.

6   71, p. 4.

7   41, p. 17.

8   47, p. 2.

9   71, p. 6.

10 71, p. 5.

11 71, p. 5.

12 71, p. 6.

13 3, p. 40.

2

Dyer's Educational Experiment in Japan

Before considering what kind of model Dyer had in mind for creating an engineering college in Japan, it will be helpful to examine the situation of technical and engineering education in various parts of the industrialized world at that time. Originally, technical schools tended to have only one department specializing in such fields as navigation, mining, civil engineering and stockbreeding. However, such schools underwent a drastic change with the advent of the idea of the 'polytechnic' that originated in the days of the French Revolution.

In France, the revolutionary assembly decided on the establishment of the *École Polytechnique* to serve as a comprehensive and professional institution to train engineers for public works. Later, more emphasis was put on the fundamental and scientific aspects for advanced and professional studies. The idea of the polytechnic soon permeated neighbouring Prussia and Switzerland, where such schools were developed as institutions of the highest level offering a variety of technical courses.

The concept eventually spread to Britain in the early 1850s. In 1852, L. Playfair authored *Industrial Instruction on the Continent*, based on the success of continental technical education that had so impressed him at the London Exposition the previous year. He directed attention to the polytechnic schools of Karlsruhe, Berlin, Dresden, Vienna, Munich, Paris, Copenhagen and other cities, but was particularly impressed with the school a Karlsruhe: 'The polytechnic school of Karlsruhe is perhaps the most efficient one in Prussia; and as its constitution and organization are probably more nearly allied to any similar institution that might arise in this country.'[1] The school was an integrated technical school in the truest sense, covering various branches including agriculture and commerce. He also cited the latest developments in Berlin, where the advanced technical school had been improving technical education in the whole field of engineering. Playfair, it should be noted in passing, would in due course become Dyer's senior at Anderson's College and exert some influence on Dyer's theory of engineering education.

Around 1870, when Dyer was about to go to Japan, more and more reports on the subject became available in Britain. A noteworthy example was a book written by J. S. Russell, *Systematic Technical Education for the English People*, published in 1869. Russell, who was a noted engineer in Scotland, pointed out the problems of British technical education and suggested possible solutions by comparing various continental examples. He made a detailed explanation of the polytechnic schools of such cities as Paris, Karlsruhe and Berlin, and gave full marks to the polytechnic school of Zurich. The book was translated into Japanese by Dairoku Kikuchi, and was published by the Department of Education under the title of *On Professional Education*, which will be discussed again later.

Another influential document was a report entitled, *The Education and Status of Civil Engineers in the United Kingdom and in Foreign Countries*, which was compiled in 1870 by the Institution of Civil Engineers based on replies to a questionnaire by intellectuals in Britain and some other countries. The report showed the actual conditions of technical education of Western nations, including the US and Canada, and giving a detailed account of the polytechnic school of Zurich. The schools listed in the above-mentioned reports can be classified into three categories.

The first is the *École Polytechnique* of France, an institution that provided a fundamental education in preparation for entry to higher institutions of applied science. Having learned rationality through mathematics, natural philosophy, chemistry and other subjects, the graduates proceeded to various areas of study, including the social and cultural sciences.

The second is the integrated technical schools of such cities as Karlsruhr and Zurich. The former was established by J. G. Tulla, a bureaucrat who had once studied in Paris, as noted by Professor Shuichi Ushiogi of Nagoya University in his book *The Birth and Transformation of Modern Colleges*. Playfair was interested in the school in its infancy, and conducted a survey that revealed it possessed two main divisions – a preparatory section with special emphasis on mathematics, and another consisting of seven specialized courses in Engineering, Architecture, Forestry, Chemistry and Technology, Mechanical

Technology, Commerce and Postal Services.[2] The Zurich school also attracted a lot of attention. According to the Institution of Civil Engineers report, it offered a preparatory course and then a specialized course. The latter had six departments: Civil Engineering, Mechanical Engineering, Architecture, Chemistry, Forestry and Agriculture and General Sciences. Except for the last one, certificates of proficiency were conferred. According to the Japanese translation of *Systematic Technical Education for the English People* by Kikuchi, Russell believed Zurich was the ideal model for Britain.

The third is the Berlin technical school. Playfair's research found that the school had integrated preparatory and specialized courses, consisting of three departments: machinery, chemistry and architecture. According to *The History of Industrial Policies in Modern Germany*, written by Professor Hideyuki Takahashi of Kobe University, the school was formerly a *Gewerbeinstitut* or Royal Technical School, which was founded by P. C. W. Beuth, chief of the commercial and industrial bureau in Germany. In 1866, the school was given a new name, *Gewerbeakademie* or technical academy. In 1871, eighteen months or so before Dyer left for Japan, the academy was developed into *Technische Hochschule*, a technical college offering courses in machinery, chemistry, metallurgy and shipbuilding. The college served as a model for other collegiate technical schools covering various fields of industry, and had twenty affiliated local schools for systematic education and training.

Now, we can turn our attention to the situation in Britain. The report by the Institution of Civil Engineers cites twelve institutions related to engineering: King's College (London), University College (London), Royal School of Mines (London), Royal School of Naval Architecture and Marine Engineering (London), University of Edinburgh, Glasgow University, Trinity College (Dublin), Royal College of Science for Ireland (Dublin), Queen's College (Cork), Owen's College (Manchester), The Royal Agricultural College (Cirencester) and Engineering Establishment of the Department of Public Works (India). However, except for the last mentioned, these institutions fell far short of polytechnic schools in concept.

After Japan was opened up to foreign contact towards the end of the Edo era, teachers came from countries with which Japan had treaty relations, promoting the systemization of modern schools and the teaching of Western arts and sciences. At that time schools of engineering were also established in Japan, and, as early as 1855, a kind of navigation school was founded in Nagasaki supported by the Dutch. In 1862, a mining school was set up in Hakodate, an open port in northern Japan, which hired two Americans. In 1865, a school was established at the Yokosuka Ironworks, which had been built with French assistance. The school's chief engineer, Verny, had intended to found a Japanese counterpart of the *École Polytechnique*, and to have its best graduates study at a naval academy in France. He was still teaching shipbuilding in Yokosuka when Dyer arrived in Japan.

☐

Prior to his assignment, Dyer had closely studied the state of engineering education of Britain and some parts of Europe. He recounted later in *Dai Nippon* that he 'had made a special study of all the chief methods of scientific and engineering study in the different countries of the world and of the organization of some of the most important institutions'.[3] He also noted: 'During my time at Glasgow University I had made a special study of the methods of training engineers in Britain, on the Continent, and in America; but they all seemed to me to be very imperfect and one-sided, and I endeavoured to draw out a scheme which would be more complete.'[4]

What were Dyer's sources of information? The Mitchell Library, a major municipal library in Glasgow, provides possible clues. The library was established in 1877, helped by £70,000 in funding bequeathed by S. Mitchell, a Scottish tobacco dealer, and is a treasure-house of valuable information on Dyer, including literature donated by him.

Thus, one can find a bibliography that Dyer drew up in his own handwriting. It is a list of the articles from newspapers and magazines he had gathered and utilized until around 1890. He made the list by ranging articles according to fields of study. The books donated by Dyer, which amount to roughly five thousand in number, are listed in another bibliography.

As regards technical education, Dyer listed about 150 articles covering nine pages. A random sampling is shown in Plate 19. Here, Dyer began by citing Russell's writings, a report by the Institution of Civil Engineers, and articles from such journals as *The Engineer* and *Engineering*.

Nearly half of the 150 articles concerning technical education had been published prior to Dyer's journey in 1873. Thus, he had a considerable amount of information to hand, which he could utilize for the foundation of the Imperial College of Engineering. Dyer collected information from a wide variety of other sources. Searching for articles on technical education, he consulted not only magazines and journals related to his area of study, but also newsletters issued by associations of engineers of both London and Scotland. Dyer's ability to collect data was that of a trained scientist; this is also true of his studies on Japan in later years.

The key question now is: which of the many ideas he collected did Dyer adopt and utilize for the Imperial College of Engineering? In order to find the answer, his subsequent statements and actions must be considered. There are three important points worthy of attention.

Firstly, it is quite probable Dyer made good and effective use of Russell's book, for he later recounted: 'A book which was of great use to me was John Scott Russell's *Systematic Technical Education for the English People*, which gave a very full account of technical education as it then existed on the Continent, and especially in Switzerland and Germany.'[5] The bibliography also lists three essays written by Russell: 'What should mechanical workmen be taught' carried in the 17 January 1859 issue of *The Engineer*, 'On the education of naval architects in England and France' that appeared in 1863 in the fourth volume of the *Transactions of the Institution of Naval Architects*, and 'On the technical education of naval architects in England' carried in its eighth volume in 1867. Dyer highly esteemed Russell, a great engineer from his homeland, so we can be fairly certain he was influenced to a large extent by Russell's writings.

Secondly, Dyer was interested in the educational systems of Germany and Switzerland. The bibliography shows two essays on engineering education in Germany, which appeared in *The Engineer* in 1867 and in *Engineering* in 1870. Dyer recounted that he had been especially impressed with the engineering education of Switzerland, on which he presumably had been informed by Russell's writings and reports from the Institution of Civil Engineers.[6] Dyer also remarked in his lecture in 1893: 'Special reference may be made to the Zurich Polytechnic, as an example of what should be done to encourage higher technical education. Even as an investment the Swiss think that their money has been well spent.'[7] In 1907, he stated in his essay: 'When in 1873, I went to Japan as Principal of the Imperial College of Engineering, I saw that something much more complete was necessary if our college was to be of any use in developing the resources of that country. I took as my model the Polytechnic of Zurich, in which there were very complete curricula in the various departments of engineering'.[8] But, although he used the Swiss educational systems and of that of other continental countries as a reference, he established quite a new kind of college that differed from these models, as I will discuss later.

Thirdly, the bibliography indicates that Dyer paid attention to education in India. He followed the news of the engineering college at Cooper's Hill, which appeared in *The Engineer* on 2 December 1870, on 10 February, 10 March, 24 March, 14 July in 1871, and on 2 August 1872, and in *Engineering* on 27 May and 16 December in 1870, and 14 July and 25 August in 1871. As I mentioned earlier, that college was founded to train engineers who would work for the Department of Public Works of India, and Morel recommended the Japanese Government to establish the Department of Public Works, which must have been modelled on that of India. Dyer also showed an interest in the situation in India, although, in Britain, there were arguments for and against the college of India, and the Institution of Civil Engineers even offered strong opposition to the concept. Dyer also expressed critical views: 'It is no reproach to the excellent staff of Cooper's Hill College, when I say that in my opinion the Government made a mistake in founding this college, for the reasons given above.'[9]

☐

Dyer left Southampton and arrived in Tokyo on 3 June 1873. Tadasu Hayashi, who had been asked by Ito to assist Dyer on his journey, accompanied him. Hayashi was one of the students sent to Britain by the Tokugawa government in its closing days, and later he would serve as the Japanese Minister in London, signing the Anglo-Japanese Alliance Treaty in 1902. On reaching Japan with Dyer, Hayashi was transferred from the Department of Foreign Affairs to the Department of Public Works, where he provided administrative and financial support for Dyer's educational challenge.

During the two-month voyage to Japan, Dyer was engaged in writing a draft of the college curriculum (in those days usually referred to as a 'Calendar'). He must have given consideration to Hayashi's advice on the situation of Japan, especially on the school that Verny had founded in Yokosuka. By the time he arrived in Japan, Dyer had completed this work. He later recounted: 'My time on the voyage was chiefly occupied in writing a draft of the Calendar of the proposed College, and on my arrival in Tokyo I was able to present it complete to the Acting Vice-Minister of Public Works, and it was accepted by the Government without change of any kind.'[10] The Acting Vice-Minister mentioned here was Yozo Yamao.

The original document that Dyer drafted on the voyage and presented to Yamao has not yet been discovered. On receiving it, however, Yamao started the process of accepting enrolment applications, making many amendments to the college programmes issued by the Department of Public Works the previous year. To cite the most significant amendment, the preparatory school that had been included in Yamao's plan was eliminated and the institution at collegiate level was set up, that is, the Imperial College of Engineering. The aim of the college was to train students in such branches of technical education as Civil Engineering, Mechanical Engineering, Telegraphy, Architecture, Practical Chemistry, Mining and Metallurgy. Shipbuilding was not included, probably out of consideration for Verny. Six years were required for graduation from the college, and students were to devote the first and second years to the preparatory course, the third and fourth years to professional studies, and the final two years to practical work. Based on the amended programme, the Department of Public Works conducted entrance examinations in August. A total of 56 students were admitted and began their studies on 1 October 1873.

Soon after classes began, the syllabus appeared in printed form (See Plate 20), containing such additions as the questions posed in the entrance examinations and the names of successful applicants. The English version was released earlier than its Japanese counterpart, which only appeared as part of the college programme in the following year, 1874. Dyer's document offers three noteworthy features considered to have come from his own original thinking.

First, the college was to cover seven branches of technical studies, as already stated. Such an extent of sub-division in engineering was unprecedented at that time. Moreover, the college was founded for engineering education exclusively, unlike the polytechnic schools in Zurich and elsewhere.

Secondly, a newly devised method of education was proposed:

> The course of training will extend over six years. During the first four years six months of each year will be spent at College, and six months in the practice of that particular branch the student may select. The last two years of the course will be spent wholly in practical work. By this alternation of theory and practice the students will be able during each working half year to make practical application of the principles acquired in the previous half year. The system of instruction will be partly what is usually termed professional and partly tutorial, consisting in the delivery of lectures, and in directions and assistance being given to the students in their work.

The alternation of theory with practice and the combination of professional and tutorial methods were both new and experimental models that Dyer created by blending the traditions of British education and Continental methods. These unique models will be discussed further in later pages.

Thirdly, special consideration was given to the educational facilities. The syllabus contains regulations on use of the Library, the Physical and Chemical Laboratories, the Workshop and the Technical Museum. To take the Physical Laboratory as an example, its special objective was 'to enable students to become practically acquainted with the fundamental laws of Physical Science, as a foundation for accurate reasoning upon physical phenomena, and the applications of the Principles of Physics to Engineering.' To take another instance, the intent of the Technical Museum is given as follows: 'Attached to each department of the College will be a hall, containing models of apparatus and works having special relation to that department. There, the students will pass hours of leisure or work, amid familiar illustrations, systematically developed and methodically arranged.' Dyer's ideal of the 'education of engineers', with which he prefaced the syllabus, found expression in those educational facilities as well.

These three ideas were realized, resulting in some of the remarkable features of the Imperial College of Engineering. On the other hand, some of the ideas were not implemented. Take diplomas as an example: in Dyer's plan, the college was to confer two levels of degree, that is to say, the Licentiate of Engineering and Master of Engineering. He had hoped to introduce into Japan the degree of the Licentiate adopted on the Continent. Instead, the Bachelor of Engineering was the degree finally introduced, in accordance with practice at the University of Tokyo and other government schools. In those days, the Faculty of Science of the University of Tokyo also covered some areas of engineering, but it only offered the degree of Bachelor of Science. Thus, by 1885, the Imperial College of Engineering was the only institution offering a Bachelor of Engineering degree to its students. The college set much stricter conditions for the degree, and by 1885 it had conferred the degree on only 61 out of 211 graduates, although the University of Tokyo gave bachelor degrees to all its graduates.

Based on the English version, the Japanese version of the syllabus was released in 1874 in the form of the college's programmes and regulations. Its explanations of the purport of Dyer's original covered the minutest detail. Thus, the English version contained 17 articles in its main text and 37 articles relating to the syllabus, along with the content of the entrance examinations and the names of successful applicants in its appendix. In the Japanese programmes and regulations, the text was divided into 79 articles. Japanese people were experienced in making these kinds of rules, as they had done for the clan schools and private schools during the Edo period. Later, quite a few additions and revisions were made to both the English and Japanese documents. Plate 21 shows two editions of Dyer's syllabus with his compliments written on their title pages that were released in 1875 and 1876, respectively.

☐

As already noted, Dyer had collected a mass of information on the engineering education of Britain and of the rest of the world. However, when working on the draft syllabus of the Imperial College of Engineering, he did not want to follow the example of any one specific country or institution – a stark contrast with Clark, the principal of Sapporo Agricultural College, who chose to implant into Japan the system of Massachusetts Agricultural College, where he was the president in active service. It may well be that Dyer did not find any institution in Britain good enough to serve as a model, and perhaps his British pride prevented him from turning to the Continent instead.

The ideal with which Dyer prefaced his prospectus centred on the 'education of engineers'; this was emphasized in his address to the first intake of students on their graduation as recorded in his book *The Education of Engineers*. It was also a phrase he often used subsequently in compiling books and papers on engineering education.

Before entering a detailed discussion of the education of engineers, we must try to clarify Dyer's definition of this breed. He stated: 'There seems to be a popular impression that an engineer is necessarily a man connected with a steam engine, and that the title "engineer" is derived from "engine". The reverse is the case, and "engineer" is derived from a word which implies the employment of one's ingenuity in the solution of any problem whatever, so that its application might be made very extensive.'[11] On another occasion, he observed: 'The Latin word *ingenium*, or the equivalent old French word *engin* means an innate or natural quality, while another old French word, *s'ingenier*, means to set one's mental powers in action to solve any problem whatever. From an etymological point of view, therefore, the name "engineer" is wide enough to include every profession, and "engineering" may be (and very often now is) applied to subjects not usually included in the work of engineers.'[12] Thus, he interpreted the word 'engineer' in a broad sense. Accordingly, when the Imperial College of Engineering was founded, its departments covered not only civil and mechanical engineering, but also various other fields. In fact, he explained the College departments as follows: 'The term "engineering" is wide enough to include all the professions connected with the great industries, and in the college in Japan I arranged for the following divisions being recognized and taught.'[13]

Dyer maintained that engineers should be members of a 'learned profession'.[14] He was determined that they should be trained just like doctors and lawyers, belonging to long-established learned professions. He insisted that the following three requirements should be met in the education of engineers.

In the first place, a great scholastic ability in a specialized field was absolutely necessary for membership of a learned profession. Dyer stated in his lecture: 'The earliest universities were organized to meet the wants of the professions, those for instance of Solerno and Bologna being distinguished as special schools for law and medicine respectively, long before they had courses for the liberal arts.'[15] He looked back on the history of universities and colleges in the world, including Scotland: 'The Scotch universities are essentially professional schools for the training of teachers, clergymen, lawyers and doctors. I do not suppose that this opinion is likely to be disputed by those who know anything about them, and I will not enter into an argument to prove it.'[16] He maintained that various areas of engineering studies were essential in college education for the establishment of a new learned profession of engineers.

In the second place, scholastic ability had to be allied with practical skill. That idea was taken as a matter of course in Scotland, as evidenced when Dyer himself engaged in an apprenticeship before going to Glasgow University. Furthermore, Rankine and Gordon had spent long years gaining practical experience before and after their college studies. However, the Japanese students of the Imperial College of Engineering, who were still proud of coming from the Edo period's uppermost social class of 'samurai', tended to dismiss the value of engaging in practical training in working clothes, which made Dyer even more emphatic about its importance. As he told the graduates:

> Unless your knowledge and skill in your profession have been gained in such a way as to train your mind to original, individual, creative ideas, you are the slave, not the master, of your learning, and it is likely to remain utterly useless to yourself and to others. It is especially necessary to impress upon Japanese students the distinction between knowledge and education.[17]

He also remarked: 'The instruction is thus made as thoroughly practical as it can be at a College, but by our connection with the Public

Works Department, we are able to make it still more so, by sending the students out to actual work, during the summer sessions of the third and fourth years.'[18] In his farewell address on leaving Japan, he recounted: 'I have always insisted on the necessity of making the education which is given in Japan at the present time of a thoroughly practical nature, as I cannot admit that any culture is worth the name which does not make a man independent of his friends or the government.'[19]

Lastly, Dyer valued general education covering a wide range of studies, since engineers were seen as prone to narrow views or actions. *The Education of Engineers* carries his lectures not only on professional education but also on 'non-professional education'. Thus:

> As I said a few days ago, you may be very well informed as to the ordinary details of your professions, but still be unfitted in a high degree, for taking a wide impartial view of matters, and all your opinions on public affairs will be apt to be biassed by professional selfishness and class prejudices. If you are entire strangers to the world of literature, philosophy and art, and to such sciences as are not immediately utilized in your profession, you will be unable to escape from the narrowness, prejudices and passions which beset most professional men.[20]

Later, he put greater emphasis on the need to provide general education for engineers, which is indicated in his theories on educational and social reforms. For example, in his essay written in later years, he stated:

> In conclusion, I should like to say that I consider one of the great defects of technical education at the present time is the want of a good general education on the part of the students. A man who has only been technically educated is, as a rule, a very poor specimen of humanity, whose interests are, for the most part, confined to his own little sphere and to making of money. Real intellectual pleasure – apart from his work – seems to be unknown to him and he is apt to degenerate both intellectually and morally.[21]

In order to realize his ideal of great scholastic ability combined with practical skill and a general education, Dyer had to create an original and elaborate plan regarding the college's educational programmes and methods. Turning to the various precedents to be found around the world, he thought that the Continental polytechnic placed too much emphasis on theoretical studies, and that engineering education in Britain overrated empirical studies. He came to believe strongly that 'it requires a judicious combination of both systems to train men who are likely to become successful engineers'.[22] Thus, he came up with the idea of dividing the six-year course into three phases of general and scientific education, professional studies and practical training. His original method of combining theory and practice is especially noteworthy. As he recounted: 'In the College itself mere book-work was made of secondary importance; and by means of drawing offices, laboratories, and practical engineering works, the students were taught the relations between theory and practice, and trained in habits of observation and logical thought.'[23]

To attain Dyer's ideal, even a six-year course was too short. Therefore, he encouraged the students to spare as many leisure hours as possible for their studies. He told the graduates that 'the time at our disposal is so short, that unless your College training be supplemented by after studies, it will not fulfil Milton's definition of a complete and generous education as "that which fits a man to perform justly, skilfully, and magnanimously all the offices, both private and public, of peace and war".'[24] Also: 'A man ought to be trained intellectually, physically and morally to perform the duties which are likely to fall to his lot, but the whole system should form something like a harmonious unity, and the result should be in the first place a man, and in the second an architect, an engineer, or anything else.'[25] The essence of Dyer's theory on engineering education was well-integrated individual growth and progress, and this should be borne in mind as the story unfolds.

☐

It took five years to complete the buildings of the Imperial College of Engineering. On 15 July 1878, the opening ceremony was finally held in the presence of Emperor Meiji. An imperial message declared that the college should promote national well-being. It should be noted that the college was meant for the welfare of the nation, not specifically for the development of armaments. In the ceremony, Dyer made a formal reply and declared that the college had proved to be a success, already enjoying fame and prosperity after only five years of operation.

In the following year, when the first student intake was about to graduate, Dyer again touched upon the college's success in two documents. One is the aforementioned record of his lecture to the graduates, *The Education of Engineers*, and the other is *The Education of Civil and Mechanical Engineers*, covering the proposals that Dyer presented to the Institution of Civil Engineering in London, which was published the following year. Both documents provide a vivid account of Dyer's deep emotion in recognizing the success of the six-year programme of study as evidenced by the graduates' ability as practising engineers. He observed: 'As our most advanced students are only in their sixth year, and have not yet received their diplomas, it is still too early to speak of results; but as far as we have gone, the progress has been very satisfactory, and I have not the slightest hesitation in saying that at the end of their course these men will be able to act as useful assistant engineers.'[26]

Soon after he returned to Glasgow in 1882, he stated in a lecture: 'Since I left Glasgow, nearly eleven years ago, I have taken the chief part in organizing and managing what is now one of the most complete Technical Colleges in existence. I think it will be admitted that I have had sufficient experience of the subject to justify my opinions being at least carefully considered.'[27] In another lecture, in 1887, he observed: 'I might have pointed to the Imperial College of Engineering in Japan, which I had the honour of organizing and in which very complete courses of instruction were given ...'[28] He was quite sure of the success of the college when he was working on *Dai Nippon*, which was published in 1904. He declared in the book that he dedicated it 'to the students of the Kobu-Daigakko who have done so much to make modern Japan', giving them the credit for Japan's modernization and industrialization.

In his lecture in 1905, Dyer was more emphatic about the success of the college, affirming that 'in five years we had one of most complete and well-equipped colleges in any part of the world.'[29] It should be noted in passing that he often used the word 'complete' in referring to the college, and he reinforced the adjective with the words 'most' or 'very'.

In this same lecture, he considered the factors that had contributed to the success as follows:

> I have always held that in educational work those responsible for it should have an ideal towards which they were working, and not be content to follow an opportunist policy without any definite plan. The difficulties in Japan were great, on account of the want of preliminary training on the part of the students; but we had the great advantage of beginning with a clean sheet, and we had no personal or vested interests to contend with. The Japanese Government gave a most hearty support to all my proposals; the professors were enthusiastic in their work, and the students were diligent and intelligent.[30]

In this quotation, he touched upon at least five factors that had worked favourably towards the success of the Imperial College of Engineering.

The first was the practical nature of the educational ideal of Dyer himself. He had high hopes of realizing his theories of engineering education coupled with humanistic education, so that engineers would be also good citizens. The second was the opportunity of starting from scratch, with the resultant freedom from conflicts of interest. Educators in Britain at that time were prone to look after their own interests, and took quite a long time to reach a consensus, which was one reason for the delayed reform of British engineering education. The third was the generous financial support from the Japanese Government, which was even out of proportion to the national budget of the time, for teachers' salaries, students' bursaries, school buildings, facilities, equipment and other expenditures. The fourth was the wholehearted support from other foreign teachers. Dyer won the cooperation of such distinguished teachers as Divers, who would succeed him as principal, Ayrton and Perry, both of whom would work for the establishment of a technical college in London, Conder of Architecture and Milne of Geology and Mining. The fifth was the intelligent and hardworking student intake. After graduation, they lived up to Dyer's expectations, exhibiting their abilities in industrial, academic and educational circles.

In addition to these five factors, Dyer placed great emphasis on the spirit of the Japanese people. He often pointed out that 'the spiritual is the parent and first cause of the practical',[31] which he found exemplified by the students of the Imperial College of Engineering. He observed in *Dai Nippon* that

[M]y own experience with Japanese students has always been, in every way, most pleasant. Eager and persevering in their studies, and with abilities which compare favourably with those of students in any part of the world, they retained a great part of their native politeness and gave no trouble to teachers in the course of their work.[32]

Dyer also perceived this great spirit in the efforts on the part of the Japanese authorities to establish a nation, and noted: 'The Japanese authorities did all in their power to bring about that success. Within five years from its institution, handsome and commodious buildings had been erected and the most improved appliances of all kinds supplied for teaching purposes.'[33] The buildings were designed by C. A. de Boinville, who was from Glasgow, of British and French descent. In 1877, the buildings in the Renaissance style were completed. W. G. Dixon, who taught English at the college, referred to the buildings as the 'handsomest which the Government has yet erected in foreign style' in the record of his personal experiences in Japan.[34] The original plan of the buildings, on which Dyer offered suggestions, is indicated in Figure 26. The auditorium was in the centre, and the left wing was not completed. There were other buildings for teachers and for students in the college precinct.

Furthermore, the facilities and equipment in the buildings were quite remarkable, as Dixon noted:

> ... the collection of engineering models is said to be the most complete in the world ... The classrooms are arranged exactly as they might be in a European College, while the various laboratories and drawing offices are furnished with the most improved appliances. Indeed, the arrangements as a whole speak volumes for the enlightened liberality of the officers of the Public Works Department, with which the college is connected. There can be no doubt that they are more complete than the arrangements usually found in the scientific colleges of England.[35]

The Library of the Imperial College of Engineering, Tokei, which I touched upon in connection with Rankine's manuals, contains 1,160 foreign books and journals, and 102 Japanese books that were available for students in 1876, three years after the college opened. In the case of foreign books in great demand, dozens of copies were made available, which must have been quite costly.

The grandeur of the buildings was inscribed in a memorial tower, which is still in the backyard of the Board of Audit, in Toranomon, Tokyo. One of the first graduates, Tatsuzo Sone, noted in the inscription that the brick two-storey buildings in the Renaissance style with museums, laboratories, works and the student centre presented a grand sight. The inscription also says that the memorial tower was built from the debris of the buildings destroyed in the 1923 Tokyo Earthquake.

Also, we should not overlook the Akabane Works, which Dyer supervised and utilized for the practical student training starting in May 1874. It was originally opened in 1871 as an ironworks, where machines presented by the Saga Clan were used. Dyer recounted:

> When I went to Japan in 1873, comparatively small mechanical engineering establishments were found in Tokyo, Yokohama, Kobe, and Nagasaki, but they were inadequate for the proper training of students, and large works were started under my management in connection with the Public Works Department at Akabane, Tokyo, in which the majority of the students of the Imperial College of Engineering spent considerable time.[36]

The Japanese authorities' determination for industrialization is also disclosed in the following remark by Dyer that the machines and fittings '. . . are of sufficient size to turn out as heavy work as likely to be required in Japan for some years. The number of workmen employed averages about 300 and the receipts for work done per annum from £20,000 to £30,000.'[37]

☐

The success of the engineering education offered was recognized not only by Dyer but by quite a few observers. Before referring to articles in newspapers and magazines in the coming section, let me quote from those who were related to the college and other impartial observers: Dyer's colleagues, his friends, his students and the Japanese authorities.

First, there is the observation by Divers, an outstanding scholar who discovered hyponitrite. He made a great contribution to the success of the Imperial College of Engineering by providing generous support for Dyer, who was eleven years younger. At the farewell party for Dyer prior to returning to Britain, Divers delivered an address on behalf of the teachers. An article of the 1 July 1882 issue of *The Japan Weekly Mail* reports: 'Dr Edward Divers, speaking in the name of his colleagues, expressed hearty admiration for the untiring zeal and earnestness of purpose which had succeeded in establishing in Japan an institution more than once publicly acknowledged to be unrivalled elsewhere in thoroughness of system and completeness of detail.'[38]

On Dyer's recommendation, Divers succeeded him as principal. After the Imperial University was founded, Divers gained a position at the College of Science and stayed in Japan until 1899. Shortly before he left Japan, an essay minimizing Dyer's achievements was carried in *The Engineer*. The writer was R. H. Smith, formerly an engineering teacher at Tokyo Kaiseigakko, the predecessor of the Imperial University. Divers contributed a long essay in refutation:

> While, as will have become plain, there are many engineers who may claim to have each done something in Japanese training – and, in individual cases sometimes very much – there is, it may truly be said, and in justice must be said, one to whom, almost alone, Japan owes its well-organized and elaborated system of engineering educa-tion, namely, to Dr Henry Dyer, of Glasgow, one of the Governors of the Glasgow and West of Scotland Technical College . . . He first arrived in Japan in June, 1873, was appointed head professor, and occupied at the same time the Chair of Civil Engineering. At this time the College was still in its infancy; and he set himself to plan the curriculum, and formulated the various College rules and regu-lations. He also planned the College buildings. As head professor he

discharged his duties with untiring diligence for the long period of almost ten years.[39]

Secondly, let me quote from two of Dyer's friends, both of whom taught at the University of Tokyo. One is J. A. Ewing of Mechanical Engineering, who later returned to Britain to become a professor at Cambridge University. It would be useful to refer to Ewing's testimonial for Dyer, which was written when the latter applied for a professorship of Glasgow University in 1886. Ewing stated:

> During a residence in Tokio for five years, I had the pleasure of knowing you and your work well. When you went to Japan to organize the Imperial College of Engineering you were exceptionally fortunate in being allowed a much freer hand than the Japanese authorities generally give their foreign officers. They let you carry out your own plans, and if you were fortunate in this respect, the Japanese were not less fortunate in the results. In a few years you created a college which is one of the best technical schools to be seen in any country. In it you presided over an able staff for ten years; and the high class work done in 'Dyer's College' (as we residents in Tokio always called it) was sufficiently evidenced by the frequent contributions to science which found their way from its laboratories to the public through the medium of the Royal, the Chemical and other Societies.

The other friend of Dyer's that I would like to mention is R. W. Atkinson of Applied Chemistry of the University of Tokyo, a British teacher known for his book on Japanese brewing. When Atkinson learned from his friend that Dyer was applying for the post at Glasgow University, he sent a testimonial to the university and observed:

> My acquaintance with Mr Dyer dates from the year 1874, when I became impressed with the value of his work in organising the Imperial College of Engineering in Tokio, Japan. In that year I entered the service of the Educational Department of the Japanese Government, Mr Dyer being in that of Public Works, and although we were not in any way connected I had frequent opportunities of knowing how the College under Mr Dyer's direction progressed. I may say that, owing to a certain amount of jealousy between the two departments of government, I had every opportunity of criticizing unfavourably, if it had been possible, the work of Mr Dyer. The College, however, was so well founded, and so ably conducted, that no opportunity was offered to its hostile critics of doing more than carping at minor details, and it gave the sincere friends of education in Japan every reason to rejoice that the care of engineering education was in such able hands.

It is interesting to note that British teachers employed by the Educational Department were jealous of the success of the Imperial College of Engineering, as is implied in Atkinson's remark and in Smith's aforementioned essay.

Thirdly, let me turn to Dyer's students, who sent him a letter of appreciation when he was leaving Japan. According to *The Japan Weekly Mail*, they wrote: 'We consider it needless to make any lengthy mention of your labours for our benefit, as it will suffice to say that mainly through your exertions the College has attained a thorough organization, and by your care and attention we have carefully completed our studies in it.'[40] The students also expressed their gratitude as follows: 'Be assured that we have a deep sense of what we personally owe to you, and that all you have done for us will be remembered by grateful hearts' (Ibid.). The writer of the article added: 'In laying these addresses before our readers, we are glad to have the opportunity of supplementing our remarks on the absence of appreciative sympathy in Japan by a most cordial testimony to the earnestness and industry of Japanese students' (Ibid.). The graduates of the Imperial College of Engineering also expressed their feelings towards Dyer in other documents related to the college and in their personal biographies.

Lastly, let me discuss the statement of Hirobumi Ito, representing the Japanese authorities. Ito worked on the negotiations for Dyer's assignment in Japan and admired his achievements greatly. In *Dai Nippon*, Dyer mentioned Ito's visit to Britain for the preliminary negotiation of the Anglo-Japanese Treaty of 1902:

> Marquis Ito was unable to visit Scotland as he had expected to do, as events called him back to Japan, but Viscount Hayashi wrote stating that the Marquis had expressed his high appreciation of my services in Japan, saying, 'That Japan can boast today of being able to undertake such industrial works as the construction of railways, telegraphs, telephones, shipbuilding, working of mines and other manufacturing works entirely by the hands of Japanese engineers is mainly attributable to the College so ably established and set in motion by you.'[41]

Dyer was the first Briton to be decorated by the Japanese Government. Due to the lack of precedents, the government went through prior consultations with its British counterpart on its own practice of decoration. Twelve documents stored at the Diplomatic Record Office of the Ministry of Foreign Affairs provide us with the details. On 20 April 1882, when Dyer was leaving Japan, Kaoru Inoue, the Minister of Foreign Affairs, was requested by the authorities to make inquiries so that Dyer would be invested with the Third Class of the Order of the Rising Sun without contradicting any British ordinances concerning decoration. Inoue conveyed the request to Arinori Mori, the Japanese envoy extraordinaire and minister plenipotentiary to Britain, who replied on 21 July that he had obtained royal permission from Britain on the matter, and even sent Inoue a copy of the document. Further negotiations were conducted by the Minister of Foreign Affairs and Minister Mori in relation to the procedures involved in the decoration, until the Order was officially bestowed via Mori on Dyer after he returned to Britain. The Ministry of Foreign Affairs documents include an outline of Dyer's career written in quite an exquisite style, and presumably by Keisuke Otori, who was the head of the Imperial College of Engineering as the director of the engineering division, expressing the sincerest admiration for Dyer. In 1908, he was elevated to the Second Class of the Order of the Sacred Treasure.

□

In the days before mass media, the first report of the opening of the Imperial College of Engineering was via diplomatic channels, namely the British Legation in Tokyo. *The Embassy and Consular Commercial Report, 1872–76*, includes the original version of the curriculum in a report entitled 'The Present Educational System of Japan' that found its way into the parliamentary papers in due course. It was forwarded from Secretary Watson at the British Legation to Minister Parkes on 30 November 1873, and from him to Earl Granville on 29 December. Plate 30 shows the opening page of its recent republication.

In an accompanying letter to Earl Granville, Parkes wrote: 'I have the honour to forward a Report which has been drawn up by Mr Watson, with great care, on the present Educational System of Japan. It details the measures adopted by the Government since they entered on a course of educational reform, based upon foreign principles; and it describes the beneficial results that can already be pointed to, and the prospects that may be anticipated in the future.' Enclosure 1 deals with Watson's report, including his letter to Parkes in which he described the difficulties in collecting information due to an undeveloped statistics system and inefficient interpreters in Japan. Enclosure 2 shows the essay that Parkes found helpful, which had appeared in *The Japan Weekly Mail*.

Watson also made in the report an abridged translation of the Education System Order promulgated by the Department of

Education the year before. In his report, Watson gave information on those aspects of Japan's educational situation to which he had access, mostly related to the Imperial College of Engineering. He would most certainly have found the syllabus helpful, since it was available in English and easy to quote.

British newspapers and magazines also carried articles on the syllabus, which was available in book form, including distinguished journals such as *Nature*, *Engineering* and *The Engineer*. For example, an article that appeared in *Nature* noted: 'A copy of the Calendar for 1873–4, of the Imperial College of Engineering, Tokei, Japan, has been forwarded us. The course of study prescribed, both general and special, theoretical and practical, and the regulations for the government of the College, appear to us to be all that at present could be desired.'[42] *The Engineer* admired both the curriculum and the quality of printing:

> As an example of what a government engineering college should be, we cannot do better than cite the institution at Tokei in Japan. The Japanese Government are in just the same position as that of India. They want engineers and they have established a college to supply them. The Calendars of this college for 1873 and 1874 lie before us, and they contain a great deal that is eminently suggestive ... [it] has been set up by Japanese compositors in the college, and printed from type cast there, and it is not too much to say that both the type and composition are thoroughly excellent, the only defects we have detected being met within some of the algebraic signs.[43]

In addition, the reports compiled by the principal and by the professors on the four years of operation from 1873 to 1877, which were published in the latter year, attracted much attention in Britain. Dyer worked on the 62-page report, that is, *General Report by the Principal for the Period 1873–77*, while the professors compiled *Class Reports by the Professors for the Period 1873–77*, extending to 72 pages. Copies are kept at the college record office of the University of Tokyo. They must have followed the example of the teachers of Tokyo Kaiseigakko, who regularly sent reports on their educational activities to the Department of Education. The reports were instrumental in making the visions and endeavours of the Imperial College of Engineering known in English-speaking countries. Their media coverage will be discussed later.

Only one of Dyer's letters written during his stay in Japan has survived. Interestingly, it deals with curriculum matters and was sent to Kiyotaka Kuroda, who directed the reclamation of Hokkaido. In it, Dyer thanked Kuroda for the first yearly report of Sapporo Agricultural

College and promised to return the favour by sending him the new edition of the syllabus of the Imperial College of Engineering, as illustrated in Plate 31. Incidentally, I have tried to locate other editions of the Calendar (curriculum) still kept in Japan, but it proved to be a long search. The National Diet Library has the original edition of 1873, the editions of 1875 and of 1876 with Dyer's signatures on them (See Plates 20 and 21), and the editions of 1878, 1879 and 1884. The National Archives have the 1881 edition, while the Department of Engineering at the University of Tokyo has the editions of 1876, 1877, 1878, 1879, 1880, 1883, 1884 and 1885, which were donated by one of the fourth-term graduates.

□

English-language newspapers issued in Japan were the most helpful source of information on Japan for British people. Newspapers such as *The Japan Punch* and *The Japan Herald* appeared in the late Edo period, and were still published after the Meiji Restoration. However, the first fully-fledged instance of mass media would have to be *The Japan Weekly Mail* of British origin, the first edition of which appeared in March 1870. Its reprinted editions, covering its first appearance through to 1917, are available in the Yokohama Archives of History and are a valuable source of information on the Imperial College of Engineering.

Even after the college was established, *The Japan Weekly Mail* did not initially record its activities, even though it did carry articles on other educational institutions in Japan. I will now refer to issues of the year 1873, when the college was founded. We can find such articles as 'Mr Mori's Letter,'[44] 'Foreign Education in Japan',[45] 'The Sunday Question in Relation to the Foreign College',[46] 'Education in Japan',[47] 'The Opening of the New Polytechnic School by Mikado',[48] 'The School of Foreign Languages in Tokei',[49] 'The Tokei Normal School',[50] and 'Education in Japan, I, Foreign Teachers'.[51] The article 'Education in Japan' is the first of a nine-part series of essays by W. E. Griffis, an American teacher at Tokyo Kaiseigakko. The series continued until 7 March of the following year, and concluded with the theme of moral education. Although the 1 November issue carried a story of a polytechnic school opened by the Emperor, it focused on Tokyo Kaiseigakko, and did not touch upon the Imperial College of Engineering. The schools described were all related to the Ministry of Education.

It was not until February 1878, that an article on the Imperial

College of Engineering finally appeared in *The Japan Weekly Mail*. It then carried articles on the college in two consecutive issues; its comments were a mixture of admiration and criticism of the syllabus of 1877 and of the reports by the principal and professors. The first article in the 9 February issue noted it had received the relevant documents 'and gladly take the opportunity thus afforded of reviewing the history and prospects of this important college, which under the able direction of its principal, Mr Henry Dyer, has already done something for the education of engineers in Japan and unquestionably possesses the capacity of doing a great deal'.[52]

Discussing the reports in the following issue of 16 February, the newspaper began with outspoken criticism on the reports by the professors. In its view, the drawing courses taught by Mr Mondy followed the narrow-minded and formal ideas that the South Kensington Science and Art Department had once adopted, and the physics classes were crippled because the time spent on teaching maths was not enough. It was also noted that the architecture course of Conder was not ready and that the museum for that subject was still to be established. Among other criticisms, the lack of the chair of Naval Architecture was also highlighted. The writer, however, did praise the classes by Ayrton and Perry for their originality and ingenuity in educational methods.

The article went on to review the principal's report, and pointed out one important problem that challenged the unqualified optimism on the college's success. The core educational philosophy of the college, in other words, the combination of theory and practice, was also criticized:

> [W]e cannot accept Principal Dyer's solution of the difficulty of judging between the old English and the French systems. He says, 'The English used to blunder stupidly, for they gave their pupils practice alone without any theory, while the French become inordinately intellectual because they theorize alone and do not condescend to practice; let us Japanese avoid the mistakes of both and content ourselves with one half of the practice of the English along with one quarter of the theory of the French.[53]

The *Weekly* noted that the Imperial College of Engineering had the six-year course of training, with the first two years spent in preparatory studies, and the last two years wholly in practical work. The third and forth years were divided equally between theory teaching and practical work, so the students had only twelve months for specialized studies of theory. In the British educational system, the course of the first two years was regarded as secondary education, and the practical work of the last two years corresponded to apprenticeship and was not to be part of the course of school education. Moreover, the term of apprenticeship in Britain extended to five or seven years, and the two-year practical work of the Imperial College of Engineering was considered too short. The article went on with its criticism to observe: 'the main object of the college, namely the scientific education of engineers, can hardly be said to be accomplished; and this for want of somewhat more earnest and profound conception of the meaning of engineering education. A broader and more liberal view must be taken of the modern relations between industry and science'.[54]

This criticism was also related to the difference between the education of the Imperial College of Engineering and that of the University of Tokyo. The name of the writer of the article is not given, but it could have been Smith or Atkinson, given that the article was probably written by a British teacher of engineering at the University of Tokyo. Indeed, Smith ignored the Imperial College of Engineering in his theory on engineering education, which is expressed in his Valedictory Address, to the Engineering Students of the University of Tokyo, July, 1877. However, Smith left Japan in July 1877 after expounding that theory, and it must have been Atkinson that wrote the article. As noted in the previous chapter, Atkinson said in his testimonial for Dyer that he had criticized Dyer's work, standing by the side of the Department of Education. The criticism that the teaching of engineering science was neglected must have struck deep into Dyer's heart.

The next account of the Imperial College of Engineering appeared in the 24 August issue of the same year, when *The Japan Weekly Mail* expressed its full admiration for the college, referring to articles in *The Engineer* and noting:

> The following highly commendatory notice of Mr Dyer's work at this institution, as recorded in his Report which was published early this year and reviewed in these columns, we take from *The Engineer* the highest English authority on these subjects ... And – a very unusual thing in the case of an English newspaper writing on Japanese matters – the praise is not undeserved nor the statement of fact exaggerated.[55]

Probably the newspaper had no choice but to reverse its previous critical views when such an authoritative British professional journal had praised it so highly. Take the coverage on financial matters as an example. In its 16 February 1878 issue, the *Weekly* voiced some tough remarks on Dyer's statement on the generous financial support he had obtained from the Department of Public Works, and on the example of the Swiss effort that the Japanese had followed. The newspaper thundered: 'We have no hesitation in saying that the evident pretensions of the college far exceed its actual performances.'[56] Six months later, however, it had adopted a much gentler tone: 'they have had their money's worth'.[57] This proved to be a major turning point in its coverage of the Imperial College of Engineering.

Its 26 October 1878 issue gave detailed information on Ayrton's physical laboratory, under the title of 'A Visit to Professor Ayrton's Laboratory.'[58] Ayrton later utilized his educational experiences at this laboratory for a technical college in London. The 15 November 1879 issue carried a story on the college's graduation ceremony held a week earlier, which was attended by members of the Imperial Family, the Prime Minister, the Minister of Finance, the Minister of Education, the Minister of Navy, the Minister of Army, the Minister of Public Works, and diplomats of various countries.[59] As previously mentioned, the address delivered by Dyer on this occasion was entitled *The Education of Engineers* and published by the college. The 1 July 1882 issue of the *Weekly*, meanwhile, gave an account of the farewell party in honour of Dyer, in which the writer observed: 'We, too, cannot allow the occasion to pass without adding our testimony to the high qualities which have deservedly won for Mr Dyer the applause of his employers and the good opinion of his colleagues.'[60]

□

Now, let us take a brief look at the comments made by the three major journals: *Nature, Engineering* and *The Engineer*.

Nature

Nature, which had developed the reputation as a reliable science journal, was quick in its newsgathering. On the day following the signing of the Agreement between Matheson and Dyer in Britain, it carried an article with the title of 'An Engineering College in Japan' in which it remarked:

> The Japanese Government, as represented by the ambassadors who visited this country last summer and autumn, have resolved upon taking example by our western civilisation, and establishing a college in the city of Yeddo for affording instruction in civil and mechanical engineering to the youth of Japan, as a strong desire has arisen in that country to make an effort to develop the great natural resources which it is known to possess. Our advice and practical

assistance in the establishment of the college have been called into requisition, owing to the ambassadors having observed during their sojourn amongst us, how intimately our eminent industrial status as a nation is dependent upon the attention which we devote to the cultivation of those sciences which are involved in the mining, metallurgical, engineering, and many manufacturing industries, and in bringing the forces of nature under the influence of man.[61]

It was more than four years before, in May 1877, the next article on the Imperial College of Engineering appeared in *Nature*. That long article, entitled 'Engineering Education in Japan', admired the fusion of theory and practice that was characteristic of the college. The writer whose name is just given as C. W. C. stated:

The technical education of engineers is a subject which has engaged public attention for a long time past and is one of great national importance. It is somewhat singular that this country, foremost as it has always been in matters of engineering enterprise, should be so behindhand in the systematic education of its engineers, there being no establishment in England devoted to that object which is recognised by the profession.[62]

Admitting that engineering education in Britain was largely dependent upon practical training, the writer declared:

The Continental system goes to the other extreme, teaching the theory and discarding the practice. It can only be by a judicious combination of the two systems, allowing science and practical experience to work hand in hand together in the education of an engineer that the best results can be looked for.

The writer went on:

While England is so far behindhand in this important question, a great work has been done by the Japanese Government in the establishment of an Imperial College of Engineering at Tokei, an institution which gives to its students a highly scientific training, combined with actual practical experience in engineering workshops which give employment at the present time to over three hundred workmen, but which are being largely increased and are turning out all classes of engineering work.[63]

Dyer could only have been encouraged by those remarks, and soon after the article appeared, he declared in *General Report* that his goal was indeed a combination of the two systems.

Nature touched upon *General Report* in July 1878. In a brief column, the 4 July 1878 issue observed:

We have received from the Imperial College of Engineering, Tokei, Japan, the Calendar for Session 1877–78, and the reports of the professors for the period 1873–77. We have already referred to this admirably conducted institution so fully already, that we need only say now that these publications confirm all we have said about the college. It is based on the best continental models, and the course of instruction is so complete, thorough, scientific, and practical.[64]

The next report on the Imperial College of Engineering appeared in *Nature* in 1886, and expressed misgivings over how the abolition of the Department of Public Works would affect the college. The 4 March issue gave concerned views, noting that it was not decided whether the college would be maintained or be merged into the University of Tokyo.[65] The 25 March issue was also apprehensive of the future, referring to the college as a 'peculiarly English' institution.[66] Then, the 10 June issue reported that Education Minister Mori had established a new university, namely, the Imperial University, and that the Imperial College of Engineering had been annexed to it.[67] The 8 July issue noted that the College of Engineering had been founded as one of the five colleges of the Imperial University.[68] Each issue indicated that the source of information was *The Japan Weekly Mail*.

Nature carried further articles on Dyer himself, which are divided into three categories. The first is reviews of Dyer's writings. *Science Teaching in Schools* was reviewed in the 15 June 1893 issue, *The Evolution of Industry* in the 22 August 1895 issue, *Dai Nippon* in the 1 December 1904 issue, and *Education and National Life* in the 19 December 1912 issue. The second is Dyer's own commentaries of books. The 27 April 1905 issue carried Dyer's review on *Japan nach Reisen und Studien* written by J. J. Rein. The third is Dyer's own essays, such as 'Education and National Efficiency in Japan' in the 15 December 1904 issue and 'Western Teaching for China' in the 25 March 1905 issue. The last article that appeared in *Nature* was Dyer's obituary of the 10 October 1918 issue.

Engineering

Engineering carried its first account on the Imperial College of Engineering, the title of which was 'Engineering Progress in Japan, Establishment of a College for Civil Engineering at Yeddo,' in its 11 April 1873 issue, eight days after *Nature* printed its first report of the college; *Engineering* gave a more detailed explanation of the college, although the information provided in the article was quite similar. It began by referring to the embassy led by Iwakura, noting that the members were impressed with the advanced industries in Britain, and that they asked Britain for help in the establishment of a college for the groundwork of industrial development in Japan. Actually, this is not necessarily true, as I remarked earlier that Japan had had its own plans for schools by that time and that Ito went to Britain with a view to asking for the recommendation of eligible teachers. *Engineering* continued: 'At the request of the representatives of the Japanese Ambassadors in this country, a scheme has been prepared by an eminent engineer for such a college, in which is displayed a comprehensive grasp of the scientific and technical course of training which should be given in that institution.'[69] The name of the eminent engineer mentioned in this quotation, which must have been Gordon, was not given in *Engineering* or in *Nature*, though such names as Rankine, Lord Kelvin and Jenkin did appear. It is still unknown whether the name of Gordon was omitted by accident or design.

Engineering also noted that Dyer was selected as the principal and professor of engineering from among the several candidates Rankine had recommended, and that Marshall and Ayrton were nominated, as *Nature* had done. However, *Engineering* gave additional information by saying: 'a first-rate model-maker has been secured in Glasgow by Professor Dyer'.[70] As this quotation shows, out of the nine British teachers who arrived in Japan first, four had been decided by that time. The model-maker mentioned here is A. King, who was later to be the chief engineer of the Ishikawajima Shipbuilding Yard. The article also touched upon the workshop, the museum and the physical and chemical laboratories, all of which were attached to the Imperial College of Engineering. Probably those facilities had to be specified first, so that the necessary equipment and fixtures could be purchased. The article concluded: 'We need scarcely say that we shall look on this movement in the Far East with a very great degree of anxiety, as it is one that is of a most hopeful character, and claims our best sympathies.'[71]

Engineering carried two more articles on the Imperial College of Engineering, in March 1875 and July 1877. The former reported the situation of the college, based on the annual reports for the previous three years. The report stated: 'There appear to be nearly 200 pupils now in the college, and judging from the percentage of marks accorded to a number of competitors at the examination of the winter session 1873–74, the efforts of the professors have been attended with no small measure of success.'[72] The latter gave Dyer credit for the successful planning of the programme of studies and buildings, highlighting the educational facilities. The writer admired Dyer's effort to overcome various difficulties surrounding the college's development, noting that he had to organize the programme of studies when Japanese industries were in their infancy, that he could not but give lectures in English, and that he was pressured not to fail as he was entrusted with a very important duty to train engineers who would work for the nation. The report also gave special attention to educational facilities such as the Akabane Works and the engineering laboratory, with the three-dimensional design and the ground plan of the buildings attached at the end. The laboratory was mentioned as especially noteworthy, as the laboratory with such a new concept had only one former example in Munich, which University College, London, had in contemplation at that time.[73]

I must add that *Engineering* showed interest in the engineering education by Smith and others at Tokyo Kaiseigakko as well. In between the two issues quoted above, it carried a long article, 'Engineering Education in Japan'. Though only a very short piece on the Imperial College of Engineering, the journal remarked: '... [its pupils] are younger than the students at the university, and do not have the same preliminary training, so that the instruction is less advanced than in the older institution'.[74] In the article, which preceded the above-mentioned report in 1877, Tokyo Kaiseigakko was referred to as the 'Imperial University' and was considered more respectable than the Imperial College of Engineering. It should be noted that the article supported Smith's unfavourable remarks on the Imperial College of Engineering.

The Engineer

The Engineer began to report on the Imperial College of Engineering later than the other two magazines. In February 1875, it carried an article with the title of 'Engineers for Asia', in which the Royal Engineering College at Cooper's Hill was given a detailed account and then the Imperial College of Engineering was mentioned as follows: 'The principal reason we refer to this college here is to show the admirable manner in which it is proposed to combine theoretical with practical instruction'.[75] We can see that *The Engineer* paid attention to the combination of theory and practice well over two years before *Nature*. The article added that 'we regret that we have no space to describe more minutely an institution which has much to recommend it'.[76]

The Engineer thus spoke very highly of the Imperial College of Engineering, and one might expect that the magazine would have covered its activities frequently. However, the next account of the college appeared two years later, in May 1877. The article remarked: '[w]e have received plans of the College buildings, which include, besides the main buildings, a museum, metallurgical, engineering, and chemical laboratories, and professors' houses. We regret we are unable from want of space to reproduce these'.[77] It also said that the course of study adopted showed 'that Mr Dyer thoroughly appreciates the necessity for an intimate combination of theory and practice'.[78] It is interesting to note that Dyer sent a letter asking for a correction of the article in September of the same year, which attests to his methodical nature. He pointed out two errors. First, in drawing up the syllabus (Calendar) mentioned in the article, Dyer had also requested other professors to submit their own drafts, and the syllabus was finally published by the officials of the Imperial College of Engineering. Secondly, it was Mr De Boinville, an architect, who had made plans of the college buildings in accordance with Dyer's overall plan.[79] In June 1878, The journal reported on the recent development of the college based on *General Report* and *Class Reports*: 'This college is not altogether like what we have in our own country, but has gone beyond us and eclipsed all that we have done in the same direction. We gather from the Calendar that practice and theory are blended, and this is as it should be.'[80]

It is quite difficult to judge from this brief overview of the three journals' reports whether the Imperial College of Engineering was given respectable media coverage in quantity or in quality. However, it cannot be denied that the journals, which did not specialize in education, carried many reports on the Imperial College of Engineering, taking note of the originality of its education and praising Dyer's achievements. It is still more difficult to judge how much of the report caught the attention of British people and exerted an influence on them. With all the information on the educational situations of such strong competitors as Germany and France available, British people still adhered to their own traditional methods of education, and this makes it difficult to conclude that they showed much interest in education in the Far East. Under such circumstances, how did Dyer's work and his colleagues benefit their homeland?

NOTES

1   Playfair, L., *Industrial Instruction on the Continent*, London, 1852, p. 22.
2   Ibid.
3   69, p. 2.
4   71, p. 6.
5   71, p. 6.
6   1, pp. 12–16.
7   59, p. 20.
8   78, p. 9.

9 3, p. 37.
10 69, p. 2.
11 2, p. 7.
12 18, p. 11.
13 5, p. 5.
14 2, pp. 8, 32; 3, pp. 7, 9.
15 39, p. 5.
16 39, p. 11.
17 2, p. 3.
18 2, p. 4.
19 4, p. 2.
20 2, pp. 47–48.
21 78, p. 9.
22 2, p. 2.
23 71, p. 8.
24 2, p. 47.
25 37, p. 2.
26 3, p. 27.
27 5, pp. 1–2.
28 18, p. 32.
29 71, p. 7.
30 71, p. 7.
31 63, pp. 122, 200, 79 p. 152.
32 69, p. 47.
33 69, p. 5.
34 Dixon, W. G., *The Land of Morning: An Account of Japan and its People based on four years' Residence in that Country*, Edinburgh, 1882, p. 170.
35 Ibid, pp. 170–171.
36 69, p. 162.
37 3, p. 27.
38 *The Japan Weekly Mail*, 1 July 1882, p. 786.
39 *The Engineer*, 6 May 1898, p. 434.
40 *The Japan Weekly Mail*, 1 July 1882, p. 787.
41 69, p. 7.
42 *Nature*, 12 March 1874, p. 373.
43 *The Engineer*, 19 February 1875, p. 134.
44 *The Japan Weekly Mail*, 3 March 1873.
45 *The Japan Weekly Mail*, 19 July 1873.
46 Ibid.
47 *The Japan Weekly Mail*, 2 August 1873.
48 *The Japan Weekly Mail*, 1 November 1873.
49 Ibid.
50 *The Japan Weekly Mail*, 8 November, 1873.
51 *The Japan Weekly Mail*, 22 November, 1873.
52 *The Japan Weekly Mail*, 9 February 1878, p. 132.
53 *The Japan Weekly Mail*, 16 February 1878, p. 154.
54 *The Japan Weekly Mail*, 16 February 1878, p. 155.
55 *The Japan Weekly Mail*, 24 August 1878, p. 847.

56 *The Japan Weekly Mail*, 16 February 1878, p. 154.
57 *The Japan Weekly Mail*, 24 August 1878, p. 847.
58 *The Japan Weekly Mail*, 26 October 1878, pp. 1129–1131.
59 *The Japan Weekly Mail*, 15 November 1879, pp. 1522–1523.
60 *The Japan Weekly Mail*, 1 July 1882, p. 786.
61 *Nature*, 3 April 1873, p. 430.
62 *Nature*, 17 May 1877, p. 44.
63 Ibid.
64 *Nature*, 4 July 1878, p. 263.
65 *Nature*, 4 March 1886, p. 424.
66 *Nature*, 25 March 1886, p. 496.
67 *Nature*, 10 June 1886, p. 131.
68 *Nature*, 8 July 1886, p. 225.
69 *Engineering*, 11 April 1873, p. 253.
70 Ibid.
71 Ibid.
72 *Engineering*, 12 March 1875, p. 212.
73 *Engineering*, 27 July 1877, pp. 74–75.
74 *Engineering*, 25 February 1876, p. 152.
75 *The Engineer*, 19 February 1875, p. 134.
76 Ibid.
77 *The Engineer*, 18 May 1877, p. 345.
78 Ibid.
79 *The Engineer*, 14 September 1877, p. 186.
80 *The Engineer*, 28 June 1878, p. 462.

The 'Boomerang Phenomenon' of Educational Experimentation

D yer took his first action for reforming engineering education in Britain when he was still in Japan. At the end of 1878, or the beginning of 1879, he sent a long list of proposals to Matheson in London with a request that they be forwarded to the Institution of Civil Engineers. Under the title of 'The Education of Civil and Mechanical Engineers', he put forward his ideas for reform, suggesting concrete measures and insisting that engineering organizations should play an active role in the process.

The origin of the Institution of Civil Engineers dates back to 1818, when engineers gathered at a coffee house in London to form a small group for the exchange and diffusion of knowledge. The group expanded and was given a Royal Charter in 1828. Its stated goal was 'the general advancement of Mechanical Science and more particularly for promoting the acquisition of these species of knowledge which constitutes the profession of Civil Engineer' (Charter of the Institution of Civil Engineers, incorporated 3 June 1828). The institution began to issue newsletters in 1837, which carried the annual report and the results of members' research. According to the annual report of 1837, the institution had 14 Honorary Members, 47 Ordinary Members, 93 Corresponding Members and 98 Associates, 252 in total who had met the high standards required for enrolment. Rankine became an associate of the institution in 1843, and began submitting his papers for publication, but he eventually left after failing to achieve full membership. With the help of his supporters Rankine then founded the Institution of Engineers in Scotland in 1857, and he was its first President.

But, to return to the Institution of Civil Engineers, the latter term originally meant engineers who were not engaged in military affairs.

However, when Dyer made his proposals, the institution was composed mostly of civil engineers in a narrow sense, since mechanical engineers had founded their own independent organization in 1848 under the presidency of Stevenson, inventor of the steam locomotive.

The institution began to work on the problems related to engineering education in 1867, as it began opening its door to students and attaching more importance not only to practical training but also to engineering education at the collegiate level. This change stemmed from the stagnation of British engineering expertise as revealed at the Paris Exposition, and to the progress of engineering education on the Continent. In opening its door to students, the institution felt it necessary to review the educational methods available to them, seeking information on engineering education of various countries by sending questionnaires to intellectuals in and outside Britain. The findings were compiled as *The Education and Status of Civil Engineers in the United Kingdom and in Foreign Countries*, which was published in 1870 (see Plate 17) and was one of the sources of information referred to by Dyer.

The report begins with background information:

> A few years ago attention was called to the state of technical education in this country, which, it was stated, had been recently shown to be so much inferior to that in other European states as to threaten seriously the industrial interests of Great Britain. The subject was taken up by the Government, and by various public bodies, and much information respecting it was collected and put on record. The Council of Institution of Civil Engineers felt it their duty to interest themselves in that part of inquiry which bore upon their own profession.[1]

The report consists of an Introductory Memorandum and three parts. Part I, 'Educational Institutions in Great Britain and Ireland, where Instruction is given bearing on the Profession of Engineering,' is about the situation of engineering education in Britain. Part II on 'Engineering Education, and the Status of Civil Engineers in Foreign Countries' provides examples of the experience of other countries. In Part III, 'Suggestions and Extracts', suggestions are offered by various individuals. In particular, there were three separate quotations from F. Jenkin, a professor of civil engineering at the University of Edinburgh. According to Professor Kita, Jenkin once accommodated a member of the embassy led by Iwakura, whose name was Koichiro Sugi. With Jenkin's guidance, Sugi learned technical drawing, and later became the first Japanese professor at the Imperial College of Engineering.

Dyer also referred to Jenkin's views and quoted some of them in his theories of engineering education. Interestingly, although it quoted others in its report, the institution itself refrained from expressing an opinion on the issues involved.

□

Several years went by, but the Institution of Civil Engineers did not take any further action on educational reform, so that Dyer decided to make specific proposals to it, encouraged by the favourable reports in British engineering journals of his educational experiment in Japan. The proposals were later published in book form, a work of forty-four pages.

He began his proposals by clarifying his intent:

> Eight years ago, the Institution of Civil Engineers published an extensive report on the education and status of engineers in the United Kingdom and in Foreign Countries. This was circulated among members without the expression of any opinion on the part of the Council, it being, doubtless, deemed preferable in the first instance to put them in profession of the particulars, as it was thought that, from the nature of the subject, various and discordant ideas would be entertained regarding it. I am not aware that any opportunity has been given to the members of expressing their opinions on the subject of the report, or that any recommendations have since been made by the Institution as a body for the education of its future members. No apology, therefore, is required for introducing the subject of the education of engineers. I wish it, however, to be understood that my object is not so much to give prominence to my own views, or to my attempts to carry them into practice, but rather to originate a discussion on the general question. It may be hoped that, as a result of such discussion, some definite steps may be taken by the Institution for placing Engineers in the same position as the members of other learned professions, by defining more clearly their relations to the public, and by taking steps to prevent unqualified men from using the title of Engineer.[2]

Before going into the contents of his proposals, Dyer defined the concept of education:

> I need scarcely say that, when I speak of education, I use the word in its conventionally restricted sense, meaning the training which a student should receive to enable him to perform the duties of assistant engineer in an intelligent manner. This training is only an introduction to his real education as an engineer, and its object should be to give him a good start in the path which he must continue through life. The second part of a man's training must be

decided almost entirely by the special circumstances under which he is placed, and by his own ability and perseverance; but I think that the first ought to be systematised to a greater extent than at present.[3]

For engineering education as described above, Dyer suggested a six-year curriculum beginning at the age of sixteen. The first three years were to be spent on theoretical studies and practical work in college, and the latter three years on practical experience through an apprenticeship, which was quite similar to the curriculum of the Imperial College of Engineering. The subjects to be taught in the first three years included civil and mechanical engineering, which again followed the curriculum of the Imperial College of Engineering. Dyer also offered suggestions on various other matters, including the engineering laboratory, workshop, examination, and diploma.

After presenting his plan for the college, Dyer went into great detail on the education at the Imperial College of Engineering, which amounted to ten pages when published in book form. He gave accounts of the six-year educational experiment, by using such subtitles as 'Short description of the course of study in the Imperial College of Engineering, Tokei, Japan', 'Entrance examinations', 'General course', 'Technical course', 'Teachers employed', 'Drawing office', 'Technical museum', 'Engineering laboratory', 'Examination', 'Higher course of study', 'Akabane Works' and 'Progress made'. He emphasized that the college was meant as just one instance: 'As I have already explained, my object in referring to this College is simply for the purpose of illustrating the views I have already enunciated, and not to hold it up as a pattern in any way.'[4] However, it is quite probable that he hoped to make the success of the Japanese experiment known in British engineering circles.

Dyer also suggested that members of the institution should be admitted after passing an examination based on its own standards for membership. He even referred to financial problems in putting his proposals into practice. In conclusion, he itemized his proposals as follows:

> 1, That the technical education of Civil and Mechanical Engineers be undertaken by existing colleges, and by new colleges of the same type, and not by special technical institutions. 2, That on the completion of the college course, those students who attain the required standard should receive a diploma for their scientific and technical knowledge. 3, That all the students should serve [an] apprenticeship of at least four-and-a-half years. 4, That on the completion of their apprenticeship they should be examined in the application of their scientific and technical knowledge to practical

problems, by a committee appointed by the Institution of Civil Engineers. 5, That no Members be appointed to the Institution of Civil Engineers who have not gone through the course indicated – except in such special cases as are mentioned above. 6, That a higher course of theoretical training and investigation be arranged for those who are able and willing to undertake it, after the completion of the above course.[5]

There are three striking features of Dyer's proposals. First, he suggested a compromise plan that both existing colleges and new colleges should work on the technical education of engineers, which is different from the case of Japan, where the national government founded an educational institution intended exclusively for engineering education. Dyer estimated that about fifteen colleges nationwide would be enough for the present, each college staffed with three professors and two instructors, and where students would undergo six months of theoretical study and six months of practical work alternately.

Secondly, he proposed that students should gain practical experience as pupils or apprentices for four-and-a-half years, that is, half of the first three-year study period and the whole of the later three-year course. This is also a compromise plan, in which he respected the British emphasis on practical experience and combined it with theoretical study.

Thirdly, he expected the Institution of Civil Engineers to conduct an examination of the practical abilities of those completing their apprenticeship, and to screen out those unqualified for institution membership. He hoped the institution would take responsibility for the improvement of the status of engineers as a learned profession through its voluntary discipline and effort.

☐

As noted, Dyer submitted his proposals via Matheson, who, in turn, received a reply from J. Forrest, the institution's secretary, dated 25 March 1879, saying they could not be accepted:

This paper is not, in the judgment of the Council, one that can be regarded as suitable for reading and discussion at an ordinary meeting of the members. The Institution, as an Institution, is not an educational body, nor has it any power to grant what are ordinarily understood as degrees. Neither has it authority to interfere with, or regulate the practice of the profession. The qualifications for admission into the several ranks of this Institution are settled by the bye-laws, and the Council feel that they would not be warranted under existing circumstances in extending their action beyond the provisions of Royal Charter of Incorporation and the bye-laws founded thereon.[6]

Matheson sent this reply to Dyer in Tokyo, who must have felt this rejection was unreasonable. He then decided to seek a wider audience by publishing the proposals in book form. As he recounted: 'The MSS. of this paper having been submitted to the several gentlemen in England who are interested practically in the education of Engineers, they expressed a strong wish that it should be published.' The names of those gentlemen are not known, but one of them must almost certainly have been Matheson. The proposals were published by E. & F. N. Spon, 46 Charing Cross, in 1880, in a cheap edition priced at one shilling. This was Dyer's first work to be published in the true sense of the word, though some of his writings had been issued by the Imperial College of Engineering.

He began by emphatically stating his feeling that the institution's reply was unreasonable,[7] especially in regard to two key points. First, the reply stated that the institution was not an educational body, while Dyer argued that his proposal was about the qualification for membership, not education. He remarked: 'At this distance from London I do not consider it advisable that I should attempt to discuss with the Council the wisdom of their resolution. I would remark, however, that I did not suppose that the Institution was an educational body. I only wished the members to re-consider the conditions of admission to the Institution.'[8] He was 'of opinion that its influence ought to be exerted in raising the profession of engineering to the same status as that of the other learned professions',[9] which required revision of the qualification criteria for institution membership. He believed that the qualification should cover theoretical studies at colleges and their applications, and that the institution should conduct examinations of practical skills before admitting new members.

Secondly, the reply noted that the action of the institution was limited to the provisions of Royal Charter of Incorporation and bye-laws, which could not, in Dyer's view, justify the rejection. He stated:

> The Institution is said to have been founded 'for the general advancement of mechanical science, and more particularly for promoting acquisition of that species of knowledge which constitutes the profession of a Civil Engineer'. Nothing is said as to the means to be adopted for attaining that end; everything is left to the members. They are allowed to 'alter, vary, revoke or make new and other bye-laws as they shall find most useful and expedient'. The

Institution *might* even become an educational body if the members so willed it, as by doing so it would 'be promoting the acquisition of that species of knowledge which constitutes the profession of a Civil Engineer' (3 p. 5, italics in original).

Not expecting the institution to be an educational body, he meant that it was unreasonable to use the bye-laws to discourage discussion on education. He also referred to the aforementioned report published by the institution in 1870:

> Eight or nine years ago the Council of the Institution published a report showing the state of engineering education in Britain and on the Continent. Was that publication specially authorised by the Charter or the bye-laws, and what was its object? If it was to show the deficiency of English engineering education, as it clearly did, I think this was unkind, unless the Council intended to do something to remedy that deficiency.[10]

Dyer expected the institution to take further steps after the report, and he must have been frustrated by its inaction.

That was the end of Dyer's contact with the Institution of Civil Engineers. Its newsletter carried index entries for various persons in 1879, 1894 and 1907, where we can find the names of Ayrton and Perry, but not the name of Dyer. Returning to Britain, he became a member of the Institution of Engineers in Scotland founded by Rankine and others. Dyer made constructive proposals on the reform of engineering education and publishing research papers. Meanwhile, the Institution of Civil Engineers was not quick in taking action even after Dyer's refutation, according to Shin Hirose, a professor at Toyama University, who has researched the history of engineering education in Britain, with emphasis on the qualification for membership of the Institution of Civil Engineers. It was not until 1888 that it recognized that theoretical knowledge had to be included in the membership qualification and only in 1897 that it began conducting examinations, testing students on general education and Associates on scientific knowledge as well as general education. This is still the situation today.

Dyer also believed that Japan needed a similar type of technical institution of engineers. In 1879, he told the first-term graduates of the Imperial College of Engineering how important this was, revealing his 'Draft Regulations for Proposed Institution of Engineers'. In his plan, the two most important goals of the 'Imperial Institution of Engineers' were to 'advance knowledge' and to 'diffuse knowledge', and the institution was to consist of Honorary Members, Fellows, Members, Graduates, Associates and Students, who were examined by the institution. Dyer was emphatic on his originality: 'In the subjoined regulations, I have followed those for the English Institutions of Civil Engineers, in so far as they relate to routine business, but the general constitution I have proposed differs very widely from any existing Institution of Engineers with which I am acquainted.'[11]

It is worth noting that the graduates of the Imperial College of Engineering founded an engineering institution that year aimed at enhancing friendship among engineers. Later, the institution opened its door to people from various circles and issued its own newsletter on engineering. This institution is the parent body of the Japan Federation of Engineering Societies of the present day, which has expanded as an academic society rather than as the technical institution Dyer had in mind.

☐

In June 1882, Dyer left Japan for Britain. He later recounted: 'for personal and family reasons, I resigned my position'.[12] Actually, he was anxious to win a position as professor at Glasgow University. This will be discussed in more detail later, but it should be noted here that he applied for the position in 1883 only to fail, primarily because his devotion to Japan for nine years had prevented him from keeping up with the rapid advances in the study of engineering. After that failure, he worked very hard on his papers trying to make up for lost time.

In November 1883, he was asked to lecture on engineering education at the Glasgow Philosophical Society. This occasion was the turning point that led him to act as an educational reformer for the rest of his life. A philosophical society was a type of gentleman's society for voluntary studies, which came into being in many parts of Britain in the middle of the eighteenth century. According to Professor Masahiro Kagawa of Sophia University, as many as 750 societies had appeared by the middle of the nineteenth century. In Scotland, which included a highly industrialized area, such societies were established quite early on by intellectuals of Glasgow University and the University of Edinburgh.

Dyer's lecture was his first speech on returning to Britain, and the audience was impressed by him as a reformer of engineering education. The lecture, 'Technical Education, with Special Reference to the Requirements of Glasgow and the West of Scotland', was carried in the society's *Proceedings*, 30 pages being allotted to it.[13] Dyer made the following statement: 'Various papers have been read at the meeting of this Society on the subject of Technical Education, during the past few years, but, so far as I know, these have always been confined to the consideration of general principles or to descriptions of Continental methods, and no one has attempted to sketch such a system as is required for Glasgow and neighbourhood'.[14] His lecture was intended to suggest a system that was needed specifically by Glasgow and its neighbourhood.

Dyer referred to the results of his educational experiment at the Imperial College of Engineering in Japan and to the situation of countries on the Continent, which he had observed soon after his return. He remarked: 'I hope to incorporate in my proposals, not only the results of my own experience, but also such parts of the Continental systems as my observation, and discussions with French and German Professors, have led me to believe are suited to our wants and conditions.'[15] He chose to speak on matters related to education which he thought were necessary for Glasgow. Touching upon his experiences in Japan, for instance, he recommended some of his methods, noting that the special courses were 'of great importance to Glasgow and the West of Scotland',[16] and that the alternation of theory and practice was 'the system which ought to be carried out in Glasgow'.[17]

He continued:

> Of all places in the world Glasgow offers the greatest number of advantages in the way of practical training in the various departments of industry; and its primary and secondary school arrangements could easily be modified to afford the preliminary education necessary for students entering an institution for training in the higher parts of their subjects; and the success of such an institution cannot be doubted, if it is judiciously arranged and managed.[18]

He believed that existing schools should be modified rather than establishing any new institution. He had already proposed the modification of schools to the Institution of Civil Engineers, but he made his point more logically in this lecture. Summing up his suggestions, he presented the following twelve points:

1. That a Technical Institute be founded to superintend all industrial education in Glasgow, and form a centre for that of the West of Scotland.
2. That it include representatives of institutions of every grade of education – from the University to the primary school – so that a connected system might be arranged whereby students who distinguish themselves in the lower grades might have opportunities of proceeding higher.

3. That it take advantage of existing institutions currently offering technical education, supplementing them where they are deficient, and arranging their courses so that there may be no waste of teaching power.
4. That the higher and professional parts of industrial education be given either in university or in institutes recognized as offering instruction leading to a degree.
5. That the secondary school curricula be modified to offer more thorough instruction in physical science, and thus prepare students who intend to study the higher parts of the subjects.
6. That Secondary Technical Schools be founded providing an introduction to technical training to those with insufficient time for the higher courses.
7. That corresponding Secondary Technical Instruction be given in evening classes to draughtsmen, foremen, and the higher class of workmen.
8. That Elementary Technical Instruction be given in evening classes to workmen.
9. That, for the most part, the practical training for the different trades be given in the workshops or manufactories.
10. That for certain trades considered suited (such as weaving, dyeing, &c.), this practical training be supplemented by instruction in special schools or classes.
11. That three grades of Diplomas or Certificates be awarded by the Technical Institute – the first for those who aim at being managers or directors, the second for draughtsmen and foremen, and the third for workmen.
12. While recognizing the actual workshops or manufactories as the chief places for practical training, that the instruction in the schools of the various grades be made more thorough by the introduction of laboratories, museums and small workshops, which will give the students opportunities to become acquainted with things themselves, instead of simply listening to lectures.[19]

Dyer delivered another lecture on the same issue in November 1893 under the title of 'Technical Education in Glasgow and the West of Scotland, a Retrospect and a Prospect'. He began with the following statement:

Almost exactly ten years ago, I had the honour of reading a paper before this Society, on 'Technical Education, with special reference to the requirements of Glasgow and the West of Scotland', and a special meeting was held for its discussion. The opinions expressed regarding the proposals which I made were, without exception, very favourable, but the speakers almost all seemed to think that they were too ideal, and not sufficiently within the range of practical efforts. One distinguished educationalist, indeed, said that they might be carried into practical effect fifty years hence; but, in his opinion, what was wanted was a practical plan which might be carried out now. It was not the first time in my experience that I had been told that my schemes were Utopian, and I have heard the same opinion many times since; but I have always held that the really practical man was not he who followed an opportunist policy from day to day, but rather the man who had carefully thought out a complete scheme, which he steadily kept in view, and tried to mould events in the direction of the ideals which he had formed.[20]

Dyer was quite confident this time, most probably because the Imperial College of Engineering in Japan had proved a success, and the technical college in Glasgow had also enjoyed admirable results. Touching upon his great contributions to the college, including the arrangement of its divisions, he noted: 'The first event of importance which I will notice is the institution of the Glasgow and West of Scotland Technical College exactly three years after my paper was read'.[21] In conclusion, he observed:

I think that a survey of what has been done during the past ten years will show that all the proposals I made have been carried out to a very considerable extent, and I have no hesitation in saying that the further developments which I have indicated are all possible within the next ten years, if gone about in an intelligent manner, and that Glasgow might then become the most important centre for scientific and industrial education in the world.[22]

In 1886, the Glasgow and West of Scotland Technical College opened, founded 'by an Order of the Queen in Council, dated 26th November, 1886, according to a Scheme framed by the Commissioners appointed under the provisions of Educational Endowments (Scotland) Act, 1882, whereby Anderson's College, the Young Chair of Technical Chemistry in connection with Anderson's College, the College of Science and Arts, Allan Glen's Institution, and the Atkinson Institution, were placed under the management of one governing body'.[23] Since the Atkinson Institution was not opened, the governing body consisted of the other four institutions. With Anderson's College as the base, the technical institutions in Glasgow were thus incorporated into the Glasgow and West of Scotland Technical College, parent body of the present-day University of Strathclyde, whose history is shown in Table 1.

After the order was issued, Dyer lost no time in disclosing his plans for the new college. In his essay 'The Glasgow and West of Scotland Technical College' carried in the 4 January issue of *The Glasgow Herald*, he remarked:

Table 1 History of Strathclyde University

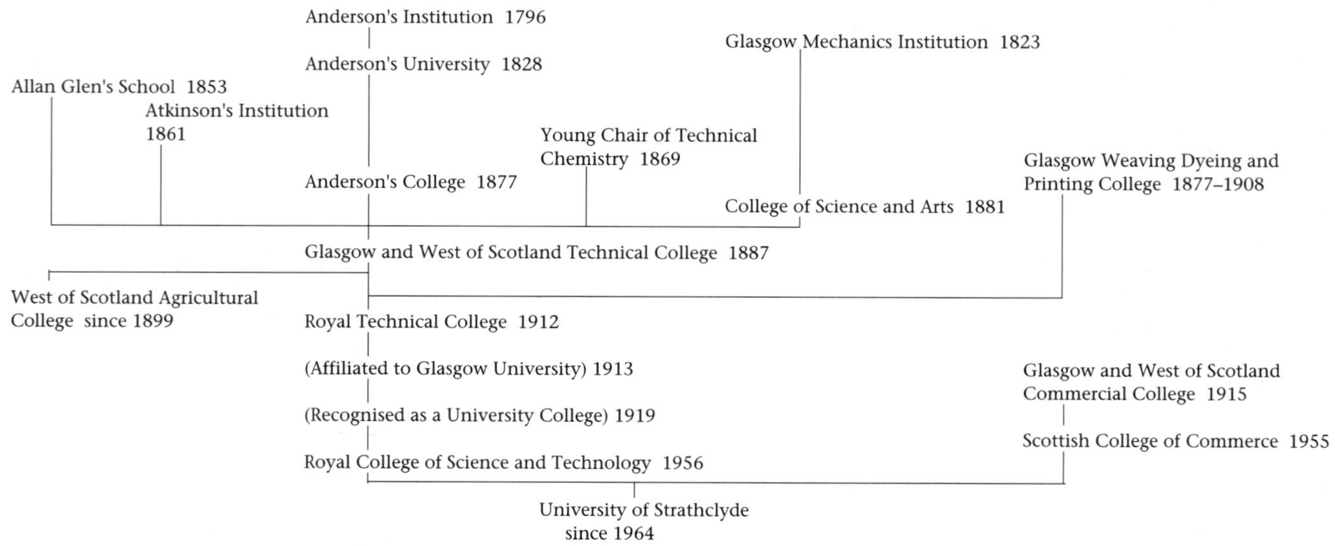

Anderson's Institution 1796

Anderson's University 1828

Glasgow Mechanics Institution 1823

Young Chair of Technical Chemistry 1869

Anderson's College 1877

College of Science and Arts 1881

Glasgow Weaving Dyeing and Printing College 1877–1908

Glasgow and West of Scotland Technical College 1887

Allan Glen's School 1853

Atkinson's Institution 1861

West of Scotland Agricultural College since 1899

Royal Technical College 1912

(Affiliated to Glasgow University) 1913

(Recognised as a University College) 1919

Royal College of Science and Technology 1956

Glasgow and West of Scotland Commercial College 1915

Scottish College of Commerce 1955

University of Strathclyde since 1964

One of the earliest duties of the governing body of the Glasgow and West of Scotland Technical College, the first meeting of which will be held in a short time, must be to consider the arrangements under which the work is to be carried on in the immediate future. If the college was an institution which was being organised for the first time it would be a comparatively simple matter to draft a constitution which would embody the results of recent educational experiences. Although the name is new the college will be made up, at least to a considerable extent at first, of institutions which have a history behind them, and the method of re-organization adopted should not be so much of the nature of a revolution as an evolution and development, so that there may be the least possible disturbance of existing arrangements and interests.[24]

Recognizing that the college was independent of the existing systems of those institutions, Dyer stated: 'It is essential that a clear idea be at once formed of the goal to be aimed at, and the general principles which should be kept in view in attempting to reach it.'[25]

According to Minutes of the Governors and Committees kept at the Archives of the University of Strathclyde, the first meeting of the Council of the Glasgow and West of Scotland Technical College was held on 21 January 1887, seventeen days after Dyer's essay appeared in *The Glasgow Herald*. Thirty members were present, all appointed by the above-mentioned or other educational institutions. Dyer was one of the six members appointed by Anderson's College.

It is not known what made Dyer print his essay in an influential newspaper before the first meeting, without holding back his name. Although we cannot tell whether he did it of his own will or at the request of the publisher, it is quite clear from the following quotations that he was confident of his own competence as the most distinguished authority on the issue:

As one who has known the Glasgow institutions for many years, and who has had special opportunities of learning what has been done in connection with technical education in various parts of the world, it may be useful, at least in beginning the discussion, if I state briefly a few of the conclusions at which I have arrived. Although a member of the governing body of the new college, it is of course understood that at present I only write as a private individual who has long taken an interest in the subjects which will engage the attention of that body.[26]

He concluded:

I trust that the suggestions I have made may at least afford a basis for the discussion, of those, not only by the governors, but also by the general public.[27]

He was quite ready to take the leadership and give suggestions for reforming the technical education of Glasgow.

On 22 February of the same year, Dyer expressed his views on his ideal technical education in a lecture at the Institution of Engineers and Shipbuilders in Scotland. The institution was formerly the Institution of Engineers in Scotland, which Rankine had established. In his lecture 'On the Education of Engineers', Dyer referred to various institutions, including the Imperial College of Engineering in Japan, the Massachusetts Institute of Technology in the United States and the *École Centrale* in Paris. Turning to the reform of technical education in Scotland, he commented on the new college in Glasgow, with reference to its specific divisions. In addition to the eight divisions he had adopted for the Imperial College of Engineering, namely, Civil Engineering, Mechanical Engineering, Naval Architecture, Electric Engineering, Architecture, Chemical Engineering, Metallurgy and Mining Engineering, he mentioned Agriculture as a subject to be taught: 'As agriculture is now so much a matter of applied science – that is, of engineering – we may without unduly stretching the meaning of the term add another division, viz.: Agriculture.'[28]

The syllabus for the first year was issued for the opening of the winter classes in October 1887. It should be noted that the nine divisions that Dyer had mentioned in his lecture in February were all adopted for the day classes without any alteration to the wording. Although Minutes of the Governors and Committees carry no detailed account of how the divisions were decided, they indicate that the members of the Committee on Teaching and Staff held a meeting on 2 February 1888 and that they appointed Dyer to head its Curriculum Sub-Committee. It was then that Dyer was officially in charge of the curriculum, and his ideas were introduced into that for the year 1888–89, which provided more detailed regulations and more organized curricula than that for the previous year. Seiichi Tejima, once the president of Tokyo Educational Museum of Japan, visited Britain and returned home with a copy of this curriculum, which is now kept in the National Diet Library in Tokyo.

In August 1888, Dyer contributed a signed account of the Glasgow and West of Scotland Technical College to *Nature* under his own name, which began with the following statement: 'At the present time, when so much is being said and done in connection with technical education, and so many new institutions are being founded, it may interest the readers of *Nature* to learn how some old ones have been reorganized to enable them more adequately to meet the requirements of the times'.[29] He also noted: 'The problem which the

1

初代 鉄道寮御雇長
エドモンド モレル
十河信二書
EDMUND MOREL
1841–1871

2

1 Relief of Edward Morel (1841–71) at Sakuragi-cho station, Yokohama
2 Bust of Yozo Yamao with saw and planes used by him as an apprentice at Napier's shipbuilding yard, Glasgow

3

3 Ei-ichibankan (first British factory in Yokohama) at the time the Choshu clan students attended in the early 1860s

4

5

6

4 Coat of arms located at the Thomas Graham Building, University of Strathclyde. Inscription: 'Mente et Manu' – ' Head and Hand'
5 Former buildings of Glasgow University in the main high street

7

MEMOIR

OF

LEWIS D. B. GORDON, F.R.S.E.

LATE REGIUS PROFESSOR OF CIVIL ENGINEERING AND MECHANICS
IN THE UNIVERSITY OF GLASGOW

For Private Circulation

EDINBURGH—MDCCCLXXVII

6 Portrait of Lewis D.B.Gordon, first professor of Engineering, Glasgow University
7 Title page of Gordon's memoir, published by Constable, London, 1877

8

A MANUAL

OF THE

STEAM ENGINE

AND OTHER

PRIME MOVERS.

BY

WILLIAM JOHN MACQUORN RANKINE,

With Numerous Engravings.

8 Portrait and signature of Dyer's mentor, Professor Macquarn Rankine of Glasgow University

9

A MANUAL

OF

CIVIL ENGINEERING.

BY

WILLIAM JOHN MACQUORN RANKINE,

With Numerous Diagrams.

SEVENTH EDITION, REVISED.

LONDON:
CHARLES GRIFFIN AND COMPANY,
STATIONERS' HALL COURT.
1871.

[*The Author reserves the right of Translation.*]

A MANUAL

OF

MACHINERY AND MILLWORK.

BY

WILLIAM JOHN MACQUORN RANKINE,

With Numerous Diagrams.

FIRST EDITION.

LONDON:
CHARLES GRIFFIN AND COMPANY,
STATIONERS' HALL COURT.
1869.

[*The Author reserves the right of Translation.*]

A MANUAL

OF

APPLIED MECHANICS.

BY

WILLIAM JOHN MACQUORN RANKINE,

With Numerous Diagrams.

SEVENTH EDITION, THOROUGHLY REVISED,

BY

EDWARD FISHER BAMBER, C.E.

LONDON:
CHARLES GRIFFIN AND COMPANY,
STATIONERS' HALL COURT.
1873.

[*The Right of Translation Reserved.*]

9 Title pages of Rankine's four student manuals

10 The new buildings of Glasgow University at Gilmorehill, shortly after their completion in 1870, when Dyer attended the university

11 Rankine's letter proposing Dyer for the Whitworth Scholarship

12 Cover of the booklet submitted by Dyer for the post of Principal of the Imperial College of Engineering, Tokyo
13 Cover of the thesis written by Dyer as a student, which won the Watt Prize
14 Portrait and signature of Lord Kelvin given to a first-year Japanese student, Rinzaburo Shida, of the Imperial College of Engineering, who studied in Britain after graduation

12

13

14

15 The first and last pages of the handwritten six-page agreement between Henry Dyer and the Japanese Ministry of Public Works, dated 2 April 1873

16

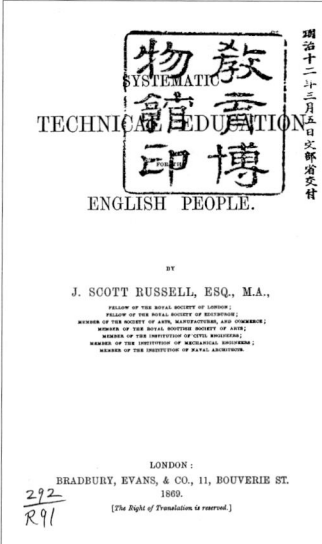

SYSTEMATIC
TECHNICAL EDUCATION

ENGLISH PEOPLE.

BY

J. SCOTT RUSSELL, ESQ., M.A.,

FELLOW OF THE ROYAL SOCIETY OF LONDON;
FELLOW OF THE ROYAL SOCIETY OF EDINBURGH;
MEMBER OF THE SOCIETY OF ARTS, MANUFACTURES, AND COMMERCE;
MEMBER OF THE ROYAL SCOTTISH SOCIETY OF ARTS;
MEMBER OF THE INSTITUTION OF CIVIL ENGINEERS;
MEMBER OF THE INSTITUTION OF MECHANICAL ENGINEERS;
MEMBER OF THE INSTITUTION OF NAVAL ARCHITECTS.

LONDON :
BRADBURY, EVANS, & CO., 11, BOUVERIE ST.
1869.
292
R91
[The Right of Translation is reserved.]

17

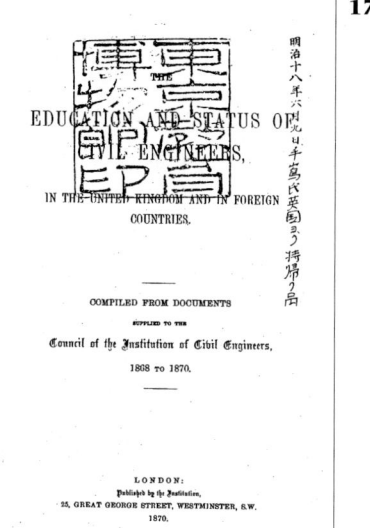

THE
EDUCATION AND STATUS OF
CIVIL ENGINEERS,
IN THE UNITED KINGDOM AND IN FOREIGN
COUNTRIES.

COMPILED FROM DOCUMENTS

SUPPLIED TO THE

Council of the Institution of Civil Engineers,

1868 TO 1870.

LONDON:
Published by the Institution,
25, GREAT GEORGE STREET, WESTMINSTER, S.W.
1870.

16 Title page of J.S.Russell's *Systematic Technical Education of the English People*, published by Bradbury, Evans & Co., 1869
17 Title page of *The Education and Status of Civil Engineers in the United Kingdom and Foreign Countries*, published by the Institution of Civil Engineers, 1870

18

18 Woodblock print of the Imperial College of Engineering by Kiyochika Kobayashi; early Meiji period

Technical Education Systematic Technical Education – Scott Russell – Bradbury & Evans 1869.
Report by Inst of C.E. (1970) on Education and Status of Engineers,
Address by Col. Greenery. at Cooper's Hall College. "Engineer" 6th Octr 1841.
Education of Engineers – Rennie's Autobiography. p 430.
Technical Education – "Engineering" Septr 1874.
The Place of Colleges in Engineering Training – Prof Kennedy, Engineering Octr 5th /78
Public Money for Public Ends – Prof Rankine. "Engineer" Vol 21 . p 299
Dangers of uniformity in Education – " " Vol 35 p. 35
Secondary Technical Education – E. B. Coxe, – American Engineering and
Mining Journal, March 1, 1879.
Gives an account of a school for miners, Oct 1874.
Higher Education of Engineers – Reid – Engineering Vol 18 . p 255 + 290
Engineering Education "Engineer" May 3rd 1861.
Explains Geo Stephenson's methods of instructing his pupils
and recommends that the Inst of C.E. hold exams for diplomas
Technical Training of Artisans – "Engineer" – Septr 8. 1965.
Gives an account of some technical schools in Belgium
Technical Education in Prussia – "Engineer" August 12. 1867.
Gives an account of the education in the Mining, Smelting
and Salt Work Department of Prussia,
Report of Commission appointed to inquire into the state of Technical
Education "Engineer" July 19. 1867. &c &c
Gives the opinions of men who had been jurors at the
Paris Exhibition
Engineering Education in India – "Engineer" August 2. 1872.
Conference at the Society of Arts,
B.A. Report 1876. – Address by Dr Andrews – "Engineer" Septr 8. 1876.
Contains some interesting remarks on education.
B.A. Report 1876 – Address by Mr Merrifield – "Engineer" Septr 15. 1876.
Art in Engineering – "Engineer" October 1876.
Reynolds – Engineering as a Profession – "Engineer" Novr 3. 1876. Very Good Any Vol 15. p 555,
Technical Education in Prussia "Engineering" 1870. A series of articles
giving an account of the training of architects and engineers,
Technical Education – "Engineering" Nov. 18. Decr 9. 1870.
Notices of Report of Inst of C.E, on Engineering Education
Fowler – Inaugural Address. Inst. C.E. January 9. 1866.
Defines the duties of a Civil Engineer see New "Engineering" October 17. 1879.
Thompson. Prof. S.J. – Apprentice schools in France – B.A. Report 1879.
Reprinted in "Building News" Aug 29. "English Mechanic" Aug 29.
Huxley – On medical education – "Critiques and Addresses. p 56.

19 An excerpt from Dyer's bibliography in his own handwriting, one of nine pages relating to technical education

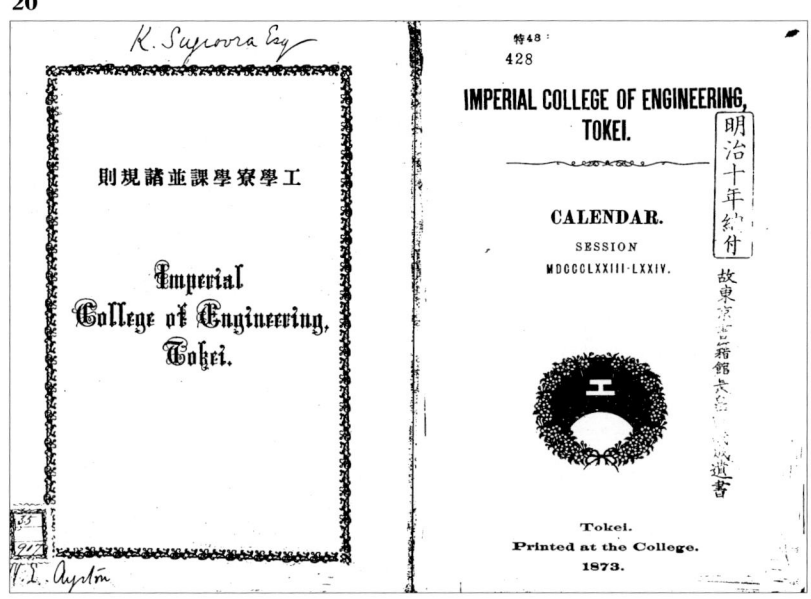

20 Cover of the first edition of the Calendar, printed in 1873, with the signature of W.E. Ayrton, Professor of Natural Philosophy, in the lower left-hand corner

21

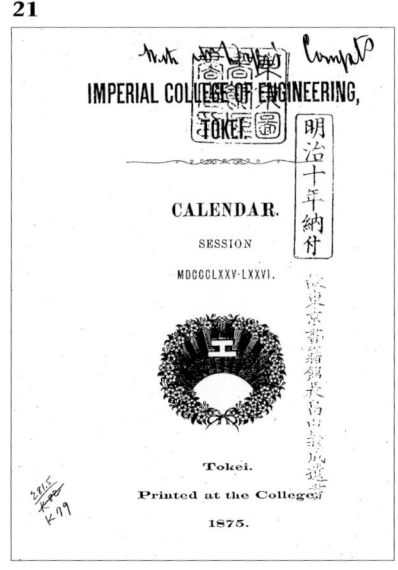

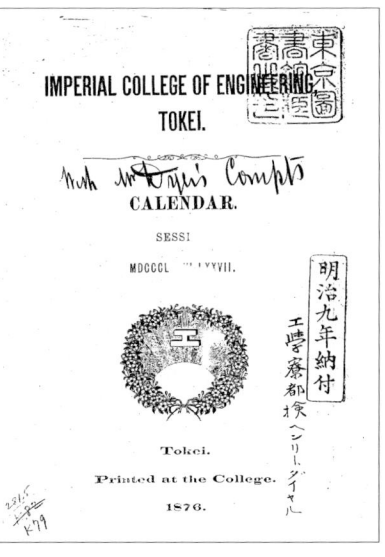

21 Title pages of the Calendars printed in 1875 and 1876, with Dyer's compliments

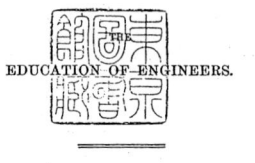

THE EDUCATION OF ENGINEERS.

明治廿年十二月九日文部省受付

BY

HENRY DYER.

C.E., M.A., B.Sc., Glasg.

Principal of the Imperial College of Engineering,
Tokei Japan.

TOKEI:

Imperial C

曩ニ工部大學校ヲ経營セシメ
今工竣ルヲ奏ス朕親カラ臨テ開
業ノ典ヲ舉ク朕惟フニ百工ヲ勸ム
ルハ経世ノ要ニシテ當今ノ急務
ナリ自今此校ニ従學スル者亹
勉シテくレテ利用厚生ノ源ヲ開
カンコヲ望ム

22 Title page of the pamphlet containing Dyer's address to the first graduates of the Imperial College of Engineering.

23 Copy of the message from Emperor Meiji delivered at the opening ceremony of the Imperial College of Engineering

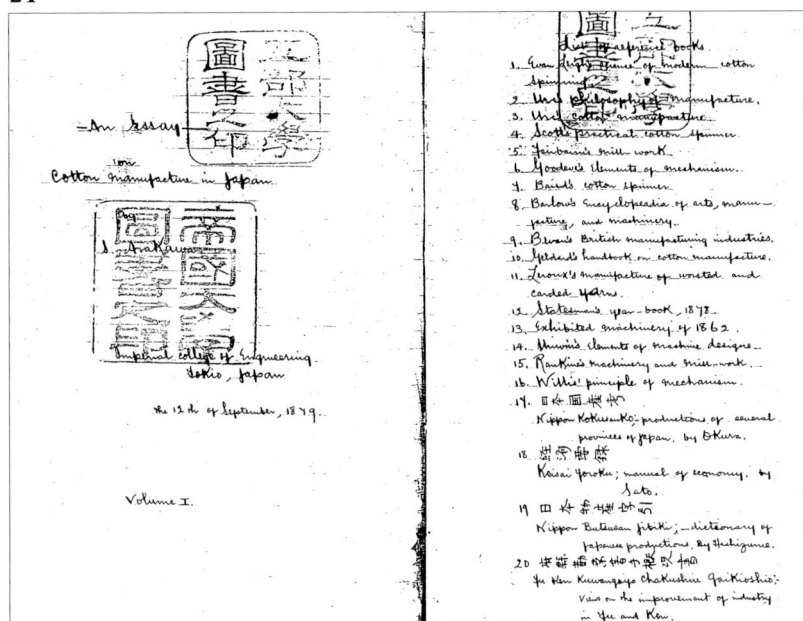

24 The cover and references of the graduation thesis 'An Essay on Cotton Industry in Japan' written by Shin'ichiro Arakawa, one of the first graduates of the Imperial College of Engineering. After graduation, Arakawa demonstrated his skills in training artisans for the textile industry in Kyoto

25

25 1880 graduation photograph of students at the Imperial College of Engineering

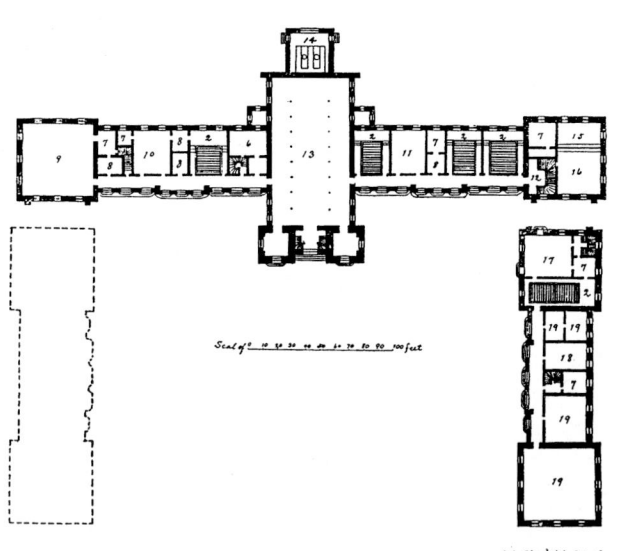

C. A. Chastel de Boinville Architect

26 Three-dimensional design and ground plan of the buildings of the Imperial College of Engineering. The left wing was never completed.

27 Photographs of the Imperial College of Engineering. *Above*: Main entrance. *Below*: back of the auditorium

(From the Graduates.)

Tokio, June 27th, 1882.

Henry Dyer Esq., M.A., B. Sc.,
Principal, Imperial College of Engineering.

Dear Sir,—As you are about to return home, we, the graduates of the Imperial College of Engineering, take the opportunity of addressing to you our heartfelt thanks for the great and numerous obligations for which we are indebted to you, and for the care and attention you have so kindly paid us, both officially and personally, for a period of over nine years, during which you have held the office of Principal of the Imperial College of Engineering.

We consider it needless to make any lengthy mention of your labours for our benefit, as it will suffice to say that mainly through your exertions the College has attained a thorough organization, and by your care and attention we have carefully completed our studies in it.

We assure you that we shall, throughout our lives, remember you with the highest feelings of gratitude, and that you carry with you our sincere wishes for your future success and prosperity.

We request that you will be pleased to accept the accompanying collection of our musical instruments in Japan.

Hoping that you and your family will enjoy a calm and pleasant passage, and that you will safely arrive at your

We are,
Dear Sir,
Yours very faithfully,
(Signatures.)

(From the Students.)

Imperial College of Engineering,
Tokei, Japan, 28th June, 1882.

Principal Dyer.

Dear Sir,—We, the students of the Imperial College of Engineering, wish to present to you a specimen of our native bronze work, as a token of our great esteem, before you leave us to fill a new position at home.

We beg to congratulate you on your prospect of returning to your native land, but are sorry that we must lose you as our principal and teacher.

Be assured that we have a deep sense of what we personally owe to you, and that all you have done for us will be remembered by grateful hearts. We hope that you will kindly accept this memento, and retain it in remembrance of your ever-attached students.

(Signatures.)

28 Memorial monument marking the opening of the Imperial College of Engineering

29 Newspaper article concering the letter of appreciation to Dyer from Imperial College of Engineering graduates and undergraduates on the occasion of his departure from Japan in June 1882

30

Japan.

*Report by Mr. Watson, Her Majesty's Secretary of Legation,
on the present Educational System of Japan.*

Sir H. Parkes to Earl Granville.

My Lord,   Yedo, December 29, 1873.
  I HAVE the honour to forward a Report which has
been drawn up by Mr. Watson, with great care, on the
present Educational System of Japan.   It details the
measures adopted by the Government since they entered
on a course of educational reform, based upon foreign
principles; and it describes the beneficial results that
can already be pointed to, and the prospects that may be
anticipated in the future.
  I think I may add to the completeness of this account
by inclosing a series of four papers on the foreign and
native teachers, the Japanese students, and the Japanese
educational officials.   These papers have been written
by the same gentleman who supplied the description of
the normal school, embodied in the Report; and it is
only due to him to say, that his personal experience of
the subject enables him to furnish a description of the
working of these new educational institutions wh[ ]
as accurate as it is attractive.
              I have, &c.
          (Signed)   HARRY S. PARK[ ]

Inclosure 1.

Mr. Watson to Sir H. Parkes.

Sir,   Yedo, November 30, 18[ ]
  IN accordance with the existing regulation, [ ]
requires that statistical Reports shall be drawn up [ ]
by Her Majesty's Secretaries of Legation, I ha[ ]
honour to lay before you the following notes and [ ]
vations in regard to the present state of educat[ ]

30 The original version of the Calendar
was reported to the British Parliament in
the year of its issuance, 1873

003

Imperial College of Engineering
3d Nov. 1888

To H.E. Kuroda Kiyotaka

Dearsir
      I beg to acknowledge
receipt of the first Annual Report
of Sapporo Agricultural College
and to thank you for the same.
  I hope in a short time
to send you in return the new
edition of the Calendar of this College
          I am
          Your obdt Servt
          Henry Dyer

31 Dyer's letter of 1888 to Kiyotaka Kuroda,
who directed the reclamation of Hokkaido.

32 Institution of Civil Engineers, London, the first British engineering organization

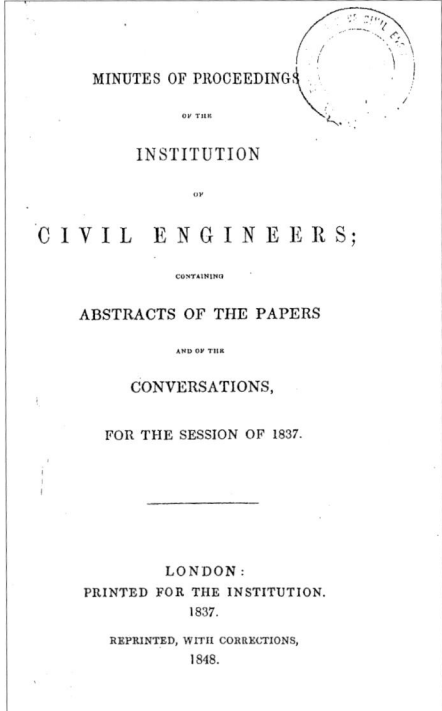

33

MINUTES OF PROCEEDINGS

OF THE

INSTITUTION

OF

CIVIL ENGINEERS;

CONTAINING

ABSTRACTS OF THE PAPERS

AND OF THE

CONVERSATIONS,

FOR THE SESSION OF 1837.

LONDON:
PRINTED FOR THE INSTITUTION.
1837.

REPRINTED, WITH CORRECTIONS,
1848.

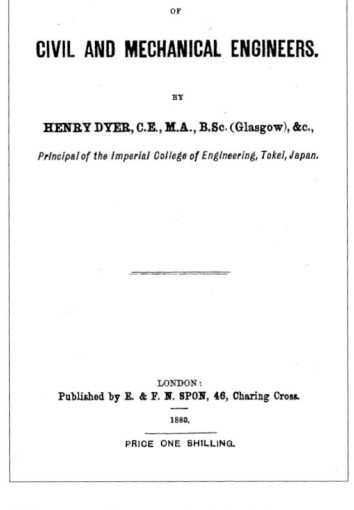

THE

EDUCATION

OF

CIVIL AND MECHANICAL ENGINEERS.

BY

HENRY DYER, C.E., M.A., B.Sc. (Glasgow), &c.,

Principal of the Imperial College of Engineering, Tokei, Japan.

LONDON:
Published by E. & F. N. SPON, 46, Charing Cross.

1880.

PRICE ONE SHILLING.

34 Dyer's first work: 'The Education of Civil and Mechanical Engineers', published by E.& F.N.Spon, London, 1880, and presented to the Institution of Civil Engineers

33 Title page of the first newsletter of the Institution of Civil Engineers, issued in 1837

35

35 Buildings of Anderson's University, the core of the Glasgow and West of Scotland Technical College, with the building for the Young Chair of Technical Chemistry on the left

36

36 The Royal Technical College in the precincts of Anderson's College, the centre of the University of Strathclyde today

37

THE

GLASGOW AND WEST OF SCOTLAND

TECHNICAL COLLEGE

CALENDAR

FOR THE YEAR

1887-88.

GLASGOW:
PRINTED FOR THE COLLEGE
BY ROBERT ANDERSON, 22 ANN STREET.
1887.

38

37 Title page of the calendar for the first year (1887–88) of the Glasgow and West of Scotland Technical College

38 The building chosen as the 'Henry Dyer Building' by the University of Strathclyde Senate, March 1986

39/40 *Left*, portrait of W.E.Ayrton (1847-1908). *Above*, portrait and signature of J.Perry (1850–1920)

41

003   Sapporo
20/4/78

To His Excellency
    Hirotake Oyushio

Sir,

In answer to your letter of yesterday :– I do not think that it will be imprudent to commence constructing the road. On receiving drawings and estimates from my students . I have directed that copies of these drawings to be sent to me in Tokio at the same time, and I shall beg leave

to make remarks to you upon them . Only that there should be little waste of time . you may wait until receiving my comments. upon the drawings, before commencing construction .

I remain

Your obedient Servant

John Perry

41 Perry's 1878 letter to the Japanese authorities, endorsing the survey by the students of the Imperial College of Engineering

43

42

42/43 Two technical colleges founded by the City and Guilds of the London Institute. Above, the Central Institution; below, the Finsbury Technical College

44

45

44 The Royal College of Science , where Perry once taught as a professor

45 Drawing of Ayrton's electrical laboratory at Finsbury Technical College

Imperial College of Engineering,

TOKEI, JAPAN.

PRINTED FOR PRIVATE CIRCULATION.

CONTENTS.

46 Title page and contents of the privately printed book that Dyer submitted in applying for the professorship of Naval Architecture at Glasgow University for the first time in 1883

"John Elder" Chair of Naval Architecture and Marine Engineering,

GLASGOW UNIVERSITY, 1886.

HENRY DYER.

CONTENTS.

47 Title page and contents of Dyer's privately printed book submitted for the second application for the professorship of Naval Architecture at Glasgow University, 1886

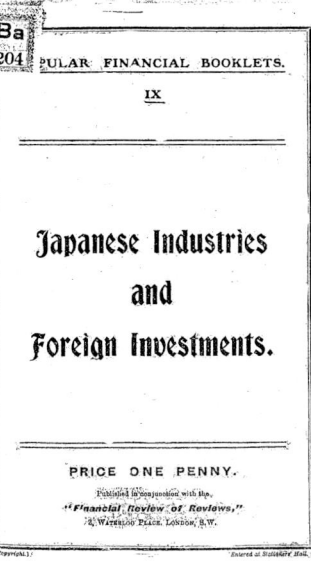

PULAR FINANCIAL BOOKLETS.

IX

Japanese Industries and Foreign Investments.

PRICE ONE PENNY.

Published in conjunction with the
"Financial Review of Reviews,"
2, Waterloo Place, London, S.W.

48 Title page of Dyer's essay on Japan's financial problems, 1906

Some Lessons from Japan.

BY HENRY DYER, C.E., M.A., D.SC.,

Emeritus Professor, Imperial University, Tokyo; Life Governor Glasgow and West of Scotland Technical College; Chairman Scottish Co-operative E.C. Association, &c., &c.

IT is universally admitted that the rise of Japan as a member of the comity of nations is the political wonder of the latter half of the nineteenth century, and it is not only the duty, but also the interest, of all the countries in the world to study the causes which have brought it about, and as far as possible to apply the lessons to be learned so that they may profit thereby. It ought, however, to be remembered that "cause" means the sum of conditions which produce a phenomenon, and that national evolution is so complex that it is impossible in a short article to state exactly the nature of the conditions or to estimate their relative importance. Moreover, conditions in different parts of the world vary so much that great care must be taken in applying the lessons to be learned from the experience of other countries. All, therefore, that I can attempt, meantime, is to mention some of the points which seem to require attention and to indicate some of the forces which have been at work to produce the changes, and especially those which have a direct bearing on the Co-operative movement. That movement is much larger and wider than is usually supposed, and the Co-operators of this country should keep their eyes open to the more general economic movements which are going on around them, and which are profoundly modifying the conditions under which their work is being carried on, and they should also note what is being done in other parts of the world. In the United States, for instance, the great development of trusts and syndicates is an illustration of what may be called an imperfect form of Co-operation in commerce and industry, the chief aim of which is the increase of the incomes of the capitalists, whereas the object of real Co-operation is the more equable and equitable distribution of the products of labour among the actual workers. Still, it is a step in the direction of Co-operation, and when the people of the United

50

49 First page of Dyer's essay, 'Some Lessons from Japan', 1908

50 Canal of the Lake Biwa project as it looks today, undertaken by Sakuro Tanabe, late 1880s, one of Dyer's graduates at the Imperial College of Engineering

51

51 Bunji Mano, one of Dyer's students, who became associate professor at the Imperial College of Engineering in 1882 and later a student at Glasgow University, returning to Japan in 1889

52

52 The Japan site of the international exposition in Vienna, 1873, with Gottfried von Wagener (1831–92) and Tsunetami Sano

53

54

53 An example of Wagener's ceramic ware known as Asahiyaki

54 Ceramic design by Kajiro Notomi, one of Wagener's outstanding pupils

55

56

57

55 The two Japanese who contributed most to Dyer's appointment in Japan, photographed in 1902: Tadasu Hayashi, who signed the 1902 Anglo-Japanese treaty, and Hirobumi Ito, the then prime minister, who received the British Order of the Bath

56 Portrait of Sakuro Tanabe, and his study with a portrait Dyer and his wife above the window.

57 Bust of Dyer, by K.Thompson, donated by the British Embassy to the University of Tokyo in 1998

governing body had to solve was to arrange a number of hitherto competing and to a certain extent opposing institutions into something like a homogeneous unity. Of course under the circumstances it is not to be expected that a perfect scheme can at once be evolved, but on the whole it will be found that a fairly good arrangement has been made.'[30] He referred to the day and evening courses of the college, and noted that 168 students attended the former and 1,771 attended the latter in 1887.[31] This article was later reprinted in the 20 October 1888 issue of *The Educational News*.

In the following year, Dyer gave two lectures on engineering education at the Institution of Engineers and Shipbuilders in Scotland. He lectured in February under the title of 'The Training of Architects', noting that 'I have taken an active part in the organization of two Colleges on opposite sides of the globe'.[32] In October, he gave a lecture 'On a University Faculty of Engineering', in which he observed: 'My proposals received a considerable amount of support from the Members, but there seemed to be a very prevalent feeling that however good they might be, they were not likely to be carried out for a considerable period ... as one of the Governors of the College, I have been able to have my proposals largely carried out.'[33]

According to Minutes of the Governors and Committees, Dyer did more than organize the divisions. As a member of the Committee on Library established on 21 September 1887, he submitted the Report on Library and Museum on 3 February of the following year. In the governors' meeting on 18 April 1888, he proposed that the Central Board for Technical Education in the West of Scotland should be set up for the supervision of engineering education in general, but his proposal was voted down for the reason that the matter was not within the committee's jurisdiction. On 17 September 1890, he moved that the Technical Schools (Scotland) Act, 1887, should be revised, and that the college should be included under the application of the act. In addition to positioning the college as an institution of engineering education, Dyer approached Glasgow University so that the college would be entitled to grant degrees. As early as 7 October 1887, he sent a long letter to the university, which was recorded in its minutes as follows: 'There was produced and read a long letter addressed to the Principal by Mr Henry Dyer, BSc, suggesting that the course of instruction in the new Glasgow and West of Scotland Technical College should be recognised by the University towards qualifying for the degree of BSc. Consideration of his letter was delayed' (Glasgow University, Minutes of Senate 1887–90, 7 October 1887).

□

Dyer recounted that his contribution to the organization of the Glasgow and West of Scotland Technical College was derived from his own experiences in the Imperial College of Engineering. In his lecture to the Glasgow Philosophical Society in 1893, for example, he observed:

> It is rather a curious fact in the history of education, that these courses are almost identical with those which I had previously arranged for the Imperial College of Engineering, Japan, and which now forms part of the Imperial University. My proposals, at first, met with considerable opposition from men whose names were well known in the educational world, who said that it was a mistake to specialise in a college or university course of engineering, and that all the students should go through practically the same curriculum. When they said this they forgot that modern engineering is not a single profession, but a group of allied professions, all, no doubt, having a common basis, but differing entirely in the nature of the preparation required for their special work.[34]

He also noted in *Dai Nippon* in 1904:

> An interesting fact in the history of education is to be found in the organisation of the Glasgow and West of Scotland Technical College. When that college was formed by the amalgamation of existing scientific institutions in Glasgow, I was able to transfer from Japan the programme of studies of Imperial College of Engineering to the Glasgow institution.[35]

Dyer's statement is endorsed by comparing the programme of studies of the Glasgow and West of Scotland Technical College with that of the Imperial College of Engineering. Based on the former's curriculum for the first year and the latter's curriculum for the year when Dyer was leaving, the specialized courses of the two colleges are shown in Table 2. The special subjects of Civil Engineering of each college are indicated in Table 3; these tables were intended for the second and third years of the three-year course of the Technical College, and for the third and fourth years of the six-year course of the Imperial College. The two tables clearly show that the results of Dyer's educational experiment in the Imperial College of Engineering were brought back to Glasgow.

Dyer utilized his experiences in Japan not only for the programme of studies but for other aspects of education, as is suggested in his lecture in 1905 at the Scientific Society of the college:

In another way Japan has not been without its influence on this country. Engineering is no longer taught as a single subject, but as a group of allied subjects depending on the general sciences; and the field which was formerly taken up by one professor or lecturer, is now divided among several, and engineering laboratories are parts of the equipment of every well-organized college. A few years ago when Lord Kelvin was inaugurating the James Watt engineering laboratory of Glasgow University, he reminded his audience that the Imperial College of Engineering, Japan, was the first educational institution which had a laboratory of this kind. The experimental

Table 2 Specialized Courses at Imperial College of Engineering and Glasgow and West of Scotland Technical College

The Imperial College of Engineering (Tokyo)	The Glasgow and West of Scotland Technical College
1. Civil Engineering	1. Civil Engineering
2. Mechanical Engineering	2. Mechanical Engineering
3. Naval Architecture	3. Naval Architecture
4. Telegraphy	4. Electrical Engineering
5. Architecture	5. Architecture
6. Practical Chemistry	6. Chemical Engineering
7. Mining	7. Mining Engineering
8. Metallurgy	8. Metallurgy
	9. Agriculture

Table 3 Special Civil Engineering Subjects at Imperial College of Engineering and Glasgow and West of Scotland Technical College

The Imperial College of Engineering (Tokyo)	The Glasgow and West of Scotland Technical College
1. Higher Mathematics	1. Higher Mathematics
2. Higher Natural Philosophy	2. Higher Natural Philosophy
3. Civil Engineering	3. Civil Engineering
4. Mechanical Engineering	4. Applied Mechanics and Steam
5. Geology	5. Geology
6. Surveying	6. Surveying
7. Drawing Office	7. Drawing Office
	8. Building Construction
	9. Laboratory
	10. One General Subject

and graphical methods introduced into every department of its course are now common in all the colleges in this country, thanks in great part to the exertions of some of my former colleagues in Japan. The method of combining theory and practice in the training of engineers which I introduced into Japan, is now being strongly recommended, and to some extent practised, under the name of the 'sandwich' system of apprenticeship.[36]

This quotation gives us three more areas where Dyer's experiences in Japan were reflected. First, as Lord Kelvin observed, an engineering laboratory originated in the Imperial College of Engineering and was adopted in many parts of Britain. Secondly, the experimental and graphical methods were invented by Dyer's colleagues and brought back to Britain. The names of the colleagues are not given, but they must have been Ayrton and Perry, as I will discuss in the following section. Thirdly, the method of combining theory and practice, introduced by Dyer into Japan, was winning a high reputation as the 'sandwich' system, which is especially noteworthy even today. I might add that the origin of the sandwich system is not certain, as is noted by Venables, a historian on British engineering education, in *Sandwich Courses*. According to the book, some believe the system was first introduced by Dyer into Glasgow, while others believe that the system had already been adopted in Glasgow University.

What now follows is an outline of the further development of the Glasgow and West of Scotland Technical College. In 1912, the college became the Royal Technical College, as we can see in Table 1, and its fine school buildings were completed in the precincts of Anderson's College. In 1913, the college was affiliated to Glasgow University, a step Dyer had long hoped to see. It was called the Royal College of Science and Technology after 1956, and it has been the University of Strathclyde since 1964. The Glasgow and West of Scotland Commercial College was incorporated into the University of Strathclyde, making it a university of engineering and commerce, while the agricultural department of the Glasgow and West of Scotland Technical College, which dated back to the foundation of the college, became independent as the West of Scotland Agricultural College in 1899.

The central building of the University of Strathclyde was built in the days of the Royal Technical College, shown in Plate 36. More and more buildings were added, until by 1984 it was made up of thirty buildings, according to the illustrated brochure on the University of Strathclyde, *Campus Development*, 1980. The buildings were named after people who contributed to the university: Anderson, Birkbeck,

Graham, Livingstone and others, but for an unknown reason Dyer's name was omitted. Having been forgotten for years, Dyer has recently been gaining attention. For example, on 18 March 1986 the Senate decided that the name of 'University of Strathclyde Centre for Industrial Innovation' should be changed to the 'Henry Dyer Building'. When I visited Glasgow in 1987, however, they still used the old name.

☐

W. E. Ayrton (1847–1908) and J. Perry (1850–1920), who taught at the Imperial College of Engineering under Dyer's leadership, achieved outstanding results through close cooperation. The college's success was due not only to Dyer's ability but also to his colleagues' support for the realization of his youthful ideals, as is pointed out rather ironically in the following quotation: 'Ayrton was then inseparable from Perry; they were known as the Japanese twins. Their association was much like that in the remarkable fish which carries a small male riveted to her side. Perry was the porpoise with which the wise fish Ayrton ever travelled. We at once took Perry into counsel and soon secured his appointment as our colleague.'[37]

We can find the biographies of Ayrton and Perry in the *Proceedings of Royal Society of London*. That of Ayrton (*Proceedings of Royal Society of London*, Vol. LXXXV, 1911, pp. i–viii) was written by Perry, and issued in book form in London. It reveals that he was born in London in 1847 and was the first student to gain a BA from University College, London. Passing examinations for the position of a telegraph engineer in India, Ayrton spent four years in the engineering service in Bombay. Back in Britain he started to work for the Great Western telegraph factory. It was then that Lord Kelvin approached him about the Japanese assignment. He transferred to Japan in 1873, teaching physics and telegraphy from the very start of the Imperial College of Engineering. His wife, Matilda Chaplin, was a noted and versatile obstetrician who authored *Child Life in Japan and Japanese Child Stories* (1879). Returning home earlier than Ayrton, Matilda submitted his curriculum vitae to his alma mater in hopes of a professorship. The cv, now kept in the Watson Library of the University of London, serves as a short biography written by his wife. According to this, his yearly salary was £1,200 at the beginning of his assignment in Japan, rising later to £1,500. Although paid less than Dyer, Ayrton nevertheless received quite preferential treatment.

Ayrton made good use of his laboratory for education at the

Imperial College of Engineering, and this made him well known. As already noted, *The Japan Weekly Mail* carried a detailed account of a visit to his laboratory in 1878, stating:

> We find it impossible to imagine that such work has been wasted. If we could share Mr. Ayrton's belief in the great power shown by some of his students, we might believe that a great school of scientific thought has been founded, and although we venture to doubt the existence of sufficient capacity in the Japanese mind for high original scientific work when unhelped, still our visit to this, the finest physical laboratory which exists perhaps in the world, has impressed us with the notion that those students whom we saw working, will yet leave an important impression of their own upon the history of science. We think that a graceful action might now be performed by the Public Works Department and without in any way annoying Professor Ayrton's successors, by officially giving his name to the laboratory which he has created. To men of science outside Japan, all future work in Natural Philosophy performed in Japan will be identified with Mr. Ayrton's name.[38]

The educational methods devised by Ayrton at the Imperial College of Engineering are rated highly even today. W. H. G. Armitage observed in *Social History of Engineering* (1961) that Ayrton's laboratory was the first in the world to offer lectures in Applied Electricity. *New Scientist* noted in its 6 November 1958 issue:

> As a professor in Tokyo (which then had been the world's biggest technical university), at the City and Guilds College, the Finsbury Technical College and the Central Technical College, South Kensington, he played a most important part in the development of technical education in applied physics and electrical engineering ... After a brief spell at the Great Western telegraph factory he went to Tokyo as professor of physics and telegraphy, and founded the first laboratory for teaching applied electricity, which served as a prototype for those that came after.[39]

Ayrton's great accomplishments are unforgettable to Japanese people. In Japan, 25 March is the Day of Electricity, which is traceable to Ayrton. On that day in 1878, Ayrton lit an arc lamp to celebrate the opening of business of the central telegraph bureau. Japanese people also remember his enthusiasm for studies. On the day when he was to leave Japan in July 1878, he stayed at the Imperial College of Engineering until the last minute, occupied with the guidance of his pupils. He then rushed to the station, only to find that he had missed his train. Heading back to the college, he continued the experiment. By the time he reached Hong Kong, he put the findings in order, sending them from Suez to the academic society in London by telegraph. Also, quite a few stories about his devotion to studies have been told by his former pupils, one being Ichisuke Fujioka, once president of a major electric company in Tokyo. Fujioka's biography shows that Ayrton valued study so much that he spent almost all hours working in his office with the exception of time for meals and sleep, describing him as a teacher who was eminent in both learning and virtue.

□

Perry came to Japan in 1875, to teach Civil and Mechanical Engineering, two years behind Ayrton. It is thought Perry was hired when Dyer returned home on leave to get married. It is interesting to note that the agreement for Perry's assignment is still on file in the Japanese Government, which is not the case with other foreign teachers. In it, Matheson acted as the Agent for the Minister of Public Works, as he had done in Dyer's assignment. Signed by Matheson and Perry in London on 2 July 1875, the document stipulated the term of three years and yearly salary of £800.

Perry was born in Ireland in 1850, and after gaining experience in an apprenticeship, he graduated from Queen's College, Belfast, as shown in his biography, 'John Perry, 1850–1920'.[40] He emulated Dyer in winning a Whitworth Scholarship, and later taught at Clifton College, where he was intent on improving the educational methods by introducing a physical laboratory and a workshop. In 1874, he became an assistant of Lord Kelvin, later taking his advice to move to Japan as a teacher.

Perry is also remembered for his enthusiasm for study at the Imperial College of Engineering. He was surprised at the remarkable laboratory equipment available, and he was so impressed with Ayrton's laboratory education that he observed in 'William Edward Ayrton' as follows: 'During his first year in Japan he arranged an electrical laboratory, which was certainly the finest then existing in the world'. Even in 1874, he was carrying out the idea that laboratory work was essential for all students, and that lectures and numerical exercise work were auxiliaries in scientific education. His students were earnest and hardworking, and they became enthusiastic about laboratory work, especially in electricity.[41] Inspired by Ayrton's example, Perry provided generous support, and he also applied Ayrton's methods to his own subject of Civil and Mechanical Engineering.

Perry made good use of practical work and field trips. Ayahiko

Ishibashi, one of the first-term graduates, recounted that Perry, on trips with his students, gave them a barrage of questions to answer. Four letters in Perry's own handwriting, written when he went on a surveying trip to Hokkaido with four students for the construction of a new road, are kept at the Northern Studies Collection at Hokkaido University. Plate 41 shows one of the letters; and it was written to assure the Japanese authorities that his students' survey map was reliable enough to be used as the groundwork for road construction:

> I do not think that it will be imprudent to commence constructing the road on receiving drawings and estimates from my students. I have directed that copies of these drawings to be sent to me in Tokio at the same time, and I shall beg leave to make remarks to you upon them. Only that there should be little waste of time, you may wait until reviewing my comments upon the drawings, before commencing construction.

We can see that Perry's educational methods had enabled his students to conduct surveys on their own. He is also well known for his introduction of the use of squared paper for mathematical education, as Kinnosuke Ogura, a notable Japanese mathematician, pointed out in his book on the history of mathematics education.

Ayrton and Perry co-authored quite a few papers and sent them to academic societies in London, earning them the sobriquet of Japanese Twins. Up to 1889, they had co-authored more than sixty-eight papers, according to the list of Ayrton's writings shown in the April 1910 issue of *The Central*, the bulletin of the Central Institution where he worked after returning home. They wrote such a large number of outstanding papers that Maxwell, the most prominent figure in electrical engineering in Britain, commented that the centre of electrical engineering had shifted from Britain to Japan, which has been quoted often.

□

Ayrton came back to London in the summer of 1878, and Perry joined him the following spring. They thus returned nearly four years ahead of Dyer. Ayrton left Japan before the graduation of his first-term students, hoping to get a position at University College, London.

This was open to people of various religious backgrounds. As noted earlier, Japanese students were admitted there in the closing days of the Tokugawa Government, assisted by A. W. Williamson, a professor of chemistry. The University of London itself was a new form of civic university, and offered, unlike Oxbridge, courses related to practical science. As early as 1841, the post of professor of civil engineering was established. The university could have even had the first chair of engineering in Britain, as the minutes of the university reveal: 'Millington, professor of Engineering and Application of Mechanical Philosophy to the Arts, was a professor at the Royal Institution, and was associated with Birkbeck and the Mechanics' Institution. He resigned the chair in 1828 on the refusal of the Council to guarantee a salary of £400 a year, but agreed to give an occasional lecture.'[42] The university, therefore, was started in 1828 without a chair of engineering, thus allowing Glasgow University the honour of being first.

In 1878, applications were invited for an additional post of professor of mechanical engineering of University College, and nine people applied, including Ayrton. According to documents kept in the Watson Library, for reasons unknown, none succeeded and instead A. B. W. Kennedy, a professor of civil engineering, held the post of mechanical engineering concurrently.

It was the City and Guilds of London Institute that made a donation for the new chair of mechanical engineering. There had been a time when neither the University of London nor other schools of such specialities as chemistry and mining in London could find effective measures to cope with industrialization. Professor Huxley of the Royal School of Mines, a leading figure in science education, wrote some papers in which he accused the association of guilds of indifference to engineering education for coming generations, and of failing to use its huge endowment for the public good. In 1878, pressured by public opinion, the City and Guilds of London Institute, offered an initial donation to the University of London.

The City and Guilds of London Institute then worked on the founding of its own self-financed college. As a preliminary, in 1879, the institute established chairs of physics and chemistry, requesting two men of science to give lectures in a room at Cowper Street School, Finsbury. In 1883, the Finsbury Technical College was inaugurated, with its new buildings completed. The institute also decided to establish a technical college of a higher standard in South Kensington, which was the site of the 1851 London Exposition and was considered quite likely to become the centre of science and technology. Construction of the school buildings began in 1881, and the college was opened as the Central Institution in 1884. Thus, the City and Guilds of London Institute secured two technical colleges in London inaugurated around the same time.

The foundation of the Finsbury Technical College was an epochal event in the history of engineering education in Britain, as endorsed by the following quotations: 'On 10th May, 1881, the foundation stone of the City College (Finsbury) was laid by Prince Leopold in the presence of distinguished company. Said the Prince: "My Lord Mayor ... I have now had the pleasure of laying the foundation-stone of the first technical college ever erected in London".'[43] Not a few people had very high opinions of the college, including Venables: 'A meeting was held at the Mansion House in 1876, resulting in a provisional committee in 1877 which brought about the foundation of the City and Guilds of London Institute for the Advancement of Technical Education in 1880, one of the most significant events in the whole of British technical education. In the following year the Finsbury Technical College was founded under the aegis of the City and Guilds of London Institute – the first college of its kind for technological studies, and later the Central Technical College which became the City and Guilds College, which is now a constituent part of the Imperial College of Science and Technology.'[44]

The Finsbury Technical College had 'a formidable teaching triplet', which was an expression by Brock. The so-called 'Finsbury Trio' were Ayrton and Perry, both returned from Japan, and H. E. Armstrong, a notable scholar who had devised a new method of science education. When lectures were given at a room at Cowper Street School, there were only two teachers, Ayrton in physics and Armstrong in chemistry. In 1882 Perry joined them, teaching mechanical engineering and applied mathematics. Armstrong declared that ... 'the Finsbury scheme was our tripartite work'.[45]

In 1884, the Central Institution, the other college owned by the City and Guilds of London Institute, named four professors, including Armstrong. However, one of them turned down the post, which was then taken by Ayrton. Here again, Armstrong and Ayrton worked together on educational plans. In 1892, Perry took up a professorship at the Royal College of Science, after ten years of teaching at the Finsbury Technical College. The Royal College of Science was established with the development of the Royal College of Chemistry. Thus, the 'Japanese Twins' became professors of two prestigious colleges vying for supremacy in London. By the Royal Charter of 1907, the two colleges and the Royal School of Mines were united as the present-day Imperial College of Science and Technology. The history of London technical colleges is shown in Table 4.

The Finsbury Trio were not monolithic in their views on engineering education. In particular, Ayrton and Armstrong often had hot arguments, of which Armstrong gave some account. For instance, he noted: '[Ayrton's] outlook, however, was definitely weighted in the

Table 4 History of London's Technical Colleges

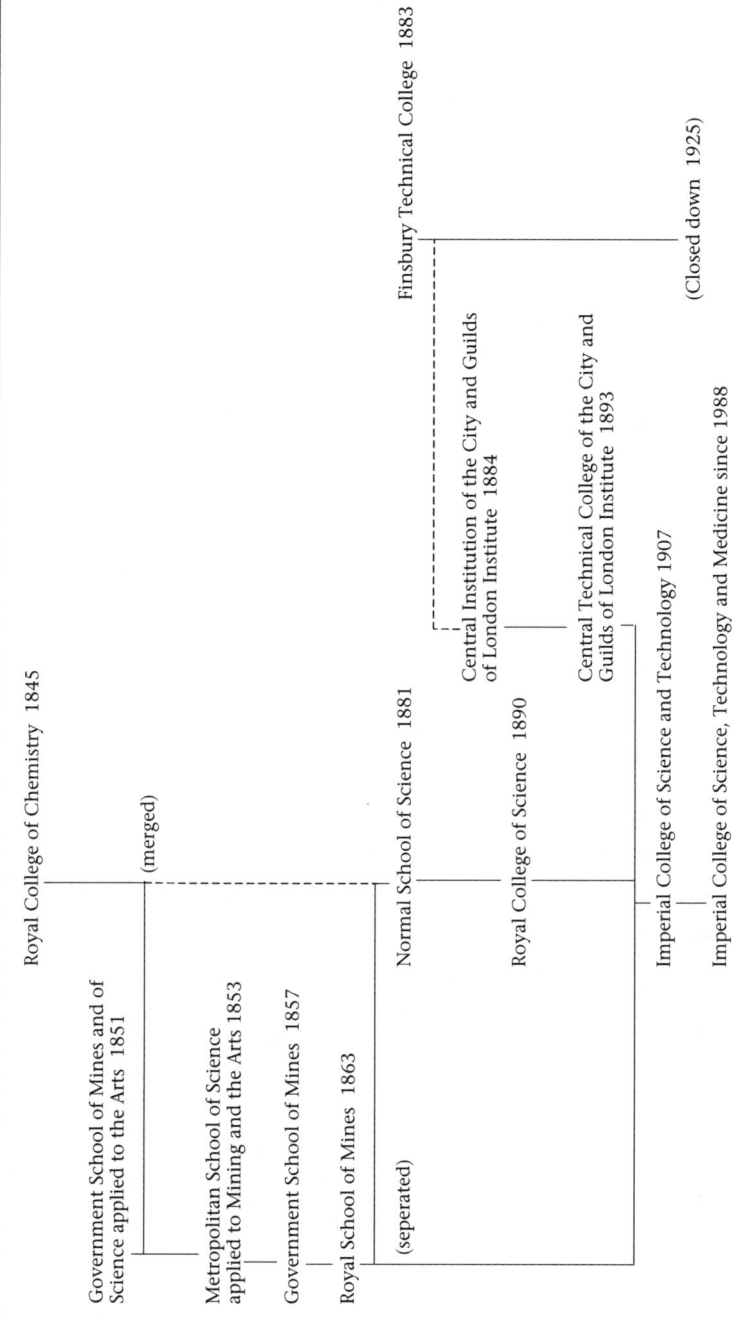

direction of commercial service and success. He always worked to industrial rather than to scientific ends, though his method of working was strictly scientific. Perry was very different.'[46] Evidently, Armstrong related to Perry more than to Ayrton, as is implied in the following quotation: 'Perry was a man of immense ability, the most delightful Irishman I have known. The burden of knowledge was not then so great. Ayrton knew little, except French and Latin, outside electricity . . . Perry knew far more than Ayrton.'[47]

It is quite probable that the arguments between Ayrton and Armstrong arose partly from their different backgrounds. Ayrton valued his five-year experience at the Imperial College of Engineering, sharing Dyer's criticism of German and French ways of education that attached more importance to theory. On the other hand, Armstrong put emphasis on his first-hand experience of German methods of education in Leipzig. Armstrong found Ayrton's educational approach too much swayed by industrial ends, as he gave priority to the practical application of theory. Further details on the arguments between Ayrton and Armstrong are given in the works of Professor Tomosuke Terakawa of Hiroshima University.

☐

The educational methods of the Imperial College of Engineering were brought back to the Finsbury Technical College and the Central Institution. The former, with the 'Japanese Twins' making united efforts, was influenced greatly by the Imperial College of Engineering.

Ayrton made the following statement in 1892, assuming the office of the president of the Institution of Electrical Engineers: 'It is only 15 years ago since I wrote from Japan to my old and valued master Dr. Hirst, then Principal of Royal Naval College, Greenwich, asking whether he thought that the time had come for starting in this country a course of applied physics somewhat on the lines of that given at the Imperial College of Engineering in Japan'.[48] Not getting a positive answer at that time, Ayrton embarked on a new educational approach after returning to Britain, by adding a laboratory emulating that of the Imperial College of Engineering to the Finsbury Technical College. Concerning this new method, Perry remarked:

> After his return to England, Professor Ayrton arranged an electrical laboratory at the Finsbury Technical College, intended for evening students who were workers in electrical engineering industries and also intended for large classes of day students . . . In 1884, when he became Professor at the College in Kensington, he, for the third time, arranged an electrical laboratory. The money available being as

great as what he had in Japan, his own experience being much
greater and quite different, and the position of the study of electricity being recognised as having become one of enormous
importance by the industrial world, it became what it now remains
– a most perfect laboratory.[49]

Ayrton's laboratory-based education in London is rated highly even
today. *New Scientist* observed that he 'played a most important part in
the development of technical education in applied physics and electrical engineering',[50] dubbing Ayrton the 'founding father of British
technical education'.[51]

Perry also earned credit for his achievements. *The Royal College of
Science Magazine* carried an article on his inauguration as professor
that observed:

> Much of his work was done in the four years which Professor Perry
> spent at the Imperial University of Japan. On returning to England
> in 1879, he devoted himself to the design of large machinery for the
> manufacture of electrical conductors, and to other practical pursuits.
> In 1882 he was appointed professor of mechanical engineering, and
> applied mechanics at the Finsbury Technical College, and delivered
> the Cantor lectures on hydraulic machinery in the same year ... As
> a teacher, Professor Perry has always been energetic and enthusiastic.
> His treatment of such subjects as Spherical Harmonics and Bessel
> Functions by graphic methods has done much to popularise these
> branches of mathematics.[52]

Perry won immortal fame in the history of mathematics education
by the utilization of squared paper for educational purposes. He
related in one of his books that this resulted from his experience at
the Imperial College of Engineering:

> Before 1876, sheets of squared paper were very expensive; they were
> only used by a few people in important work. In that year Professor
> Ayrton and I began to use it extensively in Japan, and when we
> returned to London and introduced at the Finsbury Technical
> College our methods of teaching mathematics and mechanical and
> electrical engineering and laboratory work, which have now become
> so common, we saw that one essential thing was the manufacture of
> cheap squared paper ... It is of importance that the student should
> use many sheets of squared paper, use them lavishly.[53]

Perry's great contribution to the development of mathematics
education was also pointed out in a report of the Mathematical
Association of Britain in 1926:

> Mathematics has long been recognised as an important element in
> the education of engineering and other technical students. Much
> thought has been devoted to the problem of presenting mathemat-

ical ideas in such a form that they can be readily assimilated and applied to technical problems. At one time, the presentation was undoubtedly too abstract. This tendency has now disappeared, chiefly owing to the efforts of the late Professor Perry. His methods have been adopted very widely.[54]

We can find more examples of the influence of the educational experiment at the Imperial College of Engineering on developments in London. According to Brock, the system of allocating the same first-year syllabus to all the students irrespective of their specialities was brought from Japan. In addition, the customary dependence on outsiders for examining students was replaced by the school's own management of all examinations after the style of Japan. These changes were also introduced into the technical college in Glasgow.

What was Dyer's opinion of the progress of engineering education in London? In his theories on engineering education, he often gave examples of Japan and of Continental countries, but did not make much reference to the developments in London. He did, however, take interest in the action by the City and Guilds of London Institute, which was ahead of the situation in Glasgow. In his first lecture back in Britain in 1883, which was delivered at the request of the Glasgow Philosophical Society, he stated:

> The whole programme of the City and Guilds of London Institute might be fully represented in Glasgow, not necessarily by special schools, but by classes in schools, which also afforded the students opportunities for instruction in general subjects. We have one special or trade school in Glasgow, the Weaving School, which has been very successful so far as its means would admit.[55]

He also noted in *The Evolution of Industry* in 1895: 'Those who are taking an interest in the organization of such classes should consult these syllabuses, and modify them to suit local conditions'.[56] In his lecture delivered at the Glasgow Philosophical Society in 1893, however, he noted in defence of the education in Glasgow that: 'A good many of the subjects of the programme of the City and Guilds of London Institute are now taught in Glasgow in connection with the Technical College and other organisations, although the stoppage of the grants by the Institute has recently had a damping effect upon them.'[57] This implies that he had great faith in engineering education in Glasgow. It is interesting to note that he never mentioned the names of Ayrton and Perry, even when he referred to the City and Guilds of London Institute. Was Dyer jealous of his former subordinates who enjoyed so much success and fame in London? Or, did his confidence in his work in Glasgow make him indifferent to the 'Japanese Twins'? We can only speculate.

NOTES

1   The Institution of Civil Engineers, *The Education and Status of Civil Engineers in the United Kingdom and in Foreign Countries*, London, 1870, p. v.
2   3, pp. 9–10.
3   3, p. 10.
4   3, p. 19.
5   3, pp. 43–4.
6   3, p. 3.
7   3, pp. 3–8.
8   3, p. 4.
9   3, p. 5.
10 3, p. 5.
11 2, p. 33.
12 69, p. 6.
13 5, pp. 1–30.
14 5, p. 1.
15 5, p. 2.
16 5, p. 5.
17 5, p. 8.
18 5, p. 4.
19 5, pp. 29–30.
20 59, p. 1.
21 59, p. 5.
22 59, p. 29.
23 The Glasgow and West of Scotland Technical College, *Calendar for the Year 1887–1888*, p. 15.
24 17, p. 2.
25 17, p. 2.
26 17, p. 2.
27 17, p. 2.
28 18, p. 12.
29 32, p. 428.
30 32, p. 429.
31 32, p. 429.
32 37, p. 1.
33 41, p. 1.
34 59, pp. 5–6.
35 69, p. 11.
36 71, pp. 10–11.
37 Armstrong, H. E., 'The Beginnings of Finsbury and the Central', *The Central*, Vol. XXXI, July 1934, p. 3.
38 *The Japan Weekly Mail*, 26 October 1878, p. 1131.

39 *New Scientist*, 6 November 1958, p. 1197.
40 *Proceedings of Royal Society of London*, Vol. CXI, 1926, pp. i–vii.
41 *Proceedings of Royal Society of London*, Vol. LXXXV, 1911, p. ii.
42 Bellot, H. H., *University College London 1826–1926*, London, 1929, p. 40.
43 Cardwell, D. S. L., *The Organisation of Science in England: a Retrospect*, London, 1957, p. 101.
44 Venables, P. F. R., *British Technical Education*, London, 1959, pp. 5–6.
45 *The Central*, July 1934, p. 3.
46 Armstrong, H. E., 'The Beginnings of Finsbury and the Central', *The Central*, July 1934, p. 5.
47 Ibid., p. 3.
48 *Proceedings of I.E.E.* (the Institution of Electrical Engineers), Vol. XXI, 1892, p. 2.
49 *Proceedings of the Royal Society of London*, Vol. LXXXV, 1911, pp. iii–v.
50 *New Scientist*, 6 November 1958, p. 1197.
51 *New Scientist*, 22 November 1979, p. 622.
52 *The Royal College of Science Magazine*, Vol. VIII, May 1896, p. 244.
53 Perry, J., *Elementary Practical Mathematics*, 1913, Chapter IX.
54 The Mathematical Association, *A Report on the Teaching of Mathematics to Evening Technical Students*, 1926, p. 1.
55 5, p. 25.
56 63, p. 196.
57 59, pp. 23–24.

4

Dyer's Studies on Japan: A Model of National Evolution

In 1883, a new chair of Naval Architecture was established at Glasgow University in a city already well known for its ship-building industry along the banks of the Clyde. The chronicle of the university's faculty of engineering referred to a noted ship-building engineer in Glasgow, John Elder, as 'the most brilliant mechanical engineer born on Clydeside since James Watt'.[1] He was also a close friend of Professor Rankine. After Elder's death in 1869, his widow donated £5,000 in 1872 for the chairs of civil and mechanical engineering at Glasgow University, and made another donation of £12,000 in 1883, specifically requesting that a new chair of Naval Architecture should be established. Dyer learned of this while he was in Japan, and he left for Britain in June 1882 to seek the post.

As stated earlier, Dyer recounted how he had returned home for personal and family reasons. He was still single when he first arrived in Japan, and it was while on leave in 1874 that he married Marie, a Glaswegian girl. Four children – three sons and a daughter – were born during his time in Japan: Charles Henry was born in 1877, Robert Morton in 1878, James Ferguson in 1880, and Marie Ferguson in 1882.

The time had come for Dyer to consider returning home and make his next move. For one thing, he had to think about his children's education, since his eldest son was now old enough to go to school. For another, his presence in Japan was less vital than in earlier years, especially as his leadership at the Imperial College of Engineering had enabled other teachers to stand on their own.

There is good reason to believe Dyer strongly desired to return to Glasgow University as a professor, although this assumption is based more on his actions than anything he said. He submitted his application in 1883. Observing the custom of those days, he submitted a privately printed book, entitled *Imperial College of Engineering, Tokei, Japan*, which is now kept in the university archives. Its fifteen items are divided into three categories.

The first is the recognition of his contribution by the Japanese: 'Her Majesty's Authority to accept the Insignia of the Rising Sun', 'From the Acting Minister of Public Works', 'From *The Japan Weekly Mail*, July 1, 1882', which was about his farewell party, 'From the Graduates', 'From the Students' and 'From *The Japan Weekly Mail*, November 15, 1879', which reported on the graduation ceremony of the college.

The second is the recognition of his accomplishments by people in Britain: 'From *Ross-shire Journal*, September 15, 1882', which covered Matheson's lecture, and 'From Miss Bird's *Unbeaten Tracks in Japan*'.

The third includes samples of British media coverage of the Imperial College of Engineering. They are 'From *Nature*, July 4, 1878', 'From *The Engineer*, June 28, 1878', 'From *The London and China Telegraph*, May 13, 1878', 'From *Engineering*, July 27, 1877', 'From *The Engineer*, July 20, 1877', 'From *Nature*, May 17, 1877', and 'From *Nature*, April 3, 1873'. I might add that '*The Engineer*, July 20, 1877' should have been the issue of May 18.

These published pieces explained how the success of the Imperial College of Engineering was recognized and appreciated in Japan, although no paper on Naval Architecture written by Dyer was submitted. During his stay in Japan, unlike Ayrton and Perry, Dyer did not find time for writing papers. He must have been very worried about this when he sat down to write to the Secretary of the Glasgow University Court to defend himself. His three letters are located in the university archives, but it was in the letter of 8 December 1883 that he gave a full detailed account of his ambitions in the field of Naval Architecture. He was aware that some of the strong candidates were from the Royal School of Naval Architecture and Marine Engineering, and in the letter he even expressed his critical view of that school:

> As I understood that some former students of the Royal School of Naval Architecture, and who possess its Diploma, are candidates for the 'John Elder' Professorship, and as I think it probable that they may attach undue importance to that Diploma, I send for the information of the University Court a copy of the Prospectus of the School as it existed when they were students, that is before it was combined with the Royal Naval College. I would draw the attention of the Members of the Court especially to the fact that it was possible to obtain the Diploma as a Naval Architect, with a very small knowledge of Marine Engineering, that subject only being estimated at 500 out of 10,000 marks, and as the great majority of the students came from the Government Dockyards, they confined their

attention either to Naval Architecture, or Marine Engineering. When I completed the Engineering Course of Glasgow University (which under Professor Rankine included a great deal of Naval Architecture), I proposed to become a student of the Royal School of Naval Architecture, but Professor Rankine suspended me from this as he said I had better opportunities in Glasgow of obtaining a good training in theory and practice, and in general education, as a man might pass through that school and know something about ships and engines and yet be ignorant of many subjects essential to one who was aiming at being a professor.

Information on the Royal School of Naval Architecture of those days can be found in *The Education and Status of Civil Engineers in the United Kingdom and in Foreign Countries*. When Dyer was thinking of entering the school, it was 'a School for the instruction, primarily of Admiralty pupils from the Royal Dockyards, and of Officers of the Royal Navy; and secondarily of naval architects and ship-builders in wood and iron, marine engineers, foremen of works, shipwrights, and other persons desirous of studying of Naval Architecture ... Diplomas are given to all persons, whether they have received their instruction at the School or not, who pass the final examinations of the school.'[2] Prevented from entering the school by Professor Rankine, Dyer was still making preparations for getting its diploma, when he was offered the post of the principal of the Imperial College of Engineering. It is true that he wanted to be a student of the Royal School of Naval Architecture and to study Naval Architecture, as it had been mentioned in his plan of studies submitted in 1870 for the Whitworth Scholarship. This letter indicates his pride in having had enough ability to obtain the diploma and his regret at not receiving it.

According to the minutes of Glasgow University Court, screening was carried out on 21 December 1883. There were five candidates, including Dyer. The minutes noted, 'After carefully considering the merits of the various distinguished candidates unanimously elected W. Francis Elgar in the Chair'.[3] As Dyer would have expected, they selected one of the graduates of the Royal School of Naval Architecture, who had the title of 'Consulting Naval Architect and Marine Engineer in London'. Graduating from the school in 1864, Elgar came to fame as an outstanding engineer. In 1880, he was even engaged by the Navy Department of Japan, spending more than one year giving technical advice and guidance to the Japanese concerning shipyards and harbour facilities. It cannot be denied that Elgar was a more suitable candidate than Dyer.

☐

Dyer felt that he should have written more papers, and he then devoted himself to overcoming the deficiency. Three years later, a golden opportunity came his way when Professor Elgar assumed the post of Director of Dockyards to the Admiralty, so that Glasgow University sought fresh applications for his successor.

Dyer applied for the vacancy, and he was pretty sure that he would succeed this time. The privately printed book submitted on this occasion covered, among other things, his reasons for applying, the list of his writings and letters of recommendation. He explained the reason for his application and his career in the form of a letter dated 16 August, in which he observed:

> I am strongly of opinion that so long as there is only one professor he ought to have been trained as a Mechanical Engineer, as Naval Architecture is really now a branch of Mechanical Engineering. This is especially true in the case of the chair founded in memory of John Elder, who was essentially a Mechanical Engineer, but who at the same time became a most successful shipbuilder.

He also noted:

> A distinguished professor has remarked that even the best men for the first five years after they begin teaching, teach themselves at the expense of their students. It is now more than twenty years since I commenced to train myself for such a position as is now vacant, and this I think ought to be a recommendation in my favour.

Dyer then listed his own twelve works, including the reports related to the Imperial College of Engineering and the Department of Public Works, his theories on industrial education and his papers. The theories on industrial education correspond to four of the items on the list of Dyer's writings, which appear at the end of this book, that is to say, items 2, 3, 5, and 13, while his papers correspond to six of the entries – items, 6, 8, 9, 10, 11 and 14. It is especially noteworthy that he submitted his own papers, unlike the previous occasion, when he applied without success. Four of these papers had appeared in the newsletter of the Institution of Engineers in Scotland.

He also appended letters of recommendation written for him by fifteen celebrities – each letter expressing a very favourable opinion. The letter written by Matheson is dated 5 March 1883, and is probably the same letter as was submitted in the first attempt. All the other letters were written for this second application. The fifteen writers were: H. M. Matheson, the Japanese Government's London Agent, David Rowan and Robert Mansel, who had both been president of the Institution of Engineers in Scotland, Alexander Shanks, a former manager of Napier's shipbuilding yard, J. A. Ewing, B. Sc., F. R. S. E., Professor of Engineering, University College, Dundee, who once taught at the University of Tokyo, Robert T. Napier, Shipbuilder, Yorker, who had been Dyer's fellow student at Glasgow University, Charles P. Hogg, the vice president of the Institution of Engineers in Scotland, W. Fleming Stevenson, D. D., a member of the Council of the Royal College of Ireland who once stayed in Japan, Laurence Hill, C. E., Shipbuilder, J. Murray Mitchell, M. A. LL. D., who once visited the Imperial College of Engineering, James Howden, Shipbuilding Engineer, John Turnbull, Jun., Consulting Engineer, Prof. R. W. Atkinson, F. C. S., F. I. C., etc., late Professor of Chemistry, Tokio Kaiseigakko (the parent body of the University of Tokyo), C. A. M'Vean, C. E., F. R. G. S., late Surveyor-General in Japan, and A. Allan Shand, London, late Foreign Secretary, Finance Department, Japan.

At the back of the book Dyer reproduced an article from *The Glasgow Herald*. This was about the screening process to select the right person for the principalship of the Heriot-Watt College in Edinburgh: 'A Special General Meeting of the Governors of George Heriot's Trust was held in Edinburgh yesterday afternoon to appoint a principal for the Heriot-Watt College. Lord Provost Clark, who presided, nominated Mr. Henry Dyer, M. A., B. Sc., 8 Highburgh Terrace, Dowanhill, Glasgow.'[4] It reported that Clark supported Dyer, saying, 'The curriculum of this College in Japan was very much the same as would be required in the Heriot-Watt College'.[5] In the run-off election, however, Dyer lost to F. G. Ogilvie by twelve votes to seven, according to the article. Dyer submitted this article about his unsuccessful attempt to be the principal, probably because he wanted to show that his career in Japan was appreciated and recognized outside that country.

The screening by the Court of Glasgow University was carried out on 21 September. According to the minutes, five people applied for the post, and two of them had been turned down the last time, including Dyer. One of the unsuccessful applicants of the last time, Hill, did not apply on this occasion but wrote a letter of recommendation for Dyer. In addition, he even sent another letter in support of Dyer directly to the University Court.

However, the decision was again a disappointment. 'The Secretary submitted application from the following five gentlemen. Their testimonials etc. having been previously sent to the different members of the Court ... The Court, after consideration of the various applications and testimonials, elected and hereby elect Mr. Philip Jenkins to the John Elder Chair of Naval Architecture (including Marine

Engineering) subject to the regulations laid down or to be laid down by the Senate.'[6] Jenkins's title was 'Lloyd's Surveyor'. According to Professor Kita, he distinguished himself with his work at the shipyard in Portsmouth, and he even gave lectures in place of Professor Elgar.

Dyer had lost again. He had longed to be a professor since he was a student at Glasgow University. He was an outstanding student and upon graduation had been offered the prospect of the chair of Applied Mechanics at Anderson's College. However, he opted for the Japanese assignment on the advice of Professor Rankine. He had returned home with flying colours hoping that this would meet with much recognition in Britain. But, he had failed, and must have thought he faced an important turning point in his career.

☐

Dyer felt that Glasgow University was stagnating, especially so far as the decision in favour of Jenkins was concerned. Dyer lost no time in sending a letter of protest to the University Court. The university archives contain the three letters sent to Anderson Kirkwood, the Secretary of the Glasgow University Court. The most important one, was written on 25 September, four days after the decision was made:

> I saw from the newspapers a few days ago that Mr. Philip Jenkins had been appointed to the 'John Elder' Chair of Naval Architecture and Marine Engineering in Glasgow University. I shall not dispute the wisdom of the appointment, but I wish to remark that before I became a candidate I was assured by Principal Caird that candidates should be prepared to teach both Naval Architecture and Marine Engineering. If I had not received this assurance I would not have become a candidate, knowing as I did the influence by which Mr. Jenkins was supported. When the Chair was founded three years ago, I received a similar assurance from the Principal, although not in so definite terms, as to the duties connected with it, but notwithstanding this, Marine Engineering has been simply ignored.

Thus, he was implying that Jenkins was not an expert in Marine Engineering, as well as insisting that Elder's intention should be respected for the appointment.

In the latter half of this letter, he criticized the indifference to the issues on engineering education by staff of Glasgow University, demanding that consideration should be given to improving the situation:

> When I returned from Japan I was under the impression that my special training and experience would be useful in Glasgow. Not only has this been declined by the University Authorities in connec-

tion with the John Elder Chair, but also I have had no evidence on the part of those most concerned that they feel any need for improvement in the present arrangements for the education of engineers in Glasgow. The position of professor and the salary attached to it, are matters of comparative indifference to me, but I have determined that a system of education more in keeping with the wants of the present day than the one now existing in Glasgow shall be established, and my non-election to the John Elder Chair should be no discouragement to me in my efforts. I shall try to cause the improvement to be made through the University, but if I find that impossible then it will be done outside of it.

Thus he felt compelled to express his disapproval of the University Court paying little attention to his experience and contributions in engineering education, in spite of the fact that the university was in urgent need of reforming its educational methods for engineers, and to which he was sure he was well qualified to contribute as an expert in the field.

It was not until 7 January 1887 that the University Court discussed Dyer's letter written more than three months before. Dyer had already been informed this would be the case; he then sent his second letter advising that, since he had first written:

... I have been elected a Life Governor of the Glasgow and West of Scotland Technical College, a position which will enable me to have considerable influence in connection with the matters mentioned in the latter part of that letter, and I feel convinced that if I had the support of the University Court in my efforts, I would in a comparatively short time be able to make arrangements which would do a great deal towards meeting the public wants, and that without going beyond the present powers of the Court, or throwing any additional expense on the University, or interfering in any way with existing interests.

The mention of seeking the university's support for the new college must be related to the conferment of degrees by it.

The minutes of the University Court on 7 January run as follows: 'Two letters having been received from Mr. Henry Dyer dated 25th September, 1886, and 3rd January, 1887, as to the recent appointment to the 'John Elder' Chair, and education in Marine Engineering in Glasgow. The Court were of opinion that no definite answer could be given to Mr Dyer, until he put his proposals in a more definite form, and the Secretary requested to reply to Mr Dyer in these terms.'[7] This indifferent reply made Dyer indignant. On 18 January, he sent his third letter, insisting that the University Court should give him their own view on the first half of his first letter regarding the qualifications of the rightful person for the professorship. The minutes of the University Court on 3 March noted: 'A letter from Mr Henry Dyer dated 18th Jan. 1887 was submitted to the meeting but it was not considered necessary to make any reply to it.'[8] Thus, the relationship between Dyer and Glasgow University ended in rupture.

In the third, unanswered, letter, Dyer expressed his intention to work for university extension. Indeed, a quick glance at the Dyer bibliography at the end of this book reveals a total of twelve works on the reform of universities – all were published between 1886 and 1890. He focused on the issue of university extension in some of them, for example, in *University Extension and Technical Education of 1888*,[9] *The Future of University Extension in Scotland of 1890*,[10] and *University Extension* of the same year.[11]

The movement of university extension in Britain started in the middle of the nineteenth century with the breaking of the traditional and classical concept of universities. However, Dyer looked at the problem from the standpoint of engineering education, and his goal was to revamp universities that remained unchanged and were falling behind the times. He was especially concerned about the reform of Glasgow University.

I will now outline his theories on university extension by referring to his three lectures made in 1889, when the Glasgow and West of Scotland Technical College was successfully carrying out education for the new era in stark contrast to Glasgow University.

The first of the three lectures was given to the section of architecture of the Institution of Engineering and Shipbuilders in Scotland, and its title was 'The Training of Architects'. Dyer insisted that a new chair of architecture should be established at Glasgow University and that the university should assist the new technical college in the presentation of degrees. He noted: 'I have said that in all our proposals we ought to have an ideal clearly in view, and in my opinion every educational arrangement should have for its crown a University degree. We hope before long that the Technical College will be connected with the University, and that its classes will be recognised for a great part of what is required for a degree'.[12]

The second lecture, 'A Modern University, with Special Reference to the Requirements of Science', was delivered to the Glasgow University Club. Dyer observed:

> It has always seemed to me that the University of Glasgow might attain more nearly to the standard of an ideal University than any other institution in the Kingdom. It can look back with pride on the work it has done during the past four centuries and a half, and it can

point to its flourishing schools of arts, law, medicine and theology. But if we could only get its members to rise to a proper ideal of its possibilities, the future could be made to excel both the past and the present. While encouraging and extending in length and breadth all the departments of learning which have hitherto been taught within its walls, there is a very wide field, the fringe of which only has hitherto been touched, in every department of natural and physical science, both theoretical and applied, and it is to this field I wish specially to direct attention.[13]

We can see in this quotation that Dyer asked those present to consider how teaching staff of universities should cope with the new fields of increasing importance. As one specific solution to the problem, he called for university extension with the following remark:

Between the University and the Technical College, the main departments of Pure and Applied Science are at least represented, and the latter institution is likely soon to be connected with the University in such a way as to make its classes available for degrees in the different departments of Applied Science. This is the first step towards the realisation of an ideal which I have had in my mind for a very long time, that is that the University of Glasgow should not simply be an institution situated on Gilmorehill, or even made up of various institutions is Glasgow, but that it should be an organisation, under the control of the University Court, which would include all the higher education in the West of Scotland, and that the value of that education should be estimated at its real worth, and apart from all accidents of time, place, or convenience.[14]

In his third lecture of the year, entitled, 'On a University Faculty of Engineering', he was emphatic about the necessity of the reform of Glasgow University, again speaking to members of the Institution of Engineers and Shipbuilders in Scotland. He argued:

The present time, when the University Act has been passed, is a crisis in the history of the University, and if advantage be not taken of the opportunities which have now arisen, they may be lost for ever. The inventions of James Watt revolutionized our industrial and social life, and were the direct cause of many of the problems with which we are now confronted. If it had not been for the assistance of the University of Glasgow these inventions might have been delayed for an indefinite period. To that University, therefore, the world has a right to look for the training of men who are not only thoroughly qualified to follow the scientific results of Watt's inventions, but also to assist in the solution of the social and political problems which have flowed directly from them.[15]

He expressed his firm belief that universities should adopt a positive attitude when dealing with social and political problems.

Judging from the above quotations from Dyer's lectures, it is probably not true that he criticized Glasgow University because he bore a personal grudge over being turned down. Dyer simply referred to Glasgow University as a living example, so that his theories on educational reform could take concrete shape. His arguments on university reform were largely influenced by Playfair, who was a leading figure in the field of engineering education of the time, and was once Dyer's senior at Anderson's College. Indeed, Dyer owed much to Playfair's writings, especially *Universities in their Relation to Professional Education* of 1873. Dyer shared Playfair's views that the universities in Scotland were originally started for the education and training of people of the learned professions; that universities should become involved in engineering education so that engineers would be recognised as members of the learned professions; and that universities should never neglect their primary mission of cultivating people with technical knowledge and skill.

□

In due course, Dyer fell into oblivion both in Britain and Japan. J. Stafford Ransome noted in *Japan in Transition* that Dyer returned home only to live a 'retired life'. Probably this is common ground, as no biography of Dyer has ever been written, except for the obituaries that appeared in *The Glasgow Herald* (26 September 1918), *Nature* (10 October 1918) and other print media. *Who's Who* carried his name during his lifetime, but we cannot find his name in the *Dictionary of National Biography*.

In order to discover whether Dyer really led a retired life, and to shed light on his life back in his homeland, I turned to his writings. The list of Dyer's writings is kept in the Archives of Glasgow University, and based on the list, Professor Kita cites 43 of Dyer's works. I was searching for more details on this point, when I found another list of Dyer's writings, written by himself. It was one of the materials that had been donated to the Mitchell Library. Dyer entered the list of his own writings on the right-hand pages of a large-sized notebook, and added notes on the left-hand pages when necessary. The list on the right-hand pages covered a total of nine pages and 89 different pieces of writing between 1877 and 1916 in chronological order. I have endeavoured to refer to as many of those works as possible, but there are some that I have not yet confirmed in printed form. By adding more of his writings to that handwritten list, I generated the Dyer bibliography at the end of this book.

Dyer, however, also revealed that he had contributed essays to newspapers and magazines, apart from the writings on his list. In the notes for 1896, for example, he said that he had contributed a number of essays to *Engineering, Co-operative News, Scottish Co-operator* and *The Glasgow Herald.* He made similar remarks in the notes for 1880, 1894, 1895, 1897 and 1912. By examining these newspapers and magazines it is probable that more items could be added to the bibliography.

Not counting these contributions, we can say that, rather than leading a retired life, Dyer was actively engaged in writing after his return to Britain. Indeed, following his first failure to gain the Glasgow University professorship, he worked hard on his papers. Then, when his second failure severed all links with the university, his writings took a new turn. In other words, they came to reflect his opinions and concerns in and around the following three topics: educational reform, social reform and Japanese studies.

First, let me discuss Dyer as an educational reformer. After 1887, he wrote a number of articles on educational reform, when he decided to take part in the foundation of a new technical college. As we have seen, his theories covered such issues as engineering education and university extension. In 1891, he was elected a member of Glasgow School Board, which greatly helped in the evolution of his theories on education. It was very important for people working on various reforms, including Fabians, to become members of school boards of big cities to promote these reforms. Dyer was well aware of the significance of his new position, as he remarked:

> In the matter of education especially, and therefore practically in all that refers to the welfare of the nation, it is of the greatest importance that those elected to position of school board members should be thoroughly qualified to consider all the aspects of the problems with which they are expected to deal.[16]

He even assumed the post of chairman of Glasgow School Board in 1914. Thus, he worked very hard on educational reform and in developing his theories. The word 'education' was used in the titles of 47 of the 89 items on the list of Dyer's writings.

Secondly, there is Dyer the social reformer. He was well aware of social problems becoming more serious, brought about by industry's remarkable progress. There was an urgent need to cope with increased poverty, class antagonism, deteriorating national morality and many other problems. As one step towards a solution, Dyer called for the reform of churches. He began to criticize the whole process of preaching and the preachers themselves, insisting that churches should work for the solution of social problems. He expressed his views on church reform in three essays in 1890 and 1891, and he often referred to the issue afterwards. As another step towards the solution of social problems, he turned to the co-operative movement. He believed that the welfare of the whole community should be promoted by co-operation, not by egocentric individualism. The co-operative movement of Britain owed its foundation to Robert Owen and Saint-Simon, and was influenced by socialism and dedicated to political and social reforms. Dyer became more and more inclined to support this kind of socialism. He was also greatly influenced by Sydney Webb, who was a leading figure in the Fabian Society.

Thirdly, let us consider Dyer as a scholar on Japan. He developed a fairly unique theory of national evolution, keeping the case of Japan in mind. He modelled his theory of industrial evolution after the theory of social evolution initiated by Spencer, which exerted an influence on his ideas on social reform in general. However, Dyer did not agree with Spencer's optimistic views, calling instead for the revision of the principle of laissez-faire to overcome evils caused by the development of industry and social reform based on individual choice. He also included Webb's ideas, such as those on collectivism and national efficiency in his theory of national evolution.

It should be noted that Dyer turned to an actual development that people in Britain had not yet recognized: the national evolution of Japan. In his later years he worked very hard on his studies of Japan, publishing two great works: *Dai Nippon* in 1904 and *Japan in World Politics* in 1909. The sub-title of the former is 'A Study in National Evolution'. He also wrote nine papers on various themes about Japan between 1904 and 1911. He came to Japan as a young principal with high hopes, and his efforts for Japan's industrialization and education certainly bore fruit, his contribution leading to Japan's modernization nearly thirty years after his departure. On his return to Britain, Japan must have seemed to him an ideal case of national evolution, as his efforts in Britain for social and educational reforms moved all too slowly and with much frustration.

☐

Dyer recounted in *Dai Nippon* how he took an interest in social problems soon after his return home:

> The greater part of the first year after my return was spent on the Continent of Europe in the study of educational institutions and the

inspection of engineering works. Hitherto my attention had been chiefly confined to the scientific aspect of my work, but personal knowledge of social and economic conditions in Europe soon showed me that engineering education was only a small part of the problem of education, and indeed that undue attention to it might help to intensify social problems.[17]

His first statement about social problems was made in his lecture, 'The Foundation of Social Politics', given to the Ruskin Society of Glasgow in 1889. He declared that he espoused the views of Ruskin as one of the greatest thinkers of the Victorian Age. After distinguishing himself as an art critic and then as a very influential social critic, Ruskin after Carlyle's death, was even referred to as a prophet as he advocated his ideal social reforms and opposed the principle of laissez-faire of the Manchester School. Dyer shared Ruskin's views, as is shown in the following quotation:

> What seems to me the most reasonable school of political economy is that which objects alike to social revolution and to rigid laissez faire. While rejecting the socialistic programme, its members think that the state should intervene for the purpose of mitigating the pressure of the modern industrial system on its weaker members, and extending in greater measure to the working classes the benefits of advancing civilization.[18]

He expressed his belief by noting:

> Those who wish to enter on such a path should seriously take to heart Ruskin's advice.[19]

In Dyer's opinion, one important step towards the realization of Ruskin's ideals was the reform of Christianity: 'The foundations of social politics must rest on Christianity, but it must be Christianity as Christ taught it, and especially as he lived it, and as he taught how men should live together, for the Christianity of Christ is essentially social'.[20] He believed that 'the foundations on which all our efforts at their solution must rest is in a socialized Christianity'.[21]

He made further comments on the issue of Christianity in his lecture, 'Christianity and Social Problems', which was given at Bridgeton Free Church. He began by outlining his agenda: 'My first duty is to make clear what I understand by Christianity, at least in its social relations. My second is to indicate some of the problems with which it has to deal, and how it must solve them.'[22] He went on:

> It is an inspiring ideal, which brings peace and harmony into the inner man. But while doing this it will also revolutionize social conditions, for Christ taught with great emphasis the dignity of manhood: that man is a man, and not a part of a machine for

grinding out dividends, or a mere human animal of less value than any other kind of animal. A clear realization of this principle of Christianity would in itself bring about great changes in our social arrangements, and would solve the problem which lies at the root of almost all the other problems with which we have to deal, the relations of capital and labour.[23]

He was concerned that the denial of Christianity by some socialists would estrange the working classes from Christianity; this made him emphatic about what was expected of Christianity for the attainment of 'true socialism'.[24]

As another important step to improve the welfare of people and of society as a whole, Dyer turned to the co-operative movement. He contributed essays to the annual reports of the Wholesale Co-operative Society from 1891 to 1893, supporting its activities. In the first of those essays, 'The Influence of Modern Industry on Social and Economic Conditions', he began with the following remark: 'Every age has its problems, and is entrusted with special means for their solution ... At the present time economics and the organization of industry and the problems connected with them are the most important.'[25] Then, he considered the problems that were caused by industrial development from different angles. 'Another force which is destined to have a mighty effect on the future of society is co-operation, the ideal of which is the substitution of brotherly trust and association for the cruel force of competition, which results in waste of energy and lives. For an account of its development and present position reference must be made to the *Co-operative Annual* and other publications.'[26] He maintained that the ideals of co-operation should be combined with those of State and municipal socialism:

> Measures connected with sanitation, education, and many other movements intended to improve the whole body of the people, are combinations of State and municipal socialism, and economically they are of the nature of investments of which the dividends are to be found in the improved health, happiness, comfort, and contentment of the people. Co-operative productive works are in an economic sense intermediate between the State or municipal works and those managed by private individuals.[27]

Dyer's theories of social reform culminated in his work of 1895, *The Evolution of Industry*. Instead of expressing optimistic and blind admiration of the evolution of industry, he sought ways to solve social and economic problems brought about by evolution. As he noted in the preface: 'Goethe prophesied that the great problems at the end of the nineteenth century would be the organization of mechanical industry and the social and economic questions connected therewith.'[28] He went on:

> The recognition of the processes of evolution in the natural and physical worlds, of the gradual progress from the simple to the complex, from the indeterminate to the determinate, from the uniform to the varied, from the homogeneous to the heterogeneous, and of successive integrations as the steps of this progress, has led to the application of the same methods and principles in psychology, morality and sociology, although, as we shall see presently, when we are dealing with intelligent and ethical man, great care requires to be taken in making analogies with the phenomena of the physical and natural worlds.[29]

Thus, he searched for a proper way to use the principle of natural and physical evolution for the benefit of human society. From such a viewpoint, it would be an example of evolution to opt out of the principle of individualistic competition and to opt in favour of people's well-being and co-operation. Co-operatives and trade unions would play more significant roles, and even the State and municipalities would be expected to become involved. Considering co-operatives, for instance, Dyer paid attention to efficiency, noting that 'the conditions of maximum efficiency in any organism or machine require that no energy be exerted with useless results, that friction be reduced to a minimum, and that the various parts be duly co-ordinated with each other.'[30]

Dyer concluded that the goal of future society was not a socialist revolution, but evolution by uniting various forces. 'The society of the not very distant future will have an admixture of individualism, trade unionism, co-operation, and municipal and State socialism; and not only will it be found that there is room for all, but also that all are necessary. As the evolution proceeds, these different movements will gradually approximate to each other in their results.'[31]

The book was reviewed in *Nature* as follows:

> Dr Dyer's book is an eclectic one, inasmuch as it adopts from previous writers such ideas and principles as commend themselves to the author. His frequent quotations are often followed by the remark – 'there is much truth in this' – and it is sometimes rather difficult to determine what are his own conclusions. It would not be difficult for both individualists and socialists to find support here to their own views; but the general impression made by the volume is, that the author is profoundly dissatisfied with the present state of society, and is inclined to some form of socialism as the only effective remedy.[32]

The reviewer was right in saying that Dyer was seeking measures to cope with existing social problems with his eclectic views slanted towards socialism.

□

Dyer set out on his career as an 'engineering educationalist'. His theories on education were significantly developed through his growing interest in social reform. As we have already seen, his theories on engineering education gave priority to the making of good citizens over good engineers, putting stress on general or non-professional education. His views on the importance of general education were adopted for his theories on social reform in his writings, including *The Influence of Modern Industry on Social and Economic Conditions* and *The Evolution of Industry*.

In the former, reprinted from the annual reports of the Wholesale Co-operative Society, Dyer observed: 'Modern machine industry, therefore, requires for its highest efficiency not only special manual skill, dexterity, and scientific knowledge, but also good general education to improve the intelligence of the workers and overseers, as well as special technical education in the principles and practice of their work.'[33] In the latter, he argued:

> Those engaged in industrial occupations should take a broad view of their work in the world, and assist in carrying it out in such a manner as will benefit not only those directly concerned, but also the whole community. In order that they may do this in an effective manner they should not confine themselves to those subjects which are of direct application in their work, but they should also take up those of a more general nature, which would enable them to rise above their own narrow sphere, and look at things in a broad and liberal spirit and to increase their own happiness and the welfare of humanity.[34]

The broad and liberal spirit acquired in general education was, in Dyer's views, closely connected with social reform of civic education. His most important essay on civic education is 'Education in Citizenship', which appeared in the annual report of the Wholesale Co-operative Society in 1894. He began by stating:

> One of the most remarkable signs of the times is the great change which is taking place in social ideals. It is being recognized that individual and selfish interests are insignificant when compared with those of the community, and that if we look at our own lives, and all that concerns them in their physical, intellectual, or moral

aspects, we see that we owe almost everything to the combined action of our predecessors and contemporaries ... The consequence has been a great development in social legislation, and a growth in civic spirit. Hence the necessity for such a training, that every member of the community may be able to take a fair share of the work which should fall to every citizen.[35]

To realize his goal of 'the welfare of the community as a whole' it was essential to instil people with the spirit of 'mutual help and co-operation'. He maintained: 'The education of public opinion in the right direction on all social matters is therefore a very pressing duty on all who have any influence, not only because of its direct effects, but also because public opinion in a country like ours is legislation in its nebular state.'[36]

We can also find Dyer's ideas concerning civic education in *The Evolution of Industry*. He thought that education in the duties of a citizen was imperative, especially when new political parties were expected to replace old ones and to initiate social and economic reforms:

Hence, the necessity for an education in the duties of Citizenship. As this develops and people are trained to think out the solutions of the problems, they will endeavour to become conscious helpers in the evolution of a nobler society than that of which they at present form part, and the highest ambition of every citizen will be to render efficient social service, to fill an honourable place in a well-organised community.[37]

Dyer made his theories of education more understandable to the public as he approached his declining years, writing *Education and National Life* in 1912 and *Education and Industrial Training of Boys and Girls* in 1913. The former has more to do with social reform, intended for the presentation of his views on 'the wide aspects of national education' as he himself remarked in the book. It is interesting to note that Dyer's handwritten dedication to Webb was found on the inside cover of a copy of *Education and National Life*. Finding the book in a second-hand bookstore in Britain, Yoshihito Yasuhara, a professor of Hiroshima University, purchased it. Dyer's dedication to Webb rather suggests his admiration of Fabianism.

Dyer expressed his views on general education as follows:

An engineer who is only an engineer, or indeed any professional man whose outlook is confined to his daily work, is, as a rule, a very poor specimen of humanity. All education should be liberal in the sense of fitting the students to adapt themselves to the conditions of life in which they find themselves. Specialization is, of course, necessary, but it ought to be placed on the broadest possible base.[38]

Concerning civic education, he maintained:

> It is generally admitted that the chief object of education should be the attainment of civic and social efficiency, which involves the making of good citizens in the highest sense of that term, and that the aim of all good citizens should be the promotion of the national welfare.[39]

He went on to discuss the existing obstacles to the attainment of those goals:

> The educational authorities in the past have not considered themselves charged with the training of good citizens. They were too often content that the child should become a mere grant-earning machine whose value was determined by the amount of knowledge which he could reproduce in an examination.[40]

He demanded that they should rise above 'payment by result system'.

We can safely say that Dyer was not a social revolutionist but an educational reformer, considering his contention that the problems of education were the key to the ultimate solution of social problems, as he noted in the preface to *The Evolution of Industry*:

> I believe, therefore, that the solution of the problem I have mentioned will not be brought about by a revolution, or a brand-new organisation, but by the evolution of movements at present going on, and by the development of intellectual and moral training (63, p. viii).

The reform of education was his top priority throughout his life, forming the main base from which his theories on various reforms were developed.

Dyer was appointed chairman of Glasgow School Board in 1914, as was reported in a newspaper as follows:

> A notable and thoroughly welcome and popular result of the School Board elections throughout Scotland is the appointment to the chairmanship of the largest of these School Boards – that of Glasgow – of Mr Henry Dyer, DSc, LL. D. Dr Dyer has for some time acted as vice-chairman of Glasgow School Board. He has long been perhaps its most active and efficient member, and as an educationist of life-long practical experience, whose views on the subject are of the most sane and practical character, his chairmanship is certain to mark an epoch of thorough effectiveness in the working of the machine.[41]

The article itself is a vivid and splendid account of Dyer as an educationist.

☐

Dyer devoted himself to his studies on Japan after the turn of the century, publishing his two great volumes, *Dai Nippon* and *Japan in World Politics*.

The former was intended as an analysis of the forces that successfully brought about the modernization of Japan, as Dyer stated in the preface:

> My object in the following pages has not been to give a history of modern Japan or detailed statistics of recent developments – to do that adequately would require at least a volume for the treatment of each of the main subjects mentioned in the different chapters – it has rather been to indicate the forces which have been at work in bringing about what is admitted to be the wonder of the latter half of the nineteenth century; namely, the rise of Japan as a member of the comity of nations, and to note some of the chief results.[42]

The book shows his research on various topics relating to Japan, which are reflected in the titles of its twenty chapters: 'Introductory', 'Fall of Feudalism', 'The Japanese Mind', 'Transition', 'Education', 'Army and Navy', 'Means of Communication', 'Industrial Developments', 'Art Industries', 'Commerce', 'Food Supply', 'Colonisation and Emigration', 'Constitutional Government', 'Administration', 'Finance', 'International Relations', 'Foreign Politics', 'Social Results', 'The Future' and 'Recent Events'.

Nature carried a detailed review, paying attention to the growth of Japan. Its opening remarks show that the reviewer shared Dyer's admiration of the determination and intelligence of the Japanese people who had attained their goal of modernization through education:

> The story of how Japan jumped from what she was to what she now is will always form one of the most remarkable episodes in the history of material civilisation. Not only is it this, but it is also a remarkable illustration of the results that can be achieved by occidental education fostered by and implanted on a system of oriental ethics.[43]

The reviewer also noted:

> We may give water to a horse, but to make him drink is another matter. In a similar manner we may cover a country with schools, but to induce people who have neither the ability nor desire to learn to take advantage of such schools is a formidable task. The Japanese had ability in a marked degree.

The review concluded that Japan was 'no longer a pupil, but a teacher'.[44] The book was also reviewed by such influential newspapers as *The Times*, *The Daily Telegraph*, *The Manchester Guardian*, *Daily Chronicle* and *The Glasgow Herald*, gaining a high reputation as the first book based on positive studies of Japan.

Dyer referred to the growth of Japan as a 'wonder' in his preface to *Dai Nippon*. In other writings, he used the expression 'political wonder'.[45] What did Dyer think was the most important of all the forces that had brought about the remarkable change? We can find the answer in the preceding quotations from *Nature*, while Dyer himself noted that the Japanese people's 'ardent patriotism, their high sense of personal and national honour, their keen intelligence have enabled them to work what is admitted to be the political miracle of the latter part of the nineteenth century'.[46] The use of the word 'miracle' is particularly noteworthy here.

Dyer stated that Japanese people's intelligence, their spirit and their national educational system had been combined successfully:

> The development of education in Japan during the last quarter of the nineteenth century is, without doubt, the most striking example in the history of the world of the influence of education in changing the economic, industrial and social conditions of a country.[47]

He dealt with the various aspects of Japan's growth from the sixth chapter of *Dai Nippon* onwards, attributing it to education:

> The outline which has been given of the educational organization in Japan shows that the recent developments which have taken place in that country have been laid on a solid basis of national education. The Government has taken the lead in encouraging and supporting educational institutions of all kinds, and the people have eagerly responded to the facilities which have been offered to them. All classes were quick in perceiving that from a personal and national point of view it was their duty to equip themselves in such a manner that they might be able efficiently to discharge the duties which the new conditions would place upon them ... The results of the educational arrangements which have been made in Japan will be evident from a perusal of the following chapters, dealing with the most important national developments.[48]

Above all, every part of education 'has had a more or less direct effect on the industrial development which has taken place in the country'.[49]

Five years after the publication of *Dai Nippon* came *Japan in World Politics*. The book was meant as an exploration of the role that Japan was to play in the comity of nations through further study of the topics raised in the first book, as shown by Dyer's remarks in the preface:

> The chief object of the present book is to consider some of the tendencies of the present time as illustrated by some of the important international problems which have resulted from the war between Japan and Russia as well as some of the wider aspects of the results of the economic and political development of Japan.[50]

The book was also intended to suggest a reconciliation of Eastern and Western cultures, as evidenced by Dyer's observation that:

> Thoughtful men in many countries are recognizing that the central problem of the future is the reconciliation of Western science and culture with Eastern modes of thought ... I have endeavoured to show not only the desirability but also the possibility of a reconciliation and a mutual understanding of the East and the West, and my efforts will not have been in vain if I have been successful in this, even in a very partial degree.[51]

The contents page of *Japan in World Politics* lists the following chapters: 'Meeting of the Far East and the West', 'Rise of Japan as a World-Power', 'Factors of National Life', 'Civilization of East and West', 'Japan and the Pacific Area', 'Japan and the Pacific Area – Continued', 'Japan and the West' and 'General Considerations and Conclusions'.

Japan in World Politics was intended mainly for the discussion of the fusion of the East and the West, to which I shall refer later. I now want to make the point that Dyer was more emphatic on the role of Japanese people in bringing about Japan's modernization than he had been in *Dai Nippon*.

> While it is impossible to integrate, even very approximately, the forces which have led to the success of Japan, one thing is quite clear, and that is that those of an intellectual and spiritual nature have been much more effective than the merely material ones.[52]

It seemed to Dyer that the Japanese had gained great intellectual powers by the time of the Meiji Restoration:

> What has been called the 'rise' of the Japanese in the scale of civilization has, therefore, for the most part been simply a change in the direction of their intellectual powers which has enabled them to assimilate a great deal of Western knowledge and apply it to their national affairs, without, however, giving up any of their own essential qualities ... In the course of little more than a generation the Japanese have shown that they are not only able to adapt Western science to Japanese conditions but to advance its borders by original investigation.[53]

Referring to the spirit of the Japanese in *Japan in World Politics*, Dyer paid special attention to their patriotism. He quoted General Kuropatkin, a Russian revolutionist who once studied at Glasgow University, as saying that the Russians had paid no attention to Japanese people's education in patriotism, and that Japan's victory in the Russo-Japanese War was due to this aspect.[54] Dyer admitted that the Japanese spirit was affected by various factors, but he believed that it was influenced most strongly by Shintoism and that moral instruction at Japanese schools played a very important part in the formation of that spirit.

In between the two books, he worked on other writings on Japanese studies, which are not so well known. In 1906, for example, he contributed four essays to *The Financial Review of Reviews*, a monthly magazine for British investors. Referring to Japan's growth and the Japanese spirit, he discussed the country's financial problems, which had worsened due to the Russo-Japanese War and various new enterprises. In those days, Japan had to rely on offering sterling bonds for subscription. Dyer contributed to the promotion of goodwill between Britain and Japan by making the Japanese needs known to British people.

The first essay, 'Japanese Industries and Foreign Investments', was later published in book form. In the preface, Dyer was introduced as 'the author of many works of Japan, including *Dai Nippon*, a well-known study in national evolution, and his intimate connection with Japanese industrial life during the past thirty years renders him specially qualified to speak with authority on the subject of the national industries.'[55] Standing by Japan, Dyer attributed Japan's war with Russia to 'the aggressive action of Western Powers, and especially of Russia',[56] arguing that Japan had had no choice but to countermove. He also spoke in defence of Japan, rather uncritically, that she had started on her way to modernization by the peaceful development of industry and commerce, and then gave examples of Japan's growth, including her constitutional form of government and her education. He recommended investment in Japan as follows: 'I have no hesitation in saying that, if the caution and prudence which should mark all commercial transactions is exercised, there should be no more difficulty in carrying on trade and assisting in industry in Japan than in any other country in the world,'[57] and added that the rights of foreign investors were secured by new Japanese laws.

In the second essay, 'The Commercial Morality of Japan', he pointed out that the notorious commercial morality of the Japanese was redressed, by observing that 'no unbiased witness would deny that a great improvement has taken place in recent years in the status and character of Japanese merchants, and that commerce and industry are now engaged in by men of high rank and honourable character who are exercising all the influence in their power to raise the standard of commercial morality of their fellow-countrymen.'[58]

In the third essay, 'Legal Aspects of Foreign Investments in Japan', he discussed the safety of investing in Japan in terms of her modern history. He concluded: 'Meantime there is not the slightest reason to doubt the safety of any investment which is issued with the authority of the central Government',[59] adding that 'the Japanese are too anxious to stand well with foreign countries, in every department of national life, that it is very improbable that they will dare to do anything which would lower their position among the nations of the world'.[60]

The fourth essay, 'The Japanese Loan Conversion', was about Dyer's interview with Mr Korekiyo Takahashi, the Envoy of the Japanese Government, which was requested by the editorial staff. Dyer repeated his belief blaming Russia for the outbreak of Russo-Japanese War, admiring the strength and generosity of Japan, and endorsing her sterling loans. He concluded: 'My present object being not to enter into a full discussion of economic conditions in Japan, but simply to indicate the grounds on which the Japanese found their claims to favourable terms when negotiating for the conversion of their high rated loans,'[61]

These four essays strongly suggest that Dyer was recognized as a leading scholar on Japan, and that he played an active part in promoting goodwill and understanding between Britain and Japan. Incidentally, in 1902, Japan's Department of Foreign Affairs commissioned Dyer to inform the British people of Japan's financial situation. The documents concerning that commission are still officially secret within the Diplomatic Records Office of the Ministry of Foreign Affairs of Japan.

☐

One of Dyer's best-known remarks is that 'the engineer is the real revolutionist'. He gave a specific example of engineers as revolutionists in *Dai Nippon*, by referring to the graduates of the Imperial College of Engineering making great contributions to Japan's national evolution. He noted that the most thoughtful minds in Japan:

> ... see that the engineer is the real revolutionist; for his work changes social and economic conditions and brings forces into

action which are more powerful than anything which can be done by mere legislation. The students of the Imperial College of Engineering are the men who, to a large extent, have been the means of developing engineering and industry in Japan, and it seems appropriate that a study of that remarkable evolution which has made that country a world Power should be preceded by an outline of the circumstances in which the College was founded and an indication given of the results which have followed from that evolution.[62]

He also observed:

It has been truly said that the engineer is the real revolutionist. He creates forces against which the efforts of politicians are vain, and even the actions of armies and navies are of little avail, since ultimately economic conditions determine the fate of nations.[63]

He remarked that the book, the subtitle of which is 'A Study in National Evolution', was dedicated to 'the students of the Kobu-Daigakko who have done so much to make modern Japan.'

The book was reviewed in *Nature*, from which I quoted earlier. Two weeks later, Dyer contributed an essay to *Nature*, under the title of 'Education and National Efficiency in Japan.' Concerning the development of Japan, Dyer noted:

At the root of all these developments has been the very complete system of education which has been established in the country ... The recent history of Japan is the most striking illustration of the influence of the wisely directed system of education on national affairs when those who are responsible for it are infused with high national ideals.[64]

In terms of national efficiency, Dyer called for collectivist policies by the government, especially in the field of education. He maintained that education should take the lead in such policies, citing the case of Japan as a model.

In a lecture of the following year, 1905, he stressed the role of engineers in social revolution: 'It has been remarked that the engineer is the real revolutionist, for his works bring about economic conditions which generate forces which cannot be resisted'.[65] He also stated that 'the drama which has in recent years been enacted in [the Far East], has had the engineer as the chief actor.'[66] Above all, he placed great emphasis on the Japanese victory in the war with Russia:

The success ... has been largely due to the engineering works which have been carried out in their country during the past thirty years, such as the railways, the dockyards, the shipbuilding yards, the telegraphs, and the numerous industrial establishments which made

Japan strong enough not only to withstand the aggression of Russia, but to be victorious over what was believed to be the greatest military Power in the world.[67]

He also expressed his belief that the rise of Japan as a new industrialized nation marked a new chapter in the history of the world.

In 1908, Dyer's essay 'Engineering in Japan' appeared in *The Times*. Here again, his opening remark was about the engineer as the real revolutionist, and he noted: 'The peoples of the West do not sufficiently recognize the important evolution which is going on in the Pacific area, and which will profoundly change the centre of importance, not only of the world's industry and commerce, but also of its politics.' He was convinced that 'recent events have shown that Japan will take a most important part in the further evolution which will certainly take place.' He emphasized that Japan's increasingly important role was a great credit to the Imperial College of Engineering, by quoting Hirobumi Ito as saying that the establishment of the college was 'one of the most important factors in the development of Japan today'.[68]

In *Japan in World Politics*, Dyer referred to engineers as revolutionists once again, and praised Japanese statesmen for their high hopes of building an industrialized nation. What won his greatest admiration was their extensive and effective use of educational functions, beyond the sphere of engineering education:

> While very complete arrangements have been made in every department of education which is required in industry and commerce, the Japanese Government has gone far beyond merely educational arrangements as usually understood, and it has not only shaped its national policy with the intention of developing the resources of the country, but has also directly undertaken the carrying on of work or assisted indirectly in that work, if it were of an educational nature, in the broad sense of that term. Whatever was necessary to enable Japan to attain the position at which she was aiming was considered to be part of the education of the nation.[69]

In his view, the Akabane Works programmes, as well as those of the Imperial College of Engineering, belonged to the category of 'the education of the nation'.

Frustrated with the stagnant state of industry and the perceived decline of his country in general, Dyer regarded the development of Japan as the ideal case of national evolution. His theories of social reforms dealt with industrial evolution, social evolution and then national evolution, positioning Japan as the perfect example. His views on national evolution exerted an influence on W. E. Griffis, whose studies on Japan were just as comprehensive and positive as Dyer's. After teaching at Tokio Kaiseigakko, the American scholar returned home and worked on his writings on Japan, including *The Mikado's Empire* in 1876, *The Religion of Japan* in 1895, *The Japanese Nation in Evolution* in 1907, and *The Mikado: Institution and Person* in 1915. He also wrote biographies of people who contributed to Japan's modernization: Perry, Harris, Verbeck, Brown and Hepburn. The title of the 1907 work, *The Japanese Nation in Evolution*, also shows how much Dyer influenced him.

☐

Dyer compiled his researches on Japan with the hope of throwing light on her exemplary national evolution, not only because he found it interesting as a scholar, but also because he was concerned about the situation at home and expected his works to provide pointers that would promote British social reform. As I noted earlier, Dyer remarked that he had transferred the programme of studies and educational methods of the Imperial College of Engineering to the new college in Glasgow. As he conducted further studies on Japan, he came to insist that lessons of national evolution should be sought from Japan in more areas. It was in the last chapter of *Dai Nippon* that he made his first reference to this; under the subheading 'Lessons for Great Britain', he maintained that the British should pay attention to the national educational system of Japan: 'We have seen that the educational arrangements of Japan are very complete, and that those who have had the advantage of them have been fitted to take an active and intelligent part in the great developments which have taken place.'[70] He referred to such lessons in other chapters by saying: 'Moreover, that progress is not by any means superficial, but has been built on a sound basis of education, which in some respects affords a lesson to Western nations',[71] observing that Japanese officials and students 'have laid a solid foundation for national progress in a system of education which is very complete in every department, and which, in some respects, affords lessons to Britain'.[72]

In 1908, Dyer went further in his essay, 'Some Lessons from Japan', which was contributed to the annual report of the Wholesale Co-operative Society. He noted in the opening paragraph:

> It is universally admitted that the rise of Japan as a member of the comity of nations is the political wonder of the latter half of the nineteenth century, and it is not only the duty, but also the interest, of all the countries in the world to study the causes which have

brought it about, and as far as possible to apply the lessons to be learned so that they may profit thereby.[73]

Dyer then discussed those lessons, referring to Japan as a model country of national evolution. Admitting that there were various factors that had contributed to that evolution, he picked up some important ones as subheadings: 'Life in Old Japan', 'Influence on the Character of the Japanese', 'Political Dynamics', 'Western Education in Japan', 'Administration, Government, and Legislation' and 'Developments of Industry and Commerce'. He concluded:

> What, meantime, I wish to insist upon is that the great lesson to be learned from Japan is that with nations, as with individuals, rapid and real progress is only possible when the awakened consciousness directs their energies to the attainment of truly national objects.[74]

In referring to Japan as a living model, he used the expression 'object lesson', when he noted that '[The Japanese] have given the nations of the world a striking object lesson in national efficiency'[75] and that the 'future economic evolution of Japan may afford an object lesson to the world'.[76]

Dyer touched upon lessons from Japan on many other occasions, of which the following three are instances.

First, he believed Japan's conduct in the Russo-Japanese War afforded a lesson for the world. In 'Japanese Industries and Foreign Investments', he noted:

> The standard of conduct of the Japanese statesmen, not only in politeness but also in morality and intellectual ability, in many respects afforded a lesson which the more thoughtful foreign representatives took to heart. That lesson was completed by the results of the war between Japan and Russia. In that war the Japanese soldiers and sailors displayed efficiency, skill and bravery which have won the admiration of the civilised world. They have also displayed moral qualities which may compel the peoples of the West to revise their standards of ethics and religion.[77]

In her peace treaty with Russia of 1905, Japan relinquished her demand for an indemnity, which Dyer regarded as a virtue. However, he made no mention of disgruntled and riotous Japanese people setting fire to official and private buildings in the central part of Tokyo, which is known as the 'Hibiya Incendiary Incident'. It is such discontent that led to the military gaining power and taking a hard line in subsequent decades.

Secondly, Dyer maintained that Britain should learn from Japan's moral instruction. In *Japan in World Politics* he criticized the situation in Britain, mentioning the case of Japan as a model example:

> In short, not only the syllabuses of instruction and the methods of carrying them out afford many useful lessons to educationists in Britain, where sectarian strife has too often prevented the development of education in all its aspects, including the religious, for the disputants seemed much more anxious to make men and women after their own way of thinking than good citizens inspired with a spirit which would impel them to work enthusiastically for the good of their country.[78]

In *Education and National Life*, under the subheading 'Lessons from Japan', he observed that 'at the present moment there is ample evidence to prove that the Japanese people are filled with a spirit of nationalism and patriotism of an ardour which is simply unthinkable to the British mind.'[79]

Thirdly, Dyer considered that the commercial education of Japan provided useful lessons, as well as technical education. In *Japan in World Politics*, Dyer remarked:

> Not only in technical, but also in commercial schools, Britain might learn some lessons from Japan. Our merchants still seem to think that an ordinary school education is sufficient for those who intend to follow commerce, but in Japan, as in Germany, students in this department go through a very complete course of study as well as of practical training, and we see the results in the rapidly developing commerce of these countries.[80]

He made further studies of this issue in his essay of 1910, 'Commercial Education in Japan', in which he observed:

> The Japanese were not long in recognizing, after their country was opened to foreign trade, that if they were to take a high position in world commerce they must have men who knew their business thoroughly, and while commercial education, as such, has not been developed to the same extent as what is usually called technical education, still a good deal has been done to prepare the younger men for all the different departments of their work ... I would ask the merchants of Glasgow – Have they nothing to learn from Japan in this respect?[81]

Having been unsuccessful in realizing his long-cherished dream of becoming a professor at Glasgow University, Dyer chose to push through reforms of technical education from outside the university. He then won a position as a member of an influential school board, ready to initiate reforms of the whole educational system of Glasgow. He called for social reforms, demanding reforms of churches and supporting co-operative movements. However, his efforts led to very few results, and he could not help feeling uncertain about Britain's slow progress and over her future, contrasting so vividly with the rapid progress of Japan. In Japan, his youthful efforts did bear fruit, making her modernization a great success. He regarded Japan as the living example of his ideal of national evolution, as she was still rising as the 'Britain of the East'. His studies on Japan also served as a warning to Britain, and exerted an influence on her own national evolution.

NOTES

1   Oakley, C. A., *History of Faculty*, p. 11.
2   The Institution of Civil Engineers, *The Education and Status of Civil Engineers in the United Kingdom and in Foreign Countries*, London, 1870, pp. 6–7.
3   Glasgow University, Court Minutes 1878–89, p. 230.
4   *The Glasgow Herald*, 15 May 1886.
5   Ibid.
6   Court Minutes 1878–89, p. 330.
7   Court Minutes 1878–1889, p. 332.
8   Ibid., p. 339.
9   27.
10 48.
11 51.
12 37, pp. 20–21.
13 39, p. 15.
14 39, p. 21.
15 41, pp. 21–22.
16 61, p. 310.
17 69, p. 11.
18 34, p. 26.
19 34, p. 31.
20 34, p. 18.
21 34, p. 30.
22 43, p. 3.
23 43, p. 6.
24 43, pp. 11, 13.
25 55, p. 3.
26 55, p. 33.
27 55, p. 42.
28 63, p. v.
29 63, pp. 26–27.
30 63, p. 124.
31 63, pp. 274–5.
32 *Nature*, 22 August 1895, p. 386.
33 55, p. 35.

34 63, pp. 208–9.
35 61, p. 286.
36 61, p. 305.
37 63, p. 51.
38 86, pp. 19–20.
39 86, pp. 7–8.
40 86, p. 33.
41 *Scottish County Life*, May 1914, p. 197.
42 69, p. vii.
43 *Nature*, 1 December 1904, p. 97.
44 *Nature*, 1 December 1904, p. 98.
45 79, p. 146; 82, p. 44; 84, p. 26.
46 69, p. 48.
47 69, p. 78.
48 69, p. 106.
49 69, p. 183.
50 82, p. v.
51 82, pp. vii–viii.
52 82, p. 135.
53 82, p. 120.
54 82, p. 112.
55 73, p. 3.
56 73, p. 3.
57 73, p. 10.
58 74, p. 405.
59 75, p. 116.
60 75, p. 117.
61 76, p. 336.
62 69, pp. 12–13.
63 69, p. 332.
64 70, p. 151.
65 71, p. 20.
66 71, p. 21.
67 71, p. 22.
68 80.
69 82, p. 122.
70 69, p. 426.
71 69, p. 308.
72 69, p. 342–3.
73 79, p. 146.
74 79, p. 152.
75 79, p. 165.
76 79, p. 166.
77 73, p. 4.
78 82, p. 110.
79 86, p. 39.
80 82, p. 117.
81 84.

5

Epilogue to the Original Study

All of Dyer's works are characterized by his historical and comparative approach. In other words, he developed his theories by effectively combining historical and comparative methods.

First, let me refer to his historical approach. As previously noted, Dyer showed interest in history when he was still a student. He wrote a paper 'The Influence of the Newtonian Principles on the Progress of Science during the Eighteenth Century', which won the Watt Prize. When he worked on his theories on engineering education, he insisted that historical recognition should be part of general education for engineers.

Also, he recommended Green's *History of the English People* for the students of the Imperial College of Engineering, and noted: 'The history of the constitution, the improvement of the laws, the advancement of the sciences, the vicissitudes of learning and the revolutions of the intellectual world, are of far greater importance than the personal acts of princes and rulers'.[1] In his lecture at the Institution of Engineers and Shipbuilders in Scotland, he emphasized that political recognition and historical recognition should be included in the general education of engineers. On historical recognition, he remarked: 'In the same way the historical development of the different departments of engineering could be made a most valuable means for developing the minds of the students, by showing the influence they have had on the advancing civilization of the world.'[2]

Dyer came to be known as a social reformer with the development of his theories on industrial evolution and social evolution, which resulted from his own historical approach. He believed the solution of a problem could be gained by analysing its cause from a historical point of view: 'In order that we may form an adequate idea of the effects of machinery on social and economic conditions and problems, it is necessary to look back at the days before these became very marked.'[3] In *The Evolution of Industry*, he turned to the history of industrial development, shedding light on the existing problems. Two years before the publication of that book, he had already adopted such a method in 'Education in Citizenship', in which he stated:

> A study of the evolution of industry from the earliest to the present time would be the best preparation for dealing with many of the problems which are now awaiting solution. The record of the various stages of our industrial development would not only show most distinctly the difficulties and dangers to be avoided, but also give a good idea of the possibilities of the future and the conditions which are necessary not only for the successful carrying on of trade and industry, but also for ensuring the welfare of the workers and of the community generally.[4]

In his studies on Japan, Dyer laid considerable weight on the accounts of Japanese history. In *Dai Nippon*, the first three chapters involved historical analyses. Also, the opening remark of his essay 'Some Lessons from Japan' was about the life in old-time Japan, and he noted in the essay: 'To know New Japan aright we must study Old Japan, for we cannot understand things as they are unless we know how they have become what they are.'[5] In *Japan in World Politics*, Dyer expressed his belief that the Japanese had acquired considerable intellectual qualities during the Edo Period, and he thought highly of the cultural standards in the days prior to the Meiji Restoration.

> The achievements of the Japanese since the adoption of Western methods show that under the old civilization, although there was not much in the way of what is called scholarship, there must have been intellectual qualities of a high character which prepared them for the reception of Western knowledge.[6]

Thus, Dyer was aware of the significance of the Edo period in terms of education many years before the British academic Ronald Dore made the same observation in his work *Education in Tokugawa Japan* after World War II.

Let me move on to Dyer's comparative approach, which is indicated in the following examples. When Dyer was working on the syllabus of the Imperial College of Engineering, he gave consideration to the systems of engineering education adopted on the Continent. Also, when he called for reforms of British engineering education back in Britain, he was thinking of the situation of countries on the Continent that he had visited soon after his return, and of his own educational experiment in Japan. His theories on engineering education covered not only Japan but also the rest of the world, and he maintained that engineers should keep a constant eye on developments everywhere. He observed in a lecture on engineering education at the Scientific Society of the Glasgow and West of Scotland Technical College:

> The successful man of business, in the future, must keep his eye on all parts of the world which are in any way likely to affect him. Those who do not are likely to find themselves stranded. Engineering education should, therefore, widen the sphere of vision of those who receive it, and fit them to understand the dynamics of the changing conditions, and to estimate the probable results.[7]

Dyer's comparative approach culminated in the cultural comparison of the East and the West, which I will refer to later. I will now show Dyer's emphasis on the comparative approach by the following quotation from *Japan in World Politics*:

> Our undoubted success in administering Eastern countries is imperilled from time to time by a constitutional indifference to other people's feelings, and by a neglect of the study of a comparison of the civilisations of the East and the West. That study would take us into many interesting fields of history, science, and philosophy, and all that can be attempted now is a mere outline of the subject.[8]

What is it that Dyer hoped to obtain by his methods of history and of comparison? Before he started to work on studies belonging to the sphere of social science, he was a natural scientist. In developing his theories of social science, therefore, he wanted some solid basis, even if it fell short of strict scientific rules. He referred to such a basis as 'direction' or 'the right direction' in his 'Education in Citizenship', meaning that generations and societies were on their way to evolution following in a certain direction.[9] He expanded his theories in *The Evolution of Industry* the following year, and attached more importance to finding 'the direction of the social movement',[10] which convinced him that a moderate socialism combined with collectivism was possible, through the processes of evolution and without a revolution.

☐

Dyer studied Japan as an exemplary country of national evolution with the hope of contributing to the evolution of Britain by providing useful lessons from his work. He also hoped that his own work would be of great help to Japan, as it contained advice for her future. Below are three examples of this advice to Japan.

First, he urged that Japan should not lose its own originality and identity in seeking knowledge from the West. He observed in *Dai Nippon*:

All the time I was resident in Japan I always urged that while the Japanese should take full advantage of Western science and civilization, in so far as these were necessary to make their country great and their individual lives full and complete, they should retain all the characteristics of Japanese life and character, and maintain their individuality not only nationally but also personally. The seeming reaction of recent years is therefore all in the right direction. A nation which forgets its past and gives up all its special characteristics neither deserves nor indeed is ever likely to attain true greatness.[11]

In his view, this was especially true of art industries: 'All real lovers of Japan, while admiring the energy and ability which have been displayed in the application of Western knowledge and experience to industry and commerce, and to the arts of war, would regret if, in the changes which are taking place, it lost those artistic qualities which have given it a unique position among the nations of the world.'[12] He also noted: 'I remarked that while I could not object to the arrangement and to the introduction of European art into Japan, I sincerely hoped that something would be done to prevent all that was good in Japanese art from disappearing.'[13] Dyer supported Tenshin Okakura (1862–1913), a Japanese art critic and philosopher who was known primarily for his attempt to protect and restore traditional Japanese art forms. Dyer later referred a number of times to this hope of restoration. For example, he stated: 'The modern economic conditions of Japan are having a profound effect on the art industries of the country, but it is to be hoped that amid all the changes which are taking place it will not lose those artistic qualities which have given it a unique position among the nations of the world.'[14]

Secondly, Dyer expected Japan to play the leading part in rousing Asia from sleep. He stated in *Dai Nippon*:

It is sincerely to be hoped that Japan, in her own interests, will continue her present policy, abstain from any attempt at territorial aggrandisement in Asia, and confine herself to commercial and industrial intercourse and to guidance in the rejuvenation of that vast continent ... Their duty is, therefore, to aid in the peaceful development of Asia and to give all assistance to the Chinese and the other peoples to reform their own Government and to take advantage of Western methods ... As I have frequently pointed out, this cannot be done by imposing a civilization on them from without; the impetus must come from within. Education should be developed in all its departments so that the people of China and Korea may learn what is necessary in order to hold their own in the international struggle for existence.[15]

He thought that lessons from Japan's national evolution would be of great help to Asian countries, as well as to the West. I will make further reference in due course to Dyer's belief that Japan should revitalize China and Korea, a belief he developed in *Japan in World Politics*.

Thirdly, Dyer hoped that Japan would make efforts to solve her own social problems caused by industrialization. In *The Evolution of Industry* he dealt with the invention of machinery that had changed social and economic conditions and brought about a large number of social problems, but he did not refer specifically to Japan. However, he came to be less optimistic about the evolution of Japan, observing in *Dai Nippon*:

> Those who return from Japan, especially if they have known it under the old regime, may well doubt whether the importation of Western civilization is likely to be an unmixed blessing to the people, although they will admit that it was necessary to save Japan from foreign aggression. Fortunately, the most thoughtful among the Japanese are recognizing these facts, and they are becoming more and more impressed with the necessity for attention being paid to the social and economic conditions of the people and to the problems arising therefrom.[16]

Dyer stated that the most important question was whether the people of Japan had been made better off by the shift from feudalism to modernization:

> After all, however, these developments are of small importance to the Japanese compared with the answer to the question, Have they been gainers by the changes? That is to say, Has the great body of the people been made healthier and happier and been enabled to develop their personalities to a higher degree than was possible under the old conditions?[17]

His answer was not unequivocally affirmative, and he truly hoped that Japan would not sacrifice her traditional values and culture for modernization.

☐

Dyer was undoubtedly greatly worried about the future of Britain. It seemed to him that it would suffer a downfall if his fellow countrymen remained unchanged. Above all, Dyer wanted people in

Britain to face up to the current stagnation, instead of simply looking back and taking pride in their highest stage of prosperity in the past. He said quite emphatically in 'Some Lessons from Japan':

> There are many lessons which the people of the West, and especially Co-operators, may learn from the people of Japan. First, however, it is necessary that we should get rid of some of our conceit and our ideas of superiority. In our egotism we are too much in the habit of looking upon all Easterners as uncivilised, ignorant, and bigoted, whereas in some respects they are our superiors.[18]

On several occasions, Dyer referred to the favourable circumstances that Britain had enjoyed for successful industrialization. For example: 'Great Britain owes its industrial position to its deposits of coal and iron and its geographical position, and to the fact that it had the start in the industrial race. Many of her advantages are disappearing as other countries improve their education, develop their resources, and extend their means of communication.'[19] He also observed:

> The British Empire has become great, no doubt, to a large extent through the sterling qualities of the British character, but also through a happy combination of circumstances ... Conditions, however, have changed, and are still rapidly changing, and it behoves us to consider carefully what we must do, not only to maintain our present position among the nations of the world but, it may be, our national existence.[20]

He came to believe that Britain needed more than the advantages that had once worked in her favour in order to succeed in the changing world. In his view, the rise of Japan offered a living example of what Britain needed:

> We must not be content to muddle through as we have to a large extent done in the past. We must face the altered circumstances and take full advantage of all the experience which has been gained and of all the lessons of science in the broadest sense of that term, in the same way as the Japanese have done.[21]

In other words, he expected the people to make combined efforts to overcome individualism for the national evolution of Britain.

Based on his theories and experiences, he came to the conclusion that it was crucial to arouse the spirit of the people of Britain for the sake of national evolution. In 1893, he noted in his lecture at the Glasgow Philosophical Society:

> If we wish our country to retain its position among the foremost countries of the world, we must recognize that neither technical skill nor scientific knowledge will avail much unless they are combined

with breadth of economic and political vision, and with depth of social feeling on the part of citizens. All experience and history show us that the spiritual is the parent and first cause of the practical, and that an ounce of manly pride and enthusiasm has always been worth a pound of technical skill.[22]

He made similar remarks in *The Evolution of Industry*, but he put more emphasis on the value of pride and enthusiasm, observing: 'All experience proves that the spiritual is the parent and first cause of the practical, and the economic history of the Middle Ages especially shows us that an ounce of manly pride and enthusiasm is worth more than a pound of technical skill'.[23] He also used this new comparison in another lecture.[24] He called for attention to spiritual lessons to be learned from Japan: 'The example of Japan shows how much the national spirit can achieve in the making of a nation. The want of that spirit, and the increase of selfishness and luxury in all their forms, may lead to the undoing of the British nation and of the empire.'[25]

In order to build the national spirit, education plays a very signifi-cant part. As an educational reformer, Dyer was searching for a new way of education based on British people's traditional outlook towards it until his theories on education made a unique develop-ment possible. On the Continent, the systematic education originating from Germany and France had begun to succeed. In Japan, the national educational system was quite complete in Dyer's view, playing the key role in her national evolution. However, he did not think that education for people in Britain was to be a copy of any specific nation. Rather, he sought for education that was in accord with British traits, which he referred to as 'real education'.

From the viewpoint of real education, Japan was not free from problems. In his farewell address to his students in Tokyo, he expressed his concern as follows: 'And first I would say, that in Japan the main object of education has not yet been clearly realized. Too often it is confounded with mere instruction.'[26] Back in Britain, he referred to Spencer, Huxley and other educational theorists in the country and developed his own ideas on real education as his ideal. In his lecture delivered in 1892, for instance, he quoted from Spencer and remarked: 'As Herbert Spencer has so well put it, "the essential question for us is: How to live? Not how to live in the mere material sense only, but in the widest sense".'[27] In another lecture in 1905, he observed: 'The greatest reform, however, which is required is a proper idea of the meaning and objects of education ... At the present time, especially, we must insist on the fact that man needs knowledge, not only as a means of livelihood, but also as a means of life, for it must be admitted that the majority of men and women do not live – they only exist.'[28]

Dyer's ideas on education were given their most clear and comprehensive form in one of his later works, *Education and National Life*, in which he renewed his belief that the revitalization of Britain depended on the direction of her educational reform: 'While it must be admitted that it is a great thing to teach children how to earn a living, it should be recognized that it is a far greater thing to teach them how to live.'[29] He concluded:

> An adequate system of education would ensure that the transition from the old to the new industrial and social system shall be effected almost imperceptibly and without any break of continuity, and at the same time would make our country great in the highest sense of that term, by enabling its people to realize their powers to the utmost, and to co-operate with the other people of the world in advancing the welfare of humanity.[30]

These quotations attest to his patriotism, his great faith in education and the solidity of his outlook on education.

☐

In *Japan in World Politics*, Dyer gave the following four goals that were expected of Japan as a member of the comity of nations:

First, Japan should 'prove to the world that modern civilization is not local but universal'.[31] He looked with favour on a passage from Hirobumi Ito's speech: 'Marquis (now Prince) Ito during his tour of the world in 1901 gave an interesting explanation of Japan's mission in a speech at the Metropolitan Club in New York City. "We are," said he, "the only people in the Orient who can fully understand the importance and significance of two civilizations, and I consider it a noble mission of our country to play the part of international broker in the further maintenance of the peace of the Orient"'.[32] Dyer also noted: 'All classes in Japan, from the Emperor downwards,have voiced the national aspiration of Japan to maintain permanent international peace and peaceful intercourse, commercial and political, among all nations of the East and the West',[33] which reflected how friendly Dyer's feelings were towards Japan.

Secondly, Japan was to 'harmonize Eastern and Western thought'.[34] Dyer expected Japan to work on this challenging mission: 'As has been already indicated her past history and her recent developments seem to show that Japan is peculiarly fitted to combine all that is best in philosophy and religions of the East and the West.'[35]

Thirdly, Japan should 'regenerate China and Korea'. Dyer observed: 'In former times, as we have seen, Japan owed a great deal to these two countries in the matters, not only of art and literature, but also of religion and ethics and of civilization generally, and she is now anxious to repay them as far as that is possible.'[36] He was aware of the difficulties, as he noted that Korea 'has, in a sense, become a dependency of Japan, and, as we shall see later on, the problems involved in her government are of a very complicated and difficult nature',[37] and that

> ... [the] awakening of China opens up many important questions which will require very careful consideration, on the part not only of the countries in the Far East directly concerned, but also of those of Europe and America. All the treaties which have been recently made profess a desire not only to respect the territorial integrity of China, but also to help her to take her proper place among the nations of the world, and it is to be hoped that this profession will be carried out in a spirit of brotherly co-operation and not in that of commercial or political aggression, as has unfortunately been too much the case in the past.[38]

The fourth goal for Japan was to 'promote the peace and commerce of the East'.[39] Dyer thought that Japan's success in commerce and war had raised 'a certain amount of jealousy',[40] and hoped that Japan would expand her commerce while maintaining good relations with her neighbouring countries.

In Dyer's view, these four goals were expected of Britain, as well as Japan. He hoped that Britain and Japan would work together for the realization of his ideal. We can safely say that those four goals are condensed into two important higher goals: the fusion of Eastern and Western cultures, and the attainment of world peace.

Concerning the fusion of Eastern and Western cultures, Dyer expected Japan to play the leading role and Britain to assist her. He noted in *Dai Nippon*:

> A new Power has arisen in the Far East which has not only a large share of Anglo-Saxon virility, but is also deeply imbued with Eastern thought, and it may have very important functions to perform not only in the domains of industry, commerce, and politics, but also in the realms of thought. The tendencies of the present day seem to show that Eastern philosophy streaming back to the West will produce a fundamental change in our thought and knowledge, and profoundly affect social and political conditions.[41]

Welcoming those tendencies, he used the expression 'streaming back' again in 'Some Lessons from Japan', in which he concluded:

To students of philosophy and religion it is very evident that we have much to learn from the East, and the tendencies of the present day seem to show that Eastern philosophy streaming back to the West will produce a fundamental change in our thought and knowledge, and profoundly affect social and economic conditions, and among all the nations of the Far East no one will afford us more lessons which we ought to take seriously to heart than Japan.[42]

Admitting that the fusion of Eastern and Western cultures should be promoted in such fundamental cultural spheres as philosophy, thought and religion, Dyer expected that a breakthrough would be made in the field of art, within which there seemed to be quite an East-West gap. He expressed his hope that: 'If Japanese art be guided on the right lines, it may interest every country in the world, not only from an artistic point of view, but also lead to that blending of Eastern and Western thought which, in my opinion, is necessary for the progress of the world.'[43] He also noted: 'It is to be hoped that conditions will be evolved in Japan which will allow of the free development of the artistic spirit, and lead to that blending of Eastern and Western thought which in my opinion is necessary for the true progress of the world.'[44]

In light of Japan's active adoption of Western cultures, including Western art, Dyer had no doubt that Britain should free herself from the assumption that there was 'an impassable gulf between the Eastern and the Western mind'. He wanted people in Britain to face the fact that 'the East (and especially Japan) has shown that it can imbibe Western thought and produce an amalgam which is more valuable than either of its constituents'.[45] Accordingly, he called for a shift in British attitudes towards the East:

One of the chief faults of the British people, and to a great extent of all Western peoples generally, is that they are so pleased with the advancement and excellence of their own institutions that they cannot understand why any other nation cannot be content with what contents them, and this tactless, unimaginative charity has been the main cause of their troubles in all parts of the world.[46]

Thus, he identified a problem bearing upon British international understanding.

The fusion of Western and Eastern cultures cannot be accomplished without maintaining world peace. Dyer called for Anglo-Japanese cooperation in the first place:

It will be interesting to watch how far the Britain of the East is in alliance with the Britain of the West, not only for political purposes, but also how far the two Powers are able to co-operate in the solution of the most important problems which lie in the future, and thus promote the highest welfare of the human race.[47]

Expressing his high hopes, he observed:

Japan seems to be in the way of becoming the centre of the world's politics. The treaty of alliance between Great Britain and Japan is one of the most important agreements of the kind ever made, and its results will be very far-reaching. It seems to secure peace and freedom to all the nations of the world for trade in the Far East, and also to be a great step in the direction of solidarity among the nations of the world.[48]

He anticipated the unity of not only Britain and Japan, but also of all the nations in the world, which had made him place his hopes on the second Hague Conference on World Peace of 1907. 'Although the Hague Conference failed to realize all the expectations of its earnest supporters, it at least made a beginning of an organization which, if properly developed, should be able to settle all international differences without the cruel arbitrament of war.'[49] He was convinced that the conference had made important initial steps, which would even lead to the realization of an 'International Parliament', which was his dearest wish. For the achievement of that goal, he insisted on Britain and Japan acting as mediators and peace-makers. I might add that the League of Nations, which is similar to Dyer's concept of an International Parliament, was established in 1920, eleven years after the publication of *Japan in World Politics*.

☐

Dyer harboured great expectations for Britain and Japan. It is for us to judge which was put into practice and which remains unfulfilled. No doubt this judgement should give due consideration to the situation of the early twentieth century when Dyer compiled his studies on Japan, and to the developments of world history ever since. Among various topics he discussed, let me focus on the aforementioned two important challenges, namely, the fusion of Eastern and Western cultures and the attainment of world peace.

First, let us look at the cultural fusion. Dyer regarded Japan's effort to adopt Western culture after the Meiji Restoration as a virtue. Japanese people stayed on the alert for the new developments of Western ideas and lifestyles, many of which they adopted avidly. One of the outstanding results brought about by this adoption was the unique thought of Kitaro Nishida, who succeeded in blending Eastern and Western philosophies in harmony. With the rise of the military and the aggression in China, however, such efforts were replaced by extreme nationalism, and Dyer's ideal of Eastern and Western cultures in fusion turned out to be just a daydream. As for people in Britain, their attitude towards the East did not change so easily, in spite of Dyer's assertion that they should try to understand and adopt Eastern culture, following Japan's example. They were proud and felt superior to people in the East, and the more emphatic Dyer became on the need to learn lessons from Japan, the more he alienated his fellows. Probably this is one of the reasons why he lapsed into oblivion.

Dyer's dream of world peace was shattered by Japan's invasion of China, which he had not anticipated. In *Dai Nippon*, he was emphatic about his own belief that Japan harboured no territorial ambitions:

> So far as I have been able to judge from the utterances of her statesmen, from the opinions expressed by the press and the general ideas of the people, the Japanese have no higher ambition than that their country should become the Britain of the East, resting secure in her own strength, but with no wish for territorial expansion in other parts of the world.[50]

He also noted:

> The aggressive action of Foreign Powers may indeed compel them to actions which also seem aggressive, but it is to be hoped that whatever happens, they will always be willing to grant to other Eastern nations all the rights which they have claimed for themselves, and chief among these is the right to work out their own national salvation in their own way, without foreign domination.[51]

By the aggressive action of Foreign Powers, he meant the interference of Russia, Germany and France to prevent the Japanese permanently occupying any part of the mainland of China, which Dyer thought was 'promoted by jealousy and selfish ends'.[52] Naturally, he stood by Japan on the outbreak of the Russo-Japanese War.

Likewise, Dyer did not look upon her increasing influence over other Asian countries as a form of colonization. He observed:

> Under the Chinese Government education in Formosa was almost entirely neglected, there being only two missionary schools, confined almost exclusively to the children of well-to-do parents who could afford to pay for it. The Japanese Government have been doing a good deal to encourage education, and there are now 120 Government public schools scattered throughout the island, many of them in buildings specially built for the purpose.[53]

He also justified Japan's position concerning Korea and China, maintaining that:

> In the strict sense of the term Japan has no colonies, for all the so-called colonial settlements are within the empire and under its central Government. What has been attempted is not colonization, but immigration from one part of the empire which had a surplus population to another part which was comparatively unoccupied.[54]

Five years later, however, *Japan in World Politics* showed that Dyer could not hold back his misgivings any longer. The international problems in the Far East had become so serious that such a Japan sympathizer as Dyer could not help sounding a warning. In the book, he reiterated the above-mentioned four goals expected of Japan, making the following noteworthy statement:

> If Japan is to fulfil her mission two elements in her society must be kept in check by her statesmen acting in harmony with the highest principles which inspire that mission. These are Militarism and Commercial Egotism. An army and navy are, under present conditions, necessary for the existence of the Empire, while commerce should be the chief means of her economic development. But if the soldier and the trader are not kept under some degree of statesman-like control, they are capable of becoming the most formidable, though unconscious, enemies, not only of the Japanese Empire, but also of all the countries with which she has relations, either commercial or political. The 'soul of Japan' has been able to inspire the people to deeds which have been the wonder and admiration of the world. Probably its most difficult task is to conquer that aggressive selfishness which is too often the result of the materialism of Western civilisation, and which is embodied in militarism and the equally heartless commercialism which are its greatest curses.[55]

Dyer had expressed his concern as a hypothesis, and did not mean that he had really noticed any sign of aggressive selfishness, militarism or heartless commercialism in Japan. The developments of the ensuing years, however, turned his concern into a reality. It was in 1909, when *Japan in World Politics* was published, that Hirobumi Ito, Dyer's greatest benefactor and admirer, met his death. During a tour of Manchuria, Ito was assassinated in Harbin by a Korean nationalist. In Japan in 1910, the following year, an anarchist plot to assassinate Emperor Meiji led to mass arrests of left-wing activists, while Korea was annexed by Japan. The next year the plot culminated in the execution of activists, nipping an anti-war movement in Japan in the bud.

Are we in a position to criticize Dyer for having overlooked Japan's course in the subsequent years? People must be divided in their opinion concerning that question. At least we are certain that his pro-Japanese remarks are not acceptable from the standpoint of the Korean people. In 1907, the Korean monarch secretly authorized an appeal of the protectorate treaty before the second Hague Conference on World Peace.

At that time, Japan proved not equal to the mission that Dyer had in mind, and failed to live up to his expectations of the fusion of Eastern and Western Cultures leading to the attainment of world peace. However, I would like to suggest that it is in the present day that Japan should try to meet his expectations. In this sense, Dyer had farseeing wisdom and his ideals were quite a long way ahead of his times, like those of Ruskin, whom Dyer respected very much. Dyer, therefore, is worthy of remembrance not only as a great engineer but also as an idealist philosopher of history.

NOTES

[1]   2, p. 52.
[2]   41, p. 8.
[3]   55, p. 6.
[4]   61, p. 291.
[5]   79, p. 147.
[6]   82, pp. 119–120.
[7]   71, p. 21.
[8]   82, pp. 138–9.
[9]   61, pp. 301, 305, 309, 312.
[10] 63, p. 20.
[11] 69, p. 369.
[12] 69, p. 204.
[13] 69, p. 207.
[14] 79, p. 150.
[15] 69, p. 391.
[16] 69, p. 12.
[17] 69, p. 365.
[18] 79, p. 164.
[19] 71, p. 21.
[20] 79, p. 165.
[21] 76, p. 335.
[22] 59, pp. 4–5.
[23] 63, p. 200.
[24] 71, p. 12.
[25] 86, pp. 107–8.
[26] 4, p. 2.
[27] 57, p. 4.

[28] 72, p. 30.
[29] 86, p. 48.
[30] 86, p. 109.
[31] 82, p. 169.
[32] 82, p. 169.
[33] 82, p. 169.
[34] 82, p. 169.
[35] 82, p. 169.
[36] 82, p. 170.
[37] 82, p. 170.
[38] 82, pp. 170–1.
[39] 82, p. 171.
[40] 82, p. 171.
[41] 69, p. 402.
[42] 79, p. 166.
[43] 69, p. 217.
[44] 79, p. 163.
[45] 82, p. 138.
[46] 69, p. 385.
[47] 69, p. 403.
[48] 79, p. 166.
[49] 82, p. 396.
[50] 69, p. 343.
[51] 69, p. 344.
[52] 69, p. 352.
[53] 69, p. 259.
[54] 69, p. 252.
[55] 82, pp. 171–2.

6

Dyer Revisited: Japan in the Twenty-first Century – On Her Way to Globalization

After expressing its determination that 'knowledge shall be sought for throughout the whole world' in the Charter Oath, the Meiji Government hired a large number of Westerners as teachers (*yatoi*) who were quite well paid. The number hired by government offices amounted to 213 in 1872, five years after the Meiji Restoration. As many as 153 of these were hired by the Department of Public Works, of whom 104 came from Britain – the nation exercising the strongest political influence in the Meiji Restoration, and 33 from France. By the time of the abolition of the Department of Public Works in 1885, it had hired 588 foreign teachers, including no less than 455 from Britain.

In 1873 the Department of Public Works opened the Imperial College of Engineering, with Henry Dyer as principal, and with another eight teachers, as is shown in Table 5.

After 1873, more teachers were hired, including the five teachers indicated in Table 6 who are especially well known.

These teachers devoted themselves to their duties in accordance with Dyer's educational principles. Dyer resigned in 1882 and was succeeded by Divers. Table 7 shows that the Imperial College of Engineering, which was called *Kogakuryo* or *Kobu Daigakko* in Japanese, was eventually transferred from the Department of Public Works to the Department of Education. The college was merged with *Teikoku Daigaku*, or the Imperial University (the Imperial University of Tokyo of later years), and developed as the Faculty of Engineering. This is the origin of the Faculty of Engineering of the present-day University of Tokyo. Among the staff, Divers continued teaching until 1899, Milne until 1895 and West until 1908.

Table 5 British Teachers Hired in 1873

Post/chair	Name	Educational background	Monthly salary
			yen
Principal	Henry Dyer	C. E., M. A., B. Sc., University of Glasgow	660
Natural Pholosophy	W. E. Ayrton	University College of London; Honorary Secretary for Japan of the Society of Telegraph Engineers, London	500
Mathematics	David H. Marshall	M. A., University of Edinburgh	350
Chemistry	Edward Divers	M. D., F. C. S., Queen's University, Ireland	500
Drawing	Edmund F. Mondy	A. R. S. M., Royal School of Mines, London	208
English Language & Literature	William Craigie	M. A., University of Aberdeen	208
Modeller	Archibald King		150
General Assistants	George Cawley		200
	Robert Clark		150

Table 6 Well-known Teachers Added to the Imperial College of Engineering Faculty

Chair	Name	Educational background	Monthly salary	Year of employment
			yen	
Engineering – Civil and Mechanical	John Perry	B. E., Queen's University, Ireland	333	1875
Mineralogy, Geology and Mining	John Milne	F. G. S., Associate of King's College, Royal School of Mines, London	350	1876
Architecture	Josiar Conder	A. R. B. A., University College, London	350	1877
Engineering	Thomas Alexander	C. E., University of Glasgow	350	1879
Mechanical Engineering and Naval Architecture	Charles Dickinson West	M. A., C. E., University of Dublin, Ireland, Member of Institute of Mechanical Engineers	350	1882

Table 7 History of Tokyo University

The Imperial University	The Imperial College of Engineering
1868 Kaisei Gakko	
|	
1871 Nanko	1871 Kogakuryo
|	|
1873 Kaisei Gakko	|
|	|
1877 Tokyo Daigaku*	1877 Kobu Daigakko
	1885 transferred to
1886 Teikoku Daigaku**	Ministry of Education
|	
1897 Tokyo Teikoku Daigaku	
|	
1945 Tokyo Daigaku	

* Departments of Law, Literature, Science and Medicine
** Departments of Law, Literature, Science, Engineering and Medicine

During the last thirteen years before the Imperial College of Engineering was placed under the control of the Ministry of Education, a total of 493 students were admitted, as is indicated in Table 8. The number of drop-outs totalled 111, which implies that the six-year course was so challenging that some students could not keep up. The number of graduates was 211.

Table 9 is the breakdown list of the above-mentioned 211 graduates in terms of their departments. All of them graduated when the school was called the Imperial College of Engineering, having entered during Dyer's principalship, and they were therefore influenced by his educational principles. In fact, Dyer personally tutored many of those specializing in Civil Engineering or Mechanical Engineering.

In accordance with Dyer's plan, out of the first year's crop of twenty-three graduates, eleven with outstanding records were entitled to be sent by the Japanese Government to Britain for further study. These graduates left for Britain in February 1880; four of them – Minami, Miyoshi, Shida and Takamine – studied at Glasgow University. All returned home by 1883 and were then engaged in what may be roughly divided into two categories of 'industry' and 'education'. Unfortunately, quite a few of them did not live long. Takayama returned to Japan one year earlier than the others because

Table 8 Number of Students at the Imperial College of Engineering

Year	Entry	Dropout	Death	Graduate
1873	32	3	0	–
1874	53	3	0	–
1875	53	4	0	–
1876	50	1	0	–
1877	46	13	0	–
1878	26	7	6	–
1879	25	18	2	23
1880	30	1	1	40
1881	29	8	3	38
1882	35	8	1	35
1883	50	20	4	35
1884	34	16	0	22
1885	30	9	1	18
Total	493	111	18	211

Table 9 Breakdown of Imperial College of Engineering Graduates by Department

	1879	1880	1881	1882	1883	1884	1885	Total
Civil Engineering	3	8	7	7	11	4	5	45
Mechanical Engineering	5	11	9	6	5	–	3	39
Telegraphy	1	2	6	6	5	1	–	21
Architecture	4	2	3	5	4	1	1	20
Practical Chemistry	6	5	3	2	3	4	2	25
Mining	2	11	9	8	4	9	5	48
Metallurgy	2	1	1	1	–	–	–	5
Naval Architecture	–	–	–	–	3	3	2	8
Total	23	40	38	35	35	22	18	211

of illness, with the intention of working at his old school, but died in 1886. Kondo did not survive his homeward voyage, and Shida and Kurimoto both died by 1892. The field of activity of the eleven students after their return is given in Table 10.

Table 10 Japanese Students who were Sent to Britain for Study in 1880

Name	Specialty	Major field of activity	
Kiyoshi Minami	Civil Engineering	<industry>	manager of railway company
Ayahiko Ishibashi	Civil Engineering	<industry>	pioneer of lighthouse construction
Shinrokuro Miyoshi	Mechanical Engineering	<education>	professor of Tokyo Imperial University, authority on naval architecture
Naomoto Takayama	Mechanical Engineering	<education>	professor of Tokyo Imperial University
Shin'ichiro Arakawa	Telegraphy	<industry>	leader of the spinning and weaving industry
Rinzaburo Shida	Telegraphy	<education>	professor of Tokyo Imperial University, pioneer of electric science
Kingo Tatsuno	Architecture	<education>	professor and dean of Tokyo Imperial University designer of famous buildings
Jokichi Takamine	Practical Chemistry	<industry>	discoverer of worldwide reputation
		<education>	founder of the Institute of Physical and Chemical Research
Takazo Kondo	Mining		(died on homeward voyage)
Fuyukichi Obana	Metallurgy	<industry>	pioneer of iron industry
		<education>	professor of Tokyo Imperial University, first Principal of Akita Higher School of Mines
Ren Kurimoto	Metallurgy	<industry>	mining engineer

Many of the graduates of the Imperial College of Engineering were involved in the national enterprises conducted by the Department of Public Works. By making the best use of the Western knowledge and skill acquired through British teachers, they contributed to those enterprises and helped Western expertise take root in Japan. In due course, the advent of Japan's industrial revolution increased the number of private companies and many of the graduates became prominent engineers in them. Some won credit for world-famous inventions. For example, Jokichi Takamine conducted research in the US and discovered adrenaline, diastase and others, while Masamitsu Shimose invented smokeless gunpowder, which turned out to be quite formidable in the Russo-Japanese War of 1904–5.

The graduates also contributed much in the field of education. Many were qualified enough to take the place of British teachers and became professors of the Faculty of Engineering of Tokyo Imperial University, which was the Imperial University until 1897.

Japan's technical education originated from the Imperial College of Engineering, which was intended for the education and training of top-line engineers. Later, more institutions were founded for the purpose of turning out lower-grade engineers. Those institutions of technical education in the Meiji Era (1868–1912) are divided into the following four categories:

(1) The Faculty of Engineering of the Imperial University – Tokyo (1886), Kyoto (1897) and Kyushu (1911)
(2) The Higher Technical School – Tokyo (1901), Osaka(1901), Kyoto (1902), Nagoya (1905), Kumamoto (1906), Sendai (1910), Yonezawa (1910) and Akita (1910)
(3) The Secondary Technical School – 33 schools
(4) The Apprentice, Vocational and other various Technical School – 74 schools

The principals and teachers of second category schools were provided by first category ones; schools belonging to the third or fourth category engaged principals and teachers from schools of either the first or second categories. Those who graduated from the Imperial College of Engineering played a significant role in the establishment, management and education of the schools in the first and second categories. Table 11 lists those graduates enjoying remarkable careers.

Among the educationists who were formerly Dyer's pupils, the two most outstanding figures are Sakuro Tanabe, a fifth-term graduate, and Bunji Mano, who was one of the third crop of graduates. Tanabe won fame as a young engineer who achieved success with the Lake

Table 11 Educationists who were Formerly Dyer's Pupils

Year of graduation	name	educational career
1879	Shinrokuro Miyoshi	Professor of Tokyo Imperial University (I. U.)
	Rinzaburo Shida	Professor of Tokyo I. U.
	Kingo Tatsuno	Professor and Dean of Tokyo I. U.
	Fuyukichi Obana	Professor of Tokyo I. U., first principal of Akita Higher School of Mines
1880	Yoshiaki Yasunaga	Principal of Osaka Higher Technical School
1881	Bunji Mano	Professor of Tokyo I. U. President of Kyushu I. U.
	Hatsune Nakano	Professor of Tokyo I. U.
	Osuke Asano	Professor of Tokyo I. U., Professor of Waseda University
	Yoshitatsu Kawakida	Professor of Tokyo I. U.
	Tamemasa Haga	Professor of Tokyo I. U.
1882	Hisaki Nobeji	Professor of Tokyo I. U., Principal of Iwakura Railway School
	Ariya Inokuchi	Professor of Tokyo I. U.
	Junzo Nakahara	Professor of Tokyo Higher Technical School, first principal of Kumamoto Higher Technical School, first Dean of Kyushu I. U.
	Gitaro Yamakawa	Professor of Tokyo I. U.
	Naka Matoba	Professor of Tokyo I. U., principal of Meiji Higher Technical School
	Tatsutaro Nakamura	Professor of Tokyo I. U.
1883	Sakuro Tanabe	Professor of Tokyo I. U., Dean of Kyoto I. U.
	Taki Otake	Professor of Tokyo Higher Technical School, first principal of Yonezawa Higher Technical School, first principal of Kiryu Higher Dyeing and Weaving School

Biwa Canal Project (*Biwako Sosui*) and attained the position of the Dean of Faculty of Engineering, Kyoto Imperial University. Mano became the Director of the Bureau of Industrial Education of the Education Ministry after his experiences as a professor of Tokyo Imperial University. He made great contributions as an administrator of technical education in Japan. In his later years, he was the President of Kyoto Imperial University.

SAKURO TANABE

Sakuro Tanabe was born in Edo (Tokyo) in 1861. He was a son of a vassal of the shogunate in the Tokugawa Period. After being persecuted by the Imperial Army during an ill-fated boyhood, he was employed by the Foreign Ministry of the new government. In 1877, he entered the Imperial College of Engineering, learning Civil Engineering from Dyer and other British teachers. When he was a student, Tanabe took a growing interest in the canal projects of such bodies of water as Lake Biwa which led to his graduation thesis on that subject.

The Lake Biwa Canal Project (see Plate 50) was planned by Kunimichi Kitagaki, the Governor of Kyoto Prefecture, who entrusted every detail of its technical design and execution to Tanabe. When the Emperor moved to Tokyo in the early Meiji Period, Kyoto lost its millennium-old position as the capital. In order to prevent Kyoto from falling into decline and to restore its vitality, Kitagaki and many others worked very hard on a number of important projects, including the Lake Biwa Canal Project. The purpose was to transport water from Lake Biwa to Kyoto city by building eight kilometres of tunnels and canals. It was hoped that it would provide people in Kyoto with abundant supplies of water and power from Japan's first hydroelectric power station, the Keage Power Station.

Supported by Governor Kitagaki, Tanabe made the best use of his expertise. Among other things, the project produced electricity for the mechanization of Kyoto's textile industry as well as for the first electric railway in Japan. News of the project was published in the British press quite early, with reports appearing in the 2 June 1888 issue of the *Mail* and the 20 January issue of *Industry*. On 12 July 1894, the Institution of Civil Engineers in London awarded the Telford Medal to Tanabe.

Even today, Kyoto has memorials in honour of Tanabe's contribution to the project, including a statue of the young engineer. Here are three examples of these memorials.

The first gate to lead water from Lake Biwa carries the following inscription: 'Sakuro Tanabe, Dr. Eng., Engineer-in-chief. Works commenced August 1885, completed April 1890.'

The second is the memorial erected at the junction of two rivers, the Kamo and the Takano, when a grand ceremony commemorating the project was held in July 1923. The inscription notes that the Lake Biwa Canal Project was epoch-making in Japan and unparalleled in the world, and that the project would never have been completed without Tanabe, who was so distinguished both personally and professionally.

In the third example, a memorial hall was opened in 1989 to commemorate the 100th anniversary of completion of the project. The hall has an exhibition of a number of notebooks on which Tanabe made notes of the construction process while supervising the engineering work. It is worth noting that Dyer's remark is written on the cover of each of the notebooks: 'It is not how much we did, but how well we did.' Probably Tanabe kept that in mind in carrying out the project.

Also, Tanabe stands out as a graduate from the Imperial College of Engineering which respected Dyer very much; he maintained cordial relations with Dyer even after the latter returned to Britain. In this context, I would like to recount the following five episodes.

First, Tanabe paid two visits to Dyer in Glasgow, in August 1900 and July 1914; the former visit is especially noteworthy. On that occasion, Tanabe was on a four-month tour of Russia, Europe and America, the main purpose of which was to observe the Trans-Siberian Railway. On the way, Tanabe visited Dyer at his residence in Highburgh Terrace near Glasgow University. Four years after Tanabe returned to Japan, his account of that visit appeared in a Japanese magazine, *Kogyo no Dai Nippon* (Dai Nippon of Industry), together with Dyer's photo with his own signature. Tanabe recounted, among other issues, how Dyer had been selected for the Japanese assignment, and what had made Dyer's educational trials a success.

According to the article, published in December 1904, Dyer and his wife gave a hearty welcome to Tanabe after eighteen years of separation. Dyer told his visitor how much he had been looking forward to the reunion, and that he had often seen Tanabe's name mentioned in the British media recording his success. Dyer was pleased when Tanabe told him about the remarkable careers of his other pupils. Dyer noted that he was very happy to hear every piece of news about the significant progress of Japan, encouraging Tanabe with his belief that Japanese people were expected to display their abilities in a variety of fields in the East and to spare no effort in order to demonstrate their leadership.

The table was set for Tanabe, Dyer, his wife and his four children. The eldest son was Charles, the second son Robert, the third son James and the youngest child was Marie, the daughter. According to Professor Kita, all four children graduated from Glasgow University, and made their own and very different ways through life. Unusually, none of them had any children themselves. Ian Dyer, who offered his support and cooperation to the Dyer Symposium of 1997, is Dyer's grandnephew.

Secondly, Dyer told Tanabe about his forthcoming book on this occasion, and gave him a complimentary copy. Tanabe concluded the account of his visit by saying that he was looking forward to reading Dyer's new book, *National Evolution of Japan*, which would soon be published. The book, the actual title of which Tanabe was not aware of, was, in fact, *Dai Nippon*, which was published in the same year. Dyer subsequently presented Tanabe with a complimentary copy of the volume, attached to which was the following dedicatory letter: 'To Prof. Tanabe Sakuro, a distinguished graduate of the Kobu Daigakko, who has done good service to Dai Nippon. As a mark of friendship and esteem. Henry Dyer.' This was the biggest tribute of praise to Tanabe from his respected teacher.

Thirdly, Tanabe consulted Dyer about his plan for compiling a volume on the history of Meiji industry. As a result of Dyer's encouragement, Tanabe took on the compilation after further discussion with Hirobumi Ito and other key statesmen. The project was sponsored by the Japan Federation of Engineering Societies, the first engineers' institution in Japan that owes its origins in 1879 to Dyer's suggestion. The project was delayed when necessary materials were destroyed by the 1923 Tokyo Earthquake, and it was only in 1931 that the ten volumes of *Meiji Kogyoshi* (History of Industry in the Meiji Period) were completed. Tanabe wrote the preface as chief editor, recounting his discussion with Dyer on the project.

Fourthly, Tanabe planned to invite Dyer to Japan in 1917, and was working together with his supporters on a fund-raising campaign to make it possible. However, World War I made Dyer's visit to Japan extremely difficult, and he wrote to Tanabe hoping that a delay would only be temporary. This was the last letter that Tanabe received from Dyer. It declared:

> This should reach you shortly before the New Year, and my wife and
> I send you and your wife and family our best wishes for your health,
> prosperity and happiness. A few weeks ago, I received your kind

letter of 15th Sept. with the information with regard to the progress of the History of Engineering in Japan, on which you have been engaged, for a considerable time. No doubt with the assistance of the Kogakukwai's special committee you will be able to make it very complete. I look forward to its publication with very great interest. Please keep me informed with regard to its progress, and the prospects of its publication. The graduates of the Kobudaigakuko are well represented on the Committee and no doubt they will be able to make a very complete history of the different departments of Engineering. I was very sorry to hear of the serious illness of Mr. Katayama. I hope to have better news of him in your next letter. Please give him my best wishes for his recovery and welfare. The end of dreadful war is not yet in sight and people in authority are prophesying a long war. The postponement of my visit to Japan has been a great disappointment to me. I hope the war will not last so long as to make my visit impossible.

Dyer died of illness in the following year at the age of seventy without realizing his wish to revisit Japan.

Lastly, Tanabe wrote Dyer's obituary for the *Osaka Mainichi Shinbun* on three occasions, emphasizing Dyer's great contribution to Japan's industrialization and her engineering education.[1]

Apart from distinguishing himself as the chief engineer for the Lake Biwa Canal Project and keeping friendly relations with Dyer, Tanabe was a scholar noted for his numerous scientific books and papers. It is striking that many of his scientific papers appeared in *Kogakukaishi*, the journal of Kogakkai that had originated from Dyer's suggestion. One of his most famous books is the textbook *Koshiki Kosi Hikkei* published in Kyoto in 1888, which was intended for engineers and skilled workers involved in the Lake Biwa Canal Project. In the book, Tanabe gave a simple explanation of what he had learned from Dyer and other teachers of the Imperial College of Engineering, including formulae and tables necessary for surveying and designing. The book enjoyed popularity for years among those who contributed to Japan's modern civil engineering. Tanabe also gave a concise explanation of the principle of water power generation in his book *Suiryoku* (Water Power) published in 1896.

Tanabe also taught at universities. In 1890 he became a professor at the Imperial University (Tokyo). In 1897 the second Imperial University was established in Kyoto, and he became a professor in the Department of Science and Engineering in 1900. This was divided into separate departments of Science and of Engineering in 1915, and Tanabe was the Dean of the Department of Engineering from 1916 to 1918. He died in Kyoto in 1944. In his study shown in Plate 56, a portrait of Dyer and his wife is quite noticeable, which indicates that Tanabe had respected Dyer as his mentor throughout his life.

BUNJI MANO

Like Tanabe, Mano was born to a *Bakufu* samurai family. After the Meiji Restoration of 1868, such families were forced to move from Edo to Shizuoka, where they faced a hard life; Mano's family was one of these.

In 1875, Mano went to Tokyo to attend the Imperial College of Engineering. In 1881, he graduated with honours in Mechanical Engineering. Mano was older than Tanabe by one year, and was his senior by two years at the college.

He became an associate professor at the college in 1882, and four years later, he was ordered to study in Britain. He became a student of Glasgow University, recording excellent grades. According to his Matriculation Card, which is kept at the university, he was awarded the Walker Prize, the Harvey Prize and others. The Japanese press reported that Lord Kelvin had expressed his admiration for Mano's scholastic talent. Mano then moved to Newcastle, where he engaged in practical training in the Armstrong factory. He also gained membership of the Institute of Mechanical Engineering in London. On his way back home he made an observation tour by way of Europe and America. Returning home in 1889, he was promoted to the post of professor at the Imperial University and was appointed to a governmental post of the Patent Office Examiner. In 1891, he gained a doctorate in engineering, the same year as Tanabe.

In 1899, Mano was sent to France so that he could observe and learn the latest developments in industry and science. He returned to Japan in 1901, taking up the office of Director of the Bureau of Industrial Education in the Ministry of Education. Subsequently, he spent twelve years supervising the administration of Japan's engineering education. He also taught at Tokyo Imperial University as a professor.

Mano did not write as many scientific books or papers as Tanabe, nor did he take part in any remarkable engineering project. Instead, he rendered great services in the administration of engineering education in Japan. When he was the Director of the Bureau of Industrial Education, he made the following important contributions to industrial education:

- January 1902: Revised Regulations relating to Supplementary School for Technical Instruction.

- March 1902: Established Kobe Higher Commercial School, Morioka Higher Agricultural School and Kyoto Higher School of Industrial Art.

- March 1903: Enacted Imperial Ordinance relating to Special Schools. Revised Imperial Ordinance relating to Technical Schools and designated schools for higher education as Special Technical Schools.

- February 1905: Established Yamaguchi Higher Commercial School, Nagasaki Higher Commercial School and Nagoya Higher Technical School.

- April 1906: Established Kumamoto Higher Technical School and Sendai Higher Technical School.

- June 1907: Developed Sapporo Agricultural College as the Faculty of Agriculture of Tohoku Imperial University.

- July 1907: Established Meiji Higher Technical School.

- March 1910: Established Ueda Higher Sericultural School, Otaru Higher Commercial School, Yonezawa Higher Technical School and Akita Higher School of Mines.

- January 1911: Established Kyushu Imperial University, Faculty of Technology.

- April 1912: Established the Technological College affiliated to Tohoku Imperial University.

We have seen that the system of higher industrial schools took root during Mano's time as Director. Eight new schools of technology were opened, including those related to industrial arts, mines and sericulture, four schools of commerce and one school of agriculture. Also, in addition to the ones in Tokyo and Kyoto, the third Imperial University was founded in Tohoku and the fourth in Kyushu. The Faculty of Agriculture was added to Tohoku Imperial University and the Faculty of Technology to Kyushu Imperial University. Japan's industrial education of the higher level, owing its inception to Dyer and to the Imperial College of Engineering, expanded to cover commerce and agriculture.

In 1909, Tokyo Higher Commercial School, which was one of the best institutions of commerce in Japan, suffered internal troubles over its promotion to college status. Mano was asked to become the acting principal and contributed to the settlement of the situation. In 1920, the school was authorized as the first college of commerce, which is the parent body of Hitotsubashi University, one of Japan's most prestigious universities.

We should note that Mano especially emphasized technology

education. In 1910, he remarked that he had given careful consideration to the establishment of Sendai Higher Technical School in his
speech in the graduation ceremony for the first-term students of the
school. He also stressed the importance of industry and armament for
a nation by comparing industry in peace to armament in war,
observing that it was up to engineers to strengthen their own nation,
and encouraging the students to fulfil their duties to further Japan's
prosperity. Mano hoped to inspire the students with the national
spirit that Dyer had rated so highly.

Mano was an educational administrator who not only worked for
the systemization of Japan's engineering education at higher level, but
also promoted the foundation and improvement of secondary industrial schools, which he thought were of great importance. At the end
of the Meiji Era, the number of secondary agricultural schools
amounted to 229, the number of secondary commercial schools rose
to 95, and the number of secondary technical schools reached 80,
including 47 apprentice schools for boys. Mano cited the following
four structural elements that formed the system of Japan's engineering education in the Meiji Era:

(1) Faculty of Technology(University): chief engineer, engineer
(2) Higher Technical School: assistant engineer
(3) Secondary Technical School: foreman, workman
(4) Secondary Apprentice School: workman

He understood that engineering education in Japan was expanded
from the first element down to the fourth, while in Britain the system
of apprenticeship led up to the development of universities, including
Anderson's College and the Chair of Engineering at Glasgow
University. He maintained that the third and fourth categories of
institutions should be improved for the training of efficient foremen
and workmen, pointing out that these schools were generally passed
over in Japan because the establishment of the first and second categories of institutions was considered most urgent.

He referred to those four structural elements in his essay which
appeared in *Kyoiku Jiron* (Current View on Education), one of Japan's
major educational journals at that time. In 'On Technical Education',
he noted that engineering education in Japan was almost complete
with the four structural elements and that significant changes were no
longer necessary.[2] However, he expressed concern at a serious
shortage of people trained in the schools, adding that that was especially true of people who were skilled enough to make precision
machines. In his view, it was imperative to train people skilled in

making precision machinery, because an advanced civilization was certain to increase the demand for such machines in armament, science, industry and daily life. His view is noteworthy, considering that he learned Mechanical Engineering at the Imperial College of Engineering. He went on to say that engineers and assistant engineers were trained pretty successfully in Japan, but that there was much room for improvement concerning the training of people with lower-level skills, especially workmen.

It was one of Mano's duties to promote education in commerce and agriculture, as well as engineering education. In his search of exemplary countries in these fields that Japan should keep in mind, Mano came to pay more attention to countries other than Britain.

From the beginning of the Meiji Era, Japan's education relating to commerce was modelled after business schools in the United States. And as for education in Agriculture, Sapporo Agricultural College (the Faculty of Agriculture of Hokkaido University of later days) followed the US example, while Komaba Agricultural College (the Faculty of Agriculture of Tokyo Imperial University of later days) initially used Britain as a model and then turned to Germany.

In Japan's engineering education, Britain was not the only country that set an example. In the training of people with lower-level skills that Mano worked on very hard, Germany came to be recognized as a model to the Japanese rather than Britain. The news of the success of *Fortbildungsschule* (continuation school) in Munich by Kerschensteiner aroused interest in Germany's education among many Japanese.

It was quite natural that Mano did not hesitate to turn to countries other than Britain for examples of industrial education, though his educational background owed a lot to Britain. We can safely say that he made a great contribution to the globalization of Japan's industrial education. For example, he went to Britain as an examiner of educational exhibits for the Japan-British Exhibition at White City, London, in 1910, observing the latest developments of education in Europe and America. Later, he recounted that Japan's educational system had been rated highly at the exhibition, recalling the situation in the countries he had visited. He noted that Germany had higher industrial schools like *Technische Hochschule* and industrial schools such as *Fortbildungsschule* that were in an excellent condition, and that guilds played the leading part in engineering education in Britain, while even such traditional schools as Oxford University provided elaborate extension programmes for workmen in the summer. He also referred to the United States with 390 universities and with the wealthy class willing to donate generously for the education of talented people. He believed that these were the examples that Japan was to follow.[3]

In 1913, Mano became the second president of Kyushu Imperial University. At that time the university had only two faculties of Technology and Medicine. The former faculty was founded through Mano's efforts, and it was one of his juniors, Junzo Nakahara, majoring in Mechanical Engineering at the Imperial College of Engineering, who became the first dean of that faculty.

☐

GOTTFRIED VON WAGENER

As well as Dyer, we should recognize that Gottfried von Wagener (1831–92) also played a very significant role in the foundation of Japan's industrial education. He was born in Hanover and obtained his Ph.D. from Göttingen University. For political reasons, he gave up trying to find a job in Germany and took up a teaching post in Switzerland after spending eight years in Paris. It was at the invitation of Russell & Co., which ran a soap factory in Nagasaki, that Wagener came to Japan, at the time of the Meiji Restoration of 1868.

Under the *Bakufu*, the Saga *han* (clan) had been assigned to guard Nagasaki, which was close to its traditional domain. During the national isolation, which lasted nearly three centuries, Nagasaki was the only port through which Western civilization was introduced to Japan via the Dutch enclave on the tiny man-made island of Dejima, which gave the Saga *han* a great advantage in gaining access to the study of Western sciences during the Edo period. Saga had the highest standard of expertise in iron manufacture and steamship-building in Japan. The name of the most prominent engineer in the field was Tsunetami Sano, who will be introduced later.

Learning that Wagener was in Nagasaki, young men in Saga did not miss any opportunity to learn Western sciences from him. One of them was Shigenobu Okuma, who would make a great contribution to the Meiji Restoration and would be a future prime minister. Also, Saga *han* officials asked Wagener to provide guidance for improving the skills of porcelain manufacture. Wagener went to Arita, a famous porcelain centre, and advised on what was requested in the building of the first coal-burning kiln in Japan, thereby facilitating a quantitative leap in production compared to the days of wood-burning kilns.

Okuma became one of the leading figures of the newly-established Meiji government. Wagener followed him to Tokyo at his invitation and started to teach at Tokyo Kaiseigakko, the parent body of Tokyo Imperial University, as indicated in Table 7.

It was decided that an international exposition would be held in Vienna in 1873. The Japanese Government was determined to take part in the exhibition, with a view to impressing other nations with the progress of the new Japan and also to learn the West's state-of-the-art science and technology. Okuma was in charge of that great national project as the president, with Sano as the vice president and Wagener as adviser, organizer and general manager. More than seventy Japanese left Yokohama for Vienna, just as Dyer and another eight teachers were arriving from the opposite direction. Okuma stayed in Japan to take care of the finances and other issues. The party included twenty-four artisans, as Sano placed his hope on the improvement of the traditional arts of Japan. They were offered opportunities of practical learning in Vienna through Wagener's good offices. One of these artisans was Kaijiro Notomi, a ceramic specialist from the Saga *han*, who will be discussed later.

Wagener returned to Japan in 1874. On his advice the Ministry of Education added a Manufacturing School (*Seisakugaku Kyojo*) to Tokyo Kaiseigakko with a view to teaching production and refining. This marks the beginning of technical education with its origin unrelated to the Imperial College of Engineering or Dyer. That school was closed when the University of Tokyo (Tokyo Daigaku) was established in 1877.

In 1881, in order to train assistant engineers, chief foremen and technical schoolteachers, Tokyo Technical School (Tokyo Higher Technical School, Tokyo Engineering College and Tokyo Engineering University of later days, and Tokyo Institute of Technology of our time) was established. Wagener taught ceramic industry at the new school. By using his own kiln and new kinds of pigments, he invented the art of 'Asahiyaki' based on the improvement of china manufacture.

Wagener maintained that the Japanese should continue to respect their traditional arts. He delivered his lecture 'Importance of Art' in 1887 to the members of the *Ryuchikai*, a group of artists founded by Sano in his later years. Wagener noted Japanese skills in art and ceramics and thought that the Japanese should use these skills in introducing machinery and industrial processes from abroad.[4] He made similar statements on other occasions.

Wagener was not alone in believing in the traditional arts of Japan, as a number of intellectuals were working on their revival at that time. One of them was E. F. Fenollosa, an American professor at Tokyo Imperial University. He insisted that the tradition of Japanese art should be maintained and that Japanese painting should be revived. His collection of works of Japanese traditional art was later transferred to the Museum of Fine Arts, Boston. The museum is noted for its exhibition of valuable works of art that were scattered and lost in Japan. This is similar to the Chiossoné Museum of Oriental Art, Genoa, containing items collected by E. Chiossoné, an Italian hired by the Japanese Finance Ministry who helped introduce the specialist printing methods required for producing Japanese bank notes. The most famous Fenollosa supporter was Tenshin Okakura, who was one of his students at Tokyo Imperial University. He introduced Japanese traditional art to other countries through his writings, including *The Ideals of the East, with Special Reference to the Art of Japan* (1903), *The Awakening of Japan* (1904) and *The Book of Tea* (1906).

The efforts by Fenollosa and Okakura led to the opening of Tokyo Fine Art School in 1889, which is the present-day Tokyo National University of Fine Arts and Music. Both Fenollosa and Okakura taught there as professors. The educational programme of the school covered not only fine art but also technical art.

It should be stressed that prominent figures in the education of technical art were influenced by Wagener rather than Fenollosa. These people worked hard on the foundation of technical art schools in areas renowned for their traditional technical art. Let me refer to two of Wagener's more remarkable pupils.

The first is Kaijiro Notomi, who was born in Saga. He was included by Tsunetami Sano in the party sent to Vienna. He learned Western ceramic skills from Wagener. In 1876, he was sent to the international exposition in Philadelphia, compiling a textbook for the Japanese exhibitors with the title *Onchizuroku* (Traditional Design Book of Japan). This established him as Japan's first industrial designer. In Philadelphia, he was impressed by the great popularity of Arita porcelain and felt the necessity and importance of industrialization for the purpose of exporting works of Japanese technical art.

Notomi later established four secondary technical art schools, becoming the principal of each, in areas famous for their traditional technical arts:

Kanazawa – Kanazawa Technical School, founded in 1887, and the Ishikawa Prefectural Technical School of later years. Kanazawa was famous for its technical art, including chinaware and lacquer ware, even in the Edo Period. Notomi was invited to the prefecture in 1882 and 1886, and provided technical guidance to artisans and inspired the prefectural governor and key people in each district with his belief that schools should be set up.

Takaoka – Takaoka Technical Art School, founded in 1894. Takaoka, located in Toyama Prefecture, was well known for its technical art including copperware and lacquer ware.

Takamatsu – Takamatsu Technical Art School, founded in 1898. Takamatsu, the seat of Kagawa Prefectural Office, enjoyed a reputation for its great technical art such as wood and metal crafts even in the Edo Period.

Arita – Arita Technical School, founded in 1903.

Notomi returned to his home in Saga in 1901, assuming the post of principal of Saga Prefectural Technical School, which had a branch school in nearby Arita. Notomi was also the principal of the branch school, which was developed as an independent school, Arita Technical School, in 1903. We have already seen that it was in Arita that Wagener offered guidance at the beginning of the Meiji era in the necessary skills for the first coal-burning kiln. Thirty years later, the system for the training artisans in the manufacture of Arita ware, which resulted in the international acclaim of one of Japan's most famous technical art forms, was completed by Notomi.

The other man who was greatly influenced by Wagener is Iwata Nakazawa. Born in Fukui in 1858, he was ordered to study German by Fukui *han*. In 1872, he entered the German Department of Tokyo Kaiseigakko, and then majored in chemistry at Tokyo Daigaku (the University of Tokyo). After graduation, he was employed as an assistant teacher, assisting Wagener in his studies. He was in Germany from 1883 to 1886 as a student of Berlin University. He also attended lectures at the *Technische Hochschule* and other places. In 1887, he became a professor of Practical Chemistry at Tokyo Teikoku Daigaku (Tokyo Imperial University). When Kyoto Imperial University was founded in 1897, Nakazawa assumed the position of the Dean of the Department of Science and Technology.

Nakazawa brought his ability into full play as the principal of Kyoto Higher School of Industrial Art, opened in 1902, as the first of its kind in Japan and unique until the second school of the same category, Tokyo Higher School of Industrial Art, was opened in 1921. Nakazawa contributed to the foundation of Kyoto Higher School of Industrial Art, providing guidance from the design stage. He believed that science was indispensable for the application to industry of the skills of Japanese artistic handicraft. His goal was the production of craftwork unique to Japan, by means of the fusion of art, science and technology, and the export of Japanese craftwork goods to the world market.

Kyoto had enjoyed the status of capital of Japan for a thousand years before the Meiji Restoration. Today, it is famous as a city of scenic beauty with old shrines and Buddhist temples, but it was also home to many remarkable craftsmen, who brought about the development of such traditional industries as textile manufacture and artistic handicrafts in the city. In the modernization of its traditional industry, Nakazawa made great contributions to professional education. He also published his writings on directions for technicians, including directions for his own way of making Japanese lacquer.

While Dyer's contribution brought about the success of Sakuro Tanabe, who graduated from the Imperial College of Engineering, Wagener's work led to the development of industrial art by his own pupil, Nakazawa. Having achieved success with the Lake Biwa Canal project aided by modern Western technology, Tanabe gained the position of Dean of Kyoto Imperial University. Nakazawa worked hard for education in industrial art, putting more emphasis on artistic design than on scientific technology. He became the principal of a number of Higher Schools of Industrial Art in Kyoto. The exemplary country that Nakazawa had in mind was Germany, not Britain, and he was interested in the systematic education provided by *Technische Hochschule.*

☐

As for agriculture, Western sciences and educational systems were introduced into Japan, as a predominantly agricultural country, by way of two channels. One was Sapporo Agricultural College, which was opened in 1876 by the government department called *Kaitakushi* that had been set up for the development of Hokkaido. Its teachers were all Americans, including W. S. Clark, the principal. Its educational system was modelled on the Massachusetts Agricultural College.

The other was Komaba Agricultural College, which was established by the Ministry of Home Affairs. When it was opened in 1877, its teachers came from Britain who taught such subjects as Agriculture, Agricultural Chemistry and Veterinary Science. Many of them were from the Royal Agricultural College in Cirencester. However, it was decided that Germans would replace the British teachers from 1880 onwards, due to the cultural lag between British agricultural methods and traditional Japanese rice culture, as well as because of internal problems among the British teachers.

In 1890, Komaba Agricultural College was raised to the status of the Faculty of Agriculture of Tokyo Imperial University and taught along the lines of the *Wissenschaft* of Germany.

This shift from Britain to Germany is typically embodied in Tokiyoshi Yokoi, a graduate of Komaba Agricultural College, who later became a professor at Tokyo Imperial University and a leading figure in Japan's agricultural education. His severe criticism of Britain gained the support of many Japanese concerned with agriculture. The gist of his criticism was that the national policy of Japan should be 'agriculturism' like Germany, not industrialism like Britain.

Yokoi was born in 1860 into a samurai family in Kumamoto *han* and was taught by L. L. Janes, an American, at the local Western Learning School (*Yogakko*). As a student of Komaba Agricultural College, he learned Western agricultural sciences initially from British and then from German teachers. Graduating from the college, he became the principal of Fukuoka Prefectural Agricultural School after acting as its senior teacher. In addition to establishing the educational system at secondary level, he worked hard for the improvement of rice culture.

Yokoi's new method of soaking rice seed in salt water won him great fame. A German professor at Komaba Agricultural College, M. Fesca, was so impressed with Yokoi as to recommend that he should be appointed as a technical expert at the Ministry of Agriculture and Commerce in Tokyo. However, Yokoi resigned because of his disagreement with the vice-minister and spent several years in journalism, writing critical essays on the reform of Japanese agriculture.

In 1904, Yokoi became a professor in the Faculty of Agriculture of Tokyo Imperial University and came to be known as a pioneer in the study of agronomy. The faculty had a training school for teachers of agriculture attached to it, and Yokoi as its director played the leading part in developing teaching methods. Thus, he became the most significant voice in agricultural education of Japan.

He did not hesitate to warn a large number of Japanese people, who were ardent admirers of British civilization, against what he believed was the danger of following in the footsteps of Britain. The gist of his contention was that the interminable decline of Britain was due to her neglect of agriculture and that Japan should not repeat her mistakes. Let me review three examples he cited in support of this claim.

First, he referred to a number of historical facts that showed neglect of agriculture causing national decline. In such dominant nations as Greece, Sparta, the Roman Empire, Spain, Portugal and Holland, the development of cities and people's indulgence in luxury brought about the degeneration of farming villages, leading to the decline of national power. In his view, Britain was quite likely to follow suit.

Secondly, he thought Britain had already shown signs of national decline in the Boer War, which had cost her so much to win. The main conflict occurred while Yokoi was studying in Germany, where he would have been exposed to sympathetic views towards the Boer struggle. Britain's difficulties in the Transvaal, he believed, were due largely to the decline of its agricultural base. He believed the soldiers from Ireland were stronger than those from other parts of Britain, and that this stemmed from the continued presence of more farming villages in Ireland. Japan's victory in the Russo-Japanese War, in which Yokoi praised the bravery of Japan's peasant troops, further strengthened his belief.

Thirdly, he thought that Britain would lose World War I owing to her neglect of agriculture. It seemed to him that Britain would be forced to surrender due to food shortages caused by the German submarine blockade. He was informed that Britain had only enough food supplies to last two months, again because of making light of agriculture, while Germany attached equal importance to agriculture, industry and commerce. Although German population growth was higher than those of her neighbours, the amount of her cereal production was keeping ahead of the birth rate. In the end, Yokoi's prediction did not come true as Britain emerged victorious from the war due to her diplomatic strategy in gaining support from key allies. But he attributed Germany's five-year resistance to her policies valuing agriculture.

Yokoi was sent to Germany to study in May 1899, spending one year there. He opted for Germany because he thought that her science of agriculture was more advanced than those of other countries. He respected Fesca and Kellner, who were German teachers at Komaba Agricultural College. Fesca was back in Germany when Yokoi arrived there, providing him with assistance. Fesca was the chief of the agricultural experiment station at that time.

It was A. Thaer and J. von Liebig who contributed to the establishment of German agricultural science. After that, a number of scientists took the work further, including some of Thaer's pupils, whose idea of agronomy came to Yokoi's notice. He also took notice of agricultural education in Germany. In addition to the systematic approach of the higher agricultural schools (*Hohere Landwirtschaftsschule*) and secondary agricultural schools (*Landwirt-schaftsschule*), Germany had continuation schools (*Fortbildungsschule*), which drew world attention. Yokoi was especially impressed with the latter as well as the educational institutions for girls in farming villages. These girls' schools, having a variety of names, were intended to add females to the farming population by giving lessons in domestic science and on their mission in the national community. One of the most famous schools was *Wirtschaftliche Frauenschule aus dem Lande* in Prussia. Yokoi understood that the steady development of Germany in agriculture as well as in industry and commerce was largely due to such institutions.

☐

The Education Ministry of Japan, established in 1871, gathered information on the methods of many countries for the foundation of Japan's educational systems. The ministry did not attach too much importance to any particular country. In *Kyoiku Zasshi* or Journal of Education, which the ministry issued from 1876 to 1883, information was given on the state of technical education in Britain, the United States, France and Germany. It should be noted that the journal included the fourth chapter of *Systematic Technical Education for the English People* (1869) by J. S. Russell, a British writer, and *What is Industrial and Technical Education* (1871) by J. Mill, both of which were in abridged translation.

In 1884, the ministry published the entire Russell book in Japanese, which was a voluminous work of 637 pages. It was translated by Dairoku Kikuchi, who was one of the students sent to Britain for study by the Tokugawa Government just before the Meiji Restoration, and who was to distinguish himself as a prominent figure in Japan's educational circles, assuming such important positions as Education Minister and President of the Imperial Universities of Tokyo and Kyoto.

In 1885, the ministry took on the translation of all the issues of the *Report of the Royal Commission on Technical Education of Britain*; this was completed in 1888 and amounted to twenty volumes. The original was published in Britain in 1884, dealing with the findings on the situation of technical education in Britain and on the Continent, based on a survey conducted by Commissioners appointed by Queen Victoria. It consisted of the First Report and the Second Report, including the report by Jenkin, whom Dyer respected very much. The original kept in the National Diet Library was brought from Britain by Seiichi Tejima (see below). Tejima donated the original to Tokyo's Educational Museum of those days.

It was somewhat ironical, however, that what the Japanese learned from these reports was the stagnation of Britain's technical education, which threw cold water on any Japanese admiration for a nation they had credited with advanced technical expertise. The First Report compiled by the Royal Commissioners dealt with the research of the situation in France, while the Second Report gave an account of the cases of such countries as France, Switzerland, Germany, Austria, Belgium, Holland and Italy, describing also the situation in Britain and pointing out various problems she had to solve. What impressed the Japanese was that these Western countries had not only higher technical institutions but also other schools at lower levels. In addition to such higher technical institutions for employers and managers as Japan's Imperial College of Engineering, they had evening schools available for artisans, artisans' general technical schools and apprenticeship schools, intermediate technical schools for foremen and technical managers, and women's trade and professional schools.

When the report was translated into Japanese, the Imperial College of Engineering was being developed as one of the faculties of the Imperial University, a trail-blazer in the history of universities worldwide. The next government challenge was the training of foremen, technical managers and teachers by establishing technical schools of intermediate and lower levels.

As early as 1881, the Ministry of Education set up a government technical school (*Tokyo Shokko Gakko*) to turn out foremen and teachers. From 1901, the school was called Tokyo Higher Technical School, and, in 1929, it was promoted to Tokyo Technical College, which is the present-day Tokyo Institute of Technology. Meanwhile, prefectural governments founded various secondary technical schools, including schools of weaving and industrial art. The number of such schools totalled 37 in 1900 and 135 in 1910.

SEIICHI TEJIMA

Tokyo Higher Technical School, which did not descend from the Imperial College of Engineering, was developed through the efforts of Seiichi Tejima, who contributed to the training of teachers for prefectural secondary technical schools, until he was recognized as the greatest leader of Japan's technical education. Tejima did not come from Dyer's line or from Wagener's, and established the theory and practice of technical education characteristic of Japan, by introducing the merits of both men's ideas.

Tejima was born in 1849, his father being a samurai of lower rank in Numazu *han*. Tejima became interested in the West when he was very young, learning English and mathematics at a local school of Western sciences. In 1870, just after the Meiji Restoration, he left for the United States, financed by his poor father's borrowings. The notebook that he used when he attended a university in Pennsylvania is still kept in the Archives of Tokyo Institute of Technology. When the embassy, led by Iwakura, arrived in the US in 1872 on its way to Europe, Tejima was asked to accompany them as an interpreter. He then continued his studies in Britain, returning to Japan in December 1874. It seems that he did not attend any university regularly in Britain but devoted himself to studying on his own.

Tejima returned to Japan and became a bureaucrat at the Ministry of Education. He managed the affairs of the Manufacturing School of Tokyo Kaiseigakko, where Wagener was teaching. In 1876, he was sent to the International Exposition held in Philadelphia, where he was impressed with the educational museums built in Toronto, Canada, and in various parts of the US. Back in Japan, he founded such a museum and became its curator.

Tejima went abroad many times as the person in charge of major international expositions in which the Japanese Government took part. At the government's request, he went to the Paris Exposition in 1878, the International Sanitary Exposition in London in 1884, the Columbus Exposition in Chicago in 1893, the St Louis Exposition in 1904, and the Japan-British Exhibition in 1910. He also attended the Paris Exposition of 1889, paying his own expenses. He was dubbed 'Exposition Man' of Japan, which shows that because of his first-hand experiences he was well versed in this field. After he became the principal of Tokyo Technical School in 1890, he was deeply concerned with technical education and gathered a vast amount of information on the industry and technical education of many nations.

From such information, Tejima picked out some ideas that seemed useful for Japan, with five countries most influencing him.

France

At first, Tejima paid special attention to the technical education of France, as also did people in Britain. In his essay of 1886 on technical education (*Jitsugyo Kyoiku Ron*), he noted that there were five categories of institutions of technical education in Western countries, crediting France with possessing all the categories. As I noted before, the *École Polytechnique* was founded in the days of the French Revolution, and from that time the French worked very hard to develop a system of industrial education. Their efforts led to the predominance of French industries as was demonstrated in the Paris Exposition of 1867. This brought another warning to Britain from Lyon Playfair, and this time it led to the organization of the Samuelson Commission.

Tejima thought that Japan should learn from the example of French technical education in the following three areas: the manual arts course of elementary schools, apprenticeship schools, and schools for the professional instruction of women. Japan had already established her own higher technical schools like the *École Polytechnique*. Later, Tejima strongly advocated a manual arts course, with the French model in mind.

The United States

Tejima made seven trips to the US, including his first experience of studying there. When he went again as part of the mission concerning international expositions, he stayed for some time so that he became familiar with the remarkable developments going on in that country. His first impression was that the US was an agricultural country, and he could not help marvelling at her progress as an industrial nation as demonstrated in international expositions, especially the St Louis Exposition of 1904. On this occasion, he also deepened his understanding of the background of the development of education in the US through his discussion with W. T. Harris, who became the superintendent of education of St Louis City before becoming Secretary of State for Education. Harris told Tejima to educate more people with sound judgement, and emphasized the importance of science education for sound judgement.

Tejima understood that the major factor in the industrial progress of the States was the idea of 'the right man in the right place', a principle which was very much respected and put into practice in factories as well as in other workplaces. Based on this idea, he organized an experiment of what he called talent education conducted at a technical school run by a friend of his. He also encouraged his pupils to gain practical experience in factories in the US, a country of open competition. He was sure that Japanese people could take part in the competition and gain useful experience for the development of Japanese industries.

Germany

In the meantime, Tejima became more and more interested in Germany. He made an observation tour of Britain and Germany in 1910, which made him quite certain of the superiority of the latter. On his way home in the vessel *Kaga Maru*, he wrote an essay that expressed admiration for the development of chemical engineering in Germany and the establishment of her systems of technical education. He published this essay in Japan, and in succeeding essays and speeches, he noted that Germany had the world's most organized form of technical education, which consisted of three levels: higher, secondary and lower. He emphasized that the continuation school of the lower level should be a model for Japan, which was in urgent need of that type of school. Around that time, G. M. Kerschensteiner in Munich came to the notice of more and more Japanese; Tejima was one of those who admired the developments in Munich. The City of Munich compiled *Organization und Lehrplane der obligator. Fach-u. Fortbildungsschulen für knaben in München*, the Japanese translation of which the Japanese Education Ministry published in 1916.

Britain

Having made the Industrial Revolution a success earlier than any other country in the world and having enjoyed a good reputation as the leader of industrialization, Britain was surpassed by France, the US and finally by Germany. Tejima was actively involved in the international expositions that exposed the ascendancy of these countries, maintaining a calm judgement and shifting the course of Japan's technical education towards the German ideal.

It is noteworthy that Tejima never lost his respect for Britain. Although he made no more mention of his contention that Japan was to be the 'Britain of the East', he made no critical remarks about Britain. He still repeated his belief that Japan should learn lessons from Britain, an advanced industrial nation. He took her emphasis on the cultivation of character as an example. His argument was all the more persuasive, as the Japanese industrial goods of the time were notorious for their poor quality caused by mass production. He referred to a mechanic from Leeds working at Tokyo Higher Technical School, who was a worthy gentleman that valued diligence and regular hours.

☐

I have just offered an overview of how Japanese aspirations shifted from Britain to Germany, taking the example of Seiichi Tejima, who was the leader of technical education in Japan. Germany even drew the attention of some principals of higher technical schools that were formerly Dyer's pupils. Let me take two people as examples.

One is Naka Matoba, who finished the Mining course in 1882. He took up the position of principal of Meiji Higher Technical School, a government school that had been privately founded. In 1890, he went to Germany to study at the Freiburg Mining School for two years. It is unknown why he opted for that school and not the Royal College of Mines in London, where Milne, his former teacher, had graduated. It is probable, however, that he thought that the Freiburg school was the more suitable model for Japan. I might add that Japan's first mining school was Akita Higher School of Mines, which was founded in 1910. Its first principal, Obana, was one of the first-term graduates of the Imperial College of Engineering, and, as such, he was entitled to the opportunity to study in Britain. He was also one of Milne's pupils, but he chose the Freiburg Mining School as the model for his own school.

The other Dyer pupil interested in Germany was Taki Otake, who majored in Mechanical Engineering and graduated from the Imperial College of Engineering in 1883. He spent the years from 1885 to 1889 studying in Britain, learning weaving and dyeing at Yorkshire College in Leeds. He was taught by Professor Beaumont of the Weaving School and by Professor Hummel of the Dyeing School, and won a reputation as an outstanding student, leading to more Japanese following in his footsteps there. However, in his essay of 1898, Otake expressed his belief that the country with advanced weaving schools was Germany. He observed that Germany had already had a weaving school twenty years before the first British school, Yorkshire College, was set up. He credited weaving schools in Germany with the greatest number and enrolment in the world and with the highest level of education, due to the great efforts made in the development of these schools. In 1910, Otake became the first principal of Yonezawa Higher Technical School, and in 1915, he assumed the post of the first principal of Kiryu Higher Dyeing and Weaving School. In these institutions he adopted German educational systems rather than British.

NOTES

[1] *Osaka Mainichi Shuinbun*, 5, 6, 8 October 1918.
[2] *Kyoibu Jiron*, No. 811, October 1903.
[3] *Kyoiku Jiron*, No. 925, December 1910.
[4] *Ryuchikai Hokoku*, No. 20, January 1887.

7

Retrospective

It is over one hundred and twenty years since Dyer introduced to Japan the world's best standard in the world of engineering education. His initiative urged young samurai to aspire to engineering careers and their enthusiasm has been passed down undiluted to new generations. Unlike people in Britain, the Japanese do not have much prejudice against engineers because of their social class. However, the notion that the profession of an engineer belonged to males, which is a stereotype in terms of gender, was more deeply rooted in Japan than in any other country. The influence of the 'samurai engineers' as male pioneers was dominant for many years in Japan, and, until the end of World War II, there were no female students admitted to the faculty of engineering of any university, higher technical school (college), or secondary technical school. We can safely say that Japan's successful pre-war technical education was confined to males.

I would now like to give an overview of the development of Japan's technical education after Dyer left Japan. The Imperial College of Engineering was later incorporated into Tokyo Imperial University (*Teikoku Daigaku*). Then, by the time of Japan's defeat in 1945, another six imperial universities had been founded. Six out of the seven had faculties of engineering. It should be noted that higher technical schools of the collegiate level made remarkable progress, increasing in number every year. At first, those schools were mostly governmental, reaching a total of 19 by 1925. Many secondary technical schools were prefectural or municipal and their number reached 90 by 1925; there were 11 private schools. The year 1925 marked the end of the Taisho era and the beginning of the Showa era. The institutions of technical education of 1925 are indicated in Table 12.

During World War II Japanese Government resorted to high-handed policies for the promotion of technical education in an attempt to promote the development of war industries. It is note-

Table 12 Institutions of Technical Education in 1925

Level	Institution	National*	Public**	Private	Total
Higher	Universities (faculties of engineering)	5	0	1	6
	Technical schools (colleges)	20	0	0	20
Secondary	Technical schools	0	90	11	101

* National: governmental schools
** Public: prefectural, municipal, and consolidated municipal schools

Table 13 Institutions of Technical Education in 1945

Level	Institution	National*	Public**	Private	Total
Higher	Universities (departments of engineering)	9	0	4	13
	Technical schools (colleges)	29	12	23	64
Secondary	Technical schools	0	413	135	548

* National: governmental schools
** Public: prefectural, municipal, and consolidated municipal schools

worthy that the government ordered that commercial schools for men should be changed to technical schools or girls' commercial schools; this caused the number of secondary technical schools to increase drastically. National policies also led to a drastic increase in public and private higher technical schools. As is indicated in Table 13, a large number of institutions of technical education existed on 15 August 1945, when World War II ended in the defeat of Japan. In Tokyo Prefecture, for instance, no less than 45 secondary technical schools were newly set up, seven being public higher technical schools and 38 private, and most formerly commercial schools. The conversion of schools was carried out in Japan just as the government wanted, and with such strong authority as people in Britain could hardly imagine.

After the war, the educational system underwent a drastic reform and reorganization. Secondary technical schools were incorporated into the system of secondary high schools. Many of the higher technical schools were elevated to the status of engineering universities or departments of engineering of universities. The reform and development of technical education in Japan contributed much to Japan's great economic recovery after the war.

In 2002, Japan had 99 national universities, 75 public ones and 512

Table 14 Students at Universities in Japan in 2000

Course		Total	Related to engineering	%
Undergraduate	National	455,102	139,294	30.6
(daytime)	Public	88,107	13,152	14.9
	Private	1,813,347	288,650	15.9
	Subtotal	2,356,556	441,096	18.7
Master's	National	84,129	38,374	45.6
	Public	6,493	2,272	35.0
	Private	52,208	18,430	35.3
	Subtotal	142,830	59,076	41.4
Doctorate	National	44,495	9,858	22.2
	Public	3,226	465	14.4
	Private	14,760	1,495	10.1
	Subtotal	62,481	11,818	18.9

private. The national universities included 14 medical universities and nine educational universities. Among the other 76 national universities, as many as 59 universities had faculties related to engineering. Most of the comprehensive universities in the prefectures also had faculties of engineering. These figures reflect the governmental policy that has given priority to engineering. The public universities showed a similar tendency, while the private universities, for financial reasons, had more faculties for such subjects as liberal arts and economics. In 2002, there were only 119 departments related to engineering out of a total of 512 private universities.

All things considered, however, we can safely say that engineering forms the central part of Japan's education at university level. Table 14 shows the figures from the report compiled by the Ministry of Education in 2000. We can see that 30.6% of the undergraduate students of national universities major in fields related to engineering, and that 45.6% of the students of master courses and 22.2% of the students of doctor courses major in such fields. If we group the students taking master courses at both public and private universities, 41.4% of all the students major in fields related to engineering. In Japan's education in engineering, master courses for postgraduate work play a key role.

The most influential and prestigious institution in Japan's education in engineering is the University of Tokyo. The university originated from the Imperial College of Engineering, which proved successful due to Dyer's endeavours. Now, the university has the Faculty of Engineering at undergraduate level and the Graduate School of Engineering. The number of its departments was 21 as of 1 May 1995; this rose from eight in Dyer's time as principal, and we can see from Table 15 that more priority is given to professionalization than in Dyer's time. In terms of enrolment, undergraduate courses have 2,182 students, and postgraduate courses 2,696 students. With its 118 non-degree researchers, the university has a total enrolment of 4,996. It is now a great institution with the number of students specializing in engineering alone coming close to 5,000.

It is interesting to note that the names of the eight departments founded by Dyer are still used without much change (see Table 9), such as the departments of Civil Engineering, Architecture, Mechanical Engineering, Naval Architecture and Metallurgy, which Dyer used in his syllabus. Telegraphy is now referred to as Electrical Engineering, Practical Chemistry as Applied Chemistry and Mining as Geosystem Engineering. These changes result from technological advancement, but Dyer's ideal has not been lost.

They started to reorganize the departments in 1995, and Metallurgy was incorporated into Materials Engineering in 2002. As of 1 May 2002, the university had 2,031 undergraduate students (64 foreign), 1,627 students of master courses (171 foreign), 1,070 students of doctoral courses (352 foreign) and 120 non-degree researchers (81 foreign). The total number of students was 4,848, a smaller number than that of 1995, but the number of foreign students increased from 626 to 668, while the number of students on doctoral courses rose from 994 to 1,070. Based on the policies of the Ministry of Education, the University of Tokyo is now placing more emphasis on postgraduate courses.

In Britain, technical colleges are being given the status of universities. The first British technical university is the University of Strathclyde, which was opened in 1964. As I noted earlier, the university emerged from the Glasgow and West of Scotland Technical College, which was founded through Dyer's efforts. The Robin's Report of 1963 says that as it was recommended that colleges of Advanced Technology and the Heriot-Watt College, Edinburgh, should be given university status, nine new autonomous universities of the technological type were founded. These were Battersea, Brunel, Northampton, Birmingham, Bradford, Bristol, Loughborough and Salford, and Herriot-Watt, Edinburgh, with an intake of 10,300

Table 15 Enrolments of the Faculty of Engineering of Tokyo University as of 1 May 1995

	Undergraduate	Master's	Doctorate	Research (non-degree)
Civil Engineering	118 (1)*	117 (26)	68 (48)	4 (4)
Architecture	145 (3)	127 (19)	115 (52)	17 (12)
Urban Engineering	127 (3)	70 (15)	51 (25)	6 (4)
Mechanical Engineering	107 (3)	69 (8)	27 (9)	3 (2)
Engineering Synthesis	94 (0)	54 (2)	14 (4)	8 (6)
Mechano-Informatics	97 (1)	56 (5)	13 (4)	1 (0)
Precision Machinery Engineering	127 (1)	82 (12)	32 (19)	9 (9)
Naval Architecture and Ocean Engineering	96 (0)	54 (4)	29 (11)	3 (2)
Aeronautics and Astronautics	123 (1)	106 (2)	43 (13)	10 (6)
Electrical Engineering	⎫	63 (4)	32 (13)	3 (2)
Information and Communication Engineering	⎬ 274 (8)	33 (2)	9 (4)	4 (2)
Electronic Engineering	⎭	93 (12)	69 (27)	4 (3)
Applied Physics	118 (0)	97 (0)	48 (2)	3 (1)
Mathematical Engineering and Information Physics	128 (0)	80 (1)	13 (3)	4 (2)
Quantum Engineering and Systems Science	72 (0)	77 (2)	61 (20)	2 (1)
Geosystem Engineering	61 (0)	58 (9)	11 (7)	8 (7)
Metallurgy	176 (3)	49 (2)	21 (5)	3 (2)
Material Science		57 (3)	33 (14)	6 (4)
Applied Chemistry	103 (0)	95 (12)	56 (22)	6 (4)
Chemical System Engineering	110 (1)	88 (6)	44 (14)	9 (7)
Chemistry and Biotechnology	106 (1)	107 (6)	70 (24)	4 (1)
Total	2,182 (26)	1,702 (153)	994 (364)	118 (83)

* foreign students

students in 1962–3 and probably of 21,000 in 1970.[1] In addition, the Further and Higher Education Act of 1992 hammered out plans to double the number of institutions of higher education, and polytechnics were changed into universities without degree-awarding power. Nearly 45 polytechnics became universities, and many of them have engineering departments. Still, these developments fall far short of the growth of Japan's technical education. As far as technical education is concerned, it is not an exaggeration to say that Japan has caught up with Britain, as a forefront nation.

HENRY DYER SYMPOSIUM

In the late 1990s, some eighty years after Dyer's death, an event of great interest was held in the form of the Henry Dyer Symposium in both Glasgow and Tokyo. In my original study of Dyer, 'Japan of Henry Dyer' published in 1989, I stated that Dyer had been forgotten both in Britain and Japan, but he was remembered subsequently and came to be regarded as a major figure in UK-Japan exchanges.

I was not alone in the recognition of his prominent role. At least two people were also aware of his great contribution. One is Professor W. H. Brock of Leicester University. As early as 1981, Professor Brock referred to Dyer's role in his essay 'The Japanese Connection; Engineering in Tokyo, London and Glasgow at the End of the Nineteenth Century', which was carried in the *British Journal of History of Science* (Vol. 14, No. 48). The essay was reprinted in his book, *Science for All, Studies in the History of Victorian Science and Education*.[2]

The other is Olive Checkland, formerly a Fellow of Glasgow University. Her essay 'Scotland and Japan, 1860–1914; a Study of Technical Transfer and Cultural Exchange' was carried in *Bakumatsu and Meiji* (Nish, I., ed., London School of Economic and Political Science, International Studies, 1982). Olive Checkland made further remarks on Dyer in her 1989 study, *Britain's Encounter with Meiji Japan, 1868–1912* (Macmillan).

My first paper on Dyer, written in Japanese, was carried in the *Japanese Journal of Educational Research* at a time when the studies on Dyer by Professor Brock or Olive Checkland were not known. After that, more Japanese people became interested in Dyer, including Professor Masami Kita, who carried out extensive research on Dyer's contribution to the relationship between Scotland and Japan. More of Dyer's writings were translated into Japanese. For example, 'The Education of Engineers', his essay of 1879, was translated into Japanese by Mr Noboru Umetani and Mr Tai Yamanaka. In 1999, Mr Isao Hirano's translation of *Dai Nippon* was published. Olive Checkland's aforementioned book was published in Japanese in 1996.

Today, few people dispute the fact that Dyer played a very significant role in the history of UK-Japan exchanges. Still, what surprised me about the symposium was that both the University of Strathclyde and the Faculty of Engineering of the University of Tokyo recognized Dyer as the leading figure in their foundation, and that both were determined that Dyer's ideals should be re-valued in engineering education in the twenty-first century, thus agreeing with views I had expressed over many years. The Dyer Symposium was initially planned by the University of Strathclyde and was brought about through its co-sponsorship with the University of Tokyo.

The first issue of the University of Strathclyde's *Newsletter*, which was published in June 1995, stated: 'Welcome to the first newsletter of the Henry Dyer Symposium on Industrial Globalization. This symposium is the first of two being organized jointly between the University of Strathclyde and the University of Tokyo, and will be held at the University of Strathclyde in April 1996 to mark the bicentenary of the University of Strathclyde. The two Symposia highlight the historic links between the University of Strathclyde and the University of Tokyo, established by Henry Dyer. The second symposium will be held at the University of Tokyo in March 1997.'

The origin of the University of Strathclyde is Anderson's College, which was founded in 1796. The year 1995 marked the bicentennial, and the school is renowned for its dedication to useful learning. We should note that the university held a commemorative symposium in honour of Dyer, not Anderson. Under the title of 'Who is Henry Dyer?' the issue also recording the following: 'Henry Dyer (1848–1918) was a student at Glasgow University ... He studied with a number of Japanese students who came to the UK as part of the Meiji Restoration, which proclaimed: "Knowledge shall be sought throughout the whole world". He was invited to Japan and established there the Imperial College of Engineering, which became the Faculty of Engineering in the present-day University of Tokyo, introducing educational methods which were established in Glasgow. He returned to Glasgow and became a Life Governor of the West of Scotland Technical College, the forerunner of the University of Strathclyde.'

The main theme of the Symposium in Strathclyde was 'Globalization'. The aforementioned issue set out the reasons and major questions: 'The Meiji tenet is no less important now, but has taken on a new dimension with the need for multinational working set against the increasing ease of accessing and exchanging knowledge and information. This "globalization" of information, technology, industry and business is set to make a major impact on our economies and societies as the pressure for changing increases. Major questions arising include: How should national strategies be shaped? How can companies maintain competition with collaboration? What is the impact on large, medium and small enterprises? How will our educational system respond? How can third world and developing nations keep up with the rate of change? How does IT play a role?'

The Symposium in Tokyo was held on 18–19 March 1997, and it was carried out through the efforts of Dr Hiroyuki Yoshikawa, formerly the Dean of the Faculty of Engineering and the President of the University of Tokyo. He observed in his opening address:

> While the first symposium focused on issues regarding 'Globalization,' this Second Symposium will look at 'Engineering Education'.

He also remarked:

> It is not just by chance that, at this Second Symposium almost 120 years after Henry Dyer, we will focus on engineering education … Engineering education at universities should be re-examined, revised and reconstructed. It is not just a matter of curriculum and courses, but of the whole system of engineering. To this end, Henry Dyer, who invented a revolutionary educational system and exercised it in young modernizing Japan, could be a good starting point for discussion to seek a new model of engineering education.

Speaker's Notes were issued as the report on the symposium, which began with 'Collection and Abduction' by Dr Hiroyuiki Yoshikawa, and gave an account of the fifteen themes, including the remarks on 'The Future of Engineering Education' made by Professor Yohichi Goshi, who had contributed to the symposium as the chairman of the organizing committee. Speaker's Notes also included remarks of A. Hendry, L. Hart, R. Hunter, N. Ward, B. Ion, K. MacCallum and others.

L. Hart and R. Hunter stated that they 'examined Dyer's background and factors that influenced him before, during and after his work in Japan' in their presentation, 'Henry Dyer; A man with a mission'. The following quotation from the presentation is noteworthy: 'It shows that, although he was highly respected and regarded throughout his life, his high principles, together with his clear and forthright views on a wide range of subjects, may have prevented him from achieving the recognition in his native land that he enjoyed in Japan.'

This occasion of Dyer's Symposium changed the view of the origin of the Faculty of Engineering of the University of Tokyo. In 1995, the university authorities stated in 'Brief History' that the 'roots of the School of Engineering at the University of Tokyo extend before its establishment in 1877 to educational institutions of the Edo and Meiji periods'. As I indicated in Table 7, it was supposed that the university originated from Tokyo Daigaku, which was founded in 1877 by taking over *Bakufu* educational institutions in the Edo Period and that the Imperial College of Engineering, which was established in 1873, was merged into Tokyo Daigaku.

The 2002 Overview, however, revealed the following additional information: 'Henry Dyer, who was invited from the United Kingdom in 1873, served as the first principal of the Imperial College of Engineering, forerunner to the Faculty of Engineering of the University of Tokyo, until 1882. Dyer tried to merge British engineering education, oriented towards practice, with French-style education, more oriented towards theory. This synthesis still infuses the curriculum and its success has been a foundation of the economic growth of Japan.' Although this change is epoch-making, I would like to add that the 'French-style education' in the quotation should actually be 'continental-style education'. As I have discussed in this book, Dyer turned to French educational structures but not exclusively; he also considered those of Switzerland and other countries on the Continent.

On the occasion of the symposium, the British Embassy donated a bust of Dyer to the University of Tokyo in July 1998 (See Plate 57) sculpted by K. Thomson, a Scot living in Japan. A duplicate bust was donated to the University of Strathclyde in November of the same year. The bust donated to the University of Tokyo is in the reception room of the Faculty of Engineering. It was strange that the university had statues of West and Conder in its precincts but nothing in honour of Dyer. It is fitting that Dyer was at long last given due credit.

☐   ·

It is very important that engineering education was the main theme of the Dyer Symposium in Tokyo. The report of the symposium includes a foreword by Dr Yohichi Goshi, who remarked: 'We have had many success in the past. We are now, however, moving from the twentieth century to the twenty-first century. Engineering education, again, needs some metamorphosis. Population explosion, the exhausting natural resources and environmental pollution, pose a new challenge. We have to create a new technology and a new system for engineering. These will be realized only by improving engineering education.' In addition, Dr Hiroyuki Yoshikawa, in his opening address, observed: 'The Imperial College of Engineering under Henry

Dyer's initiative had a unique educational system, even by today's standards.'

Now, it is for us to ask how Dyer's legacy should be passed down in terms of the standards of the twenty-first century. Let me suggest the following three significant points.

(1) *Ideal of Social Revolution*
Dyer encouraged and inspired his students by referring to engineers as real revolutionists, who exerted a profound impact. It is true, however, that the revolution issues in the society of his time differ greatly from those of our rapidly-changing society of the twenty-first century, and the first and foremost step for new engineering education should be to find out what roles engineers as revolutionaries are expected to play for the 'social revolution' which Dyer referred to so often.

Here, let me turn to Professor Naomasa Nakajima of the Faculty of Engineering of the University of Tokyo, who expressed the following two visions in 2000 in 'Engineering Visions – from the University of Tokyo' (in Japanese). First, he maintained that engineering should be responsible for society and the environment of the twenty-first century, preserving the environment of our planet, developing our civilization, enriching our life and culture, and contributing to the world from a global point of view. Secondly, he insisted that engineering should develop new industries and civilizations through constant efforts at innovation, searching for new frontiers and new findings, providing more opportunities for industries and societies with advanced technologies of information and intelligence, and making a paradigm shift by harmonizing the knowledge and skill of engineering. These visions are basically consistent with the theme of Dyer's Symposium at Strathclyde, 'Globalization'. In Dyer's time, 'national evolution' was the top priority, and he valued the Japanese people's national spirit as the greatest factor that had made their nation's industrialization a success. The 'samurai engineers' of those days were without exception enthusiastic patriots. After World War II, more emphasis was put on individuals than on the nation, a historic turnaround, which made people less motivated to contribute to social revolution. A large number of young people nowadays hope to become engineers, but I am afraid that they have lost sight of the mission of engineers. I believe that the ideal of engineers, on which Dyer commented so frequently, should be the first item to be considered with regard to Dyer's legacy.

(2) *Synthesis of Theory and Practice*

Students under Dyer's educational system spent their first two years in preparatory and elementary studies, the middle two years in specialized studies including a great deal of laboratory work, and the last two years in practical work necessary for Japan's modernization. Dr Yoshikawa referred to this system as a 'revolutionary educational system'.

The system originates in the sandwich course that had been used in Britain, to which Dyer gave a new twist. The excellence of the system was proven by the remarkable practical abilities that Dyer's students displayed, which he referred to as 'the power of applying knowledge'. Sakuro Tanabe of the Lake Biwa Canal Project is a good example. Also, we can learn from the list of the graduation essays of the first-term and second-term graduates (1879–80) of the Imperial College of Engineering, which were written in English, that they worked on practical issues that were closely connected with Japan's industrial modernization. The list is carried in the catalogue of the college library for 1880. These essays might seem to be of an elementary level from the viewpoint of engineering of the present day, but they clearly show that these students respected Dyer's ideal and tried to live up to his expectations.

Even today, the principle of Dyer's system exerts an influence on the University of Tokyo. In the four-year undergraduate course, for instance, two years of general education are followed by two years of specialization with lectures and laboratory together with engineering work. Students of some departments are encouraged to work as interns in an engineering-related company during the summer recess in their senior years. Nevertheless, it is out of the question for Japan today to adopt Dyer's sandwich system just as it was.

Accordingly, we should pay attention to the aforementioned engineering visions. They include the synthesis of theory and practice, based on the belief that the essence of engineering for the twenty-first century should be to organize new engineering theories which would enable us to harmonize, supervise and operate various complicated systems. Dr Yoshikawa calls this '*gijutsuchi*' or technological wisdom.

When Japan's great post-war economic recovery caused considerable labour shortages, enterprises employed a large number of college graduates, providing in-house education and training to make them efficient and essential engineers. People of many countries thought it was this in-house education that gave rise to Japan's great economic recovery. However, university education did come to be considered more important, as Japan had new leading-edge technologies and interdisciplinary fields. Now, an increasing number of universities are promoting cooperation with private enterprises and offering various educational programmes for company employees.

Dyer involved his students in new projects of the Ministry of Public Works, which helped them develop and improve their practical abilities. In the twenty-first century, practical abilities are in great demand not only in public works but also in private enterprises.

In relation to engineers in private enterprises, Japan received good news in 2002, when the Nobel Prize in chemistry was awarded to a Japanese researcher and engineer, Mr Koichi Tanaka, who worked for Shimadzu Corporation, a Japanese private company. Nobel Prize winners in chemistry and physics include specialists related to engineering, which is not an independent category for the prize. Japan had Nobel Prize winners in chemistry for three years in a row, as Mr Tanaka followed Dr Ryoji Noyori, the winner in 2001, who had followed Dr Hideki Shirakawa, the 2000 winner. Mr Tanaka was an undergraduate student of the Faculty of Engineering of Tohoku University, which was descended from Sendai Higher Technical School founded in 1906. Dr Noyori is from the doctoral course of the Faculty of Engineering of Kyoto University, which originated from Kyoto Imperial University founded in 1897. And Dr Shirakawa attended the doctoral course of Tokyo Institute of Technology, which stems from Tokyo Technical School founded in 1881. We can see that these winners come from first-rate Japanese institutions of engineering education, which must have enabled them to distinguish themselves. I might add that Mr Tanaka was on loan to the company's subsidiary in Britain on two occasions, thus gaining first-hand experience of living in the country.

(3) The Importance of Character and Culture
Dyer attached importance not only to professional education for an engineer but also to non-professional education. He believed that engineers should be 'good and true men' in the first place, prior to being 'real revolutionists'. He was afraid that too much stress on professionalism was certain to bring professional selfishness, which would make them enslaved to narrowness, prejudices and passions. He came to the conclusion that non-professional education was indispensable for engineers to be respected as members of the learned professions. Therefore, Dyer allotted the first two years of study at the Imperial College of Engineering to the general and scientific course, and this consideration of his is greatly esteemed in the University of Tokyo even today.

When Dyer was the principal of the Imperial College of Engineering, the students were deeply impressed by him in a number of respects. They were especially moved by his treatment of his students as gentlemen and by his own behaviour as a model. Over Japan's long feudal era, people had come to take it for granted that teachers should control students, based on a relationship of superiority and inferiority. Dyer's education was grounded upon a more human relationship between teachers and students. For one thing, he showed respect for his students by calling them 'Mister'. For another, he opted for requests rather than imperatives or prohibitions, putting up a notice stating: 'You are requested not to walk on the grass.'

Many of Dyer's students became principals of technical schools, as I mentioned earlier. They emulated Dyer in his ideals, including his attitude towards students. Take Junzo Nakahara, for example, who in 1906 was appointed principal of Kumamoto Higher Technical School. He adopted Dyer's method of gentleman education in the British way. He remarked in his address at the entrance ceremony that his students were to be treated as gentlemen. He also observed in the graduation ceremony that they should not forget the importance of their own professions and that they were expected to be worthy, honourable and dignified at all times. Taki Otake was also one of those who followed Dyer's example and valued human education. He became the principal of Yonezawa Higher Technical School in 1910, and in his address at the entrance ceremony he made it clear that his students were to be respected as gentlemen.

It should be noted that Dyer turned to reward, not punishment, in order to encourage students to study. He himself was honoured when he won the Watt Prize and other prizes at Glasgow University, and as the principal of the Imperial College of Engineering he awarded prizes to the best achievers. According to the regulation of 1877, during the summer session three students of each grade were offered seven-yen, eight-yen and a ten-yen prizes. Also, the top two students were offered a twenty-yen and thirty-yen prize. In most cases, these prizes were foreign books that were very expensive at that time. Sakuro Tanabe received *Chamber's Encyclopaedia*, which had just been published, as his prize. Yoshiaki Yasunaga, a second-term student, was presented with a book written by Rankine, which is still kept at the University of Tokyo. Inside the book, there is the following inscription and Dyer's signature:

Imperial College of Engineering, Tokei,
At the pass examination in the General and Scientific Course held
    in March 1876

The *First* Prize was awarded to *Yasunaga Yoshiaki*
Henry Dyer Principal
(The words in italics are handwritten.)

It should also be noted that Dyer encouraged his students to take part in sports. After classes were dismissed at four p.m., the students had an hour for sporting activities. The regulation of 1878 indicates that they had opportunities to practise a variety of sports with Japanese teachers as their coaches – twelve physical exercises including running and swimming, and a number of ball games including football, baseball and cricket. They say that it was Dyer who introduced football into Japan.

Lifelong learning is considered more and more important today, and it is remarkable that Dyer emphasized the importance of continuing education ahead of his time. It is also noteworthy as well that he induced his students to form a professional society, which was realized in 1879 when *Kogakkai*, or the Japan Society of Engineering, was established with a membership of 23 graduates. The society expanded year after year, until it was recognized as the core of engineering societies in Japan. The society is now functioning as the coordinator of a number of sub-divided societies of various disciplines. It played an active role and obtained support from twelve engineering societies in its alliance when Sakuro Tanabe had the ten volumes of *Meiji Kogyoshi* ('History of Industry in the Meiji Period') published in 1931.

People interested in engineering education must read 'Professional Education' and 'Non-professional Education', which were two addresses delivered by Dyer in 1879. The latter is especially noteworthy, expressing the British ideal of liberal education and serving as a warning to Japan's education for being prone to placing too much value on utility and conformity.

NOTES

[1]   Green H. H., *The Universities*, Pelican Books, 1969, p. 315.
[2]   Variorum Collected Studies Series, 518, Ashgate Publishing Limited, 1996.

Afterword

What I have mentioned in these paragraphs covers just a few examples of the great many issues in Dyer's legacy that call for our attention and consideration. For example, he insisted that Japan should be the leader in Asia and work for the fusion of Eastern and Western civilizations, the discussion about which would require a great volume on its own.

My next challenge is to be a reconsideration of Japan's education by turning to Dyer and Sir Hugh Cortazzi, whom I respect very much. Sir Hugh has expressed his strong concern and criticism about the educational situation in Japan in a number of outstanding studies. I hope to find out what it is that Japanese people have been unable to learn from Britain in spite of their strenuous efforts, or what the gulf could be.

I should feel greatly rewarded for my efforts if this book should serve as something like a milestone in the studies on foreign teachers hired in Japan an in the historical research of cultural and educational exchanges, both of which are quite likely to be increasingly important.

NOBUHIRO MIYOSHI
April 2004

Sources of Photographs
and Illustrations

1 Photographed by the author.
2 The photo of the bust is from Kenjiro Kumamoto's book, *Meiji Shoki Raicho Itaria Bijutuka no Kenkyu* or A Study on Italian Artists who Came to Japan in the Early Meiji Era (Sanseido, 1940). The tools belong to Mr. Shin-ichi Yamao, a grandson of Yozo Yamao's.
3 From the fifth issue of *Tamakusu* issued by Yokohama Archives of History in 1987, p. 26.
4 Photographed by the author.
5 Moss, M. and Hume, J., *Glasgow as it was*, Vol. I, 1975.
6 Constable, T., *Memoir of Lewis D. B. Gordon*, 1877.
7 Kept in Glasgow University Library.
8 Channel, D. F., *Rankine*, 1986.
9 *A Manual of the Steam Engine and other Prime Movers* is kept at the Department of Engineering of the University of Tokyo, while the others are kept in the University's General Library.
10 Channel, D. F., *Rankine*, 1986.
11 Kept in Glasgow University Archives.
12 Kept in Glasgow University Archives.
13 Kept in Glasgow University Archives.
14 Fumio Shida, *Ko-Shida Rinzaburo Do-Tomiko Kinenroku*, or Bibliography of late Rinzaburo Shida and His Wife, 1927.
15 Kept at the Northern Studies Collection of Hokkaido University.
16 Kept in the National Diet Library of Japan.
17 Kept in the National Diet Library of Japan.
18 Kept in the National Diet Library of Japan.
19 Kept in the Mitchell Library.
20 Kept in the National Diet Library of Japan.
21 Kept in the National Diet Library of Japan.
22 Kept in the National Diet Library of Japan.
23 Kept in the Archives of the University of Tokyo.
24 Kept at the Department of Engineering of the University of Tokyo.
25 From *Kyu Kobu Daigakko Shiryo* or the Historical Materials on the Imperial College of Engineering.
26 From *Kyu Kobu Daigakko Shiryo* or the Historical Materials on the Imperial College of Engineering.
27 From *Kyu Kobu Daigakko Shashin Cho* or the Photographs of the Imperial College of Engineering.

28   Photographed by the author.
29   Kept in Yokohama Archives of History.
30   Kept in the National Diet Library of Japan.
31   Kept at the Northern Studies Collection of Hokkaido University.
32   Photographed by the author.
33   Kept in the library of the Institution of Civil Engineers (London).
34   Kept in the British Museum.
35   University of Strathclyde, *Campus Development*, p.2.
36   University of Strathclyde, *Campus Development*, p.3.
37   Kept in the Archives of the University of Strathclyde.
38   Photographed by the author.
39   *The Central*, Vol.VII, No.21, April, 1910. Kept in the Archives of the Imperial
     College of Science and Technology.
40   Kept in the Archives of the Imperial College of Science and Technology.
41   Kept at the Northern Studies Collection of Hokkaido University.
42   Tomosuke Terakawa's book, *Armstrong no Rika Kyoiku Ron no Kenkyu* or A Study
     on Armstrong's Theory on Science Education 1985.
43   *Centenary of the Imperial College of Science and Technology*, p.17.
44   Photographed by the author.
45   *New Scientist*, Nov. 22, 1979, p.622.
46   Kept in Glasgow University Archives.
47   Kept in Glasgow University Archives.
48   Kept in the National Diet Library of Japan.
49   Kept in Glasgow University Library.
50   Tokyo Electric Power Co., *Illume*, No.23, 2000.
51   *Kyoiku Jinbutsu Jiten* or Directory of Educationists, Vol.1, 1912.
52   Kept in Arita Archives of History.
53   Kept in Kyoto National Museum.
54   Kept in Tokyo National Museum.
55   Left: *Ito Hirobumi Den*, or Biography of Hirobumi Ito, 1940. Right: Morinosuke
     Kazima's book, *Nippon Gaikoshi*, or History of Japanese Diplomacy, Vol. 6,
     1970.
56   *Kogyo no Dai Nippon* or Japan of Engineering, Vol.6, No.2, 1909.
57   Kept in the reception room of the Faculty of Engineering of the University of
     Tokyo.

Dyer's Writings

1   1877. Imperial College of Engineering (KOBU-DAIGAKKO), *General Report by the Principal for the Periods 1873–77*, published by the Imperial College of Engineering, Tokyo (62 pages).

2   1879. *The Education of Engineers*, published by the Imperial College of Engineering, Tokyo (60 pages).

3   1880. *The Education of Civil and Mechanical Engineers*, E. & F. N. Spon, London (44 pages).

4   1882. *Valedictory Address to the Students of the Imperial College of Engineering*, published by the Imperial College of Engineering, Tokyo (6 pages).

5   1883. 'Technical Education, with Special Reference to the Requirements of Glasgow and the West of Scotland', lecture given at the Glasgow Philosophical Society. Carried in the society's newsletter, *Proceedings*, on 21 November (30 pages).

6   1884. 'On Energy and Entropy and their Applications to the Theories of Air and Steam', lecture delivered at the Institution of Engineers in Scotland. Carried in the institution's newsletter, *Transactions*, on 25 November.

7   1885. 'German Universities', *Fifeshire Journal*, 19 February.

8   1885. 'On the Propulsion of Steam Ships, Discussion on Mr. Denny's Paper', lecture delivered at the Institution of Engineers in Scotland. Carried in the institution's newsletter, *Transactions*, on 24 February.

9   1885. 'On the Present State of the Theory of the Steam Engine and Some of its Bearings on Current Marine Engineering Practice', lecture delivered at the Institution of Engineers in Scotland. Carried in the institution's newsletter, *Transactions*, on 24 November.

10 1885. 'On Construction in Earthquake Countries, Discussion on Mr. Milne's Paper', Minutes of Proceedings of the Institution of Civil Engineers (London), Vol. 83.

11 1886. 'On Some Properties of Cast Iron and other Metals, Discussion on Mr. Millar's Paper', lecture delivered at the Institution of Engineers in Scotland. Carried in the institution's newsletter, *Transactions*, on 23 March.

12 1886. 'On a Peculiar Form of Corrosion in Steel and Iron Propeller Shafts, Discussion on Mr. Davison's Paper', lecture delivered at the

Institution of Engineers in Scotland. Carried in the institution's newsletter, *Transactions*, on 27 April.

13   1886. 'Universities and Engineering.' Presented in serial form in the 2 July issue and the five succeeding issues of *Industries*.

14   1886. 'On the Two Chief Laws of Thermodynamics.' Presented in serial form in the 9 July issue of *Industries* and in the succeeding three issues. Published as a pamphlet by the Indian Government.

15   1886. 'On the Development of Marine Engine', lecture given at the Glasgow Philosophical Society. Carried in the society's newsletter, *Proceedings*, on 3 November.

16   1886. 'University Organisation I', *The Glasgow Herald*, 7 December.

17   1887. 'The Glasgow and West of Scotland Technical College', *The Glasgow Herald*, 4 January.

18   1887. 'On the Education of Engineers', lecture delivered at the Institution of Engineers in Scotland. Carried in the institution's newsletter, *Transactions*, on 22 February (37 pages).

19   1887. 'University Organisation II', *The Glasgow Herald*, 5 March.

20   1887. 'University Evening Classes', *The Glasgow Herald*, 11 March.

21   1887. 'University Classes for Merchants I/II', *The Glasgow Herald*, 28 March/11 April.

22   1887. 'A Notable French Technical School', *The Glasgow Herald*, 9 June.

23   1887. 'The Technical Schools (Scotland) Act.' Presented in serial form in the 28 September issue of *The Glasgow Herald* and in the succeeding two issues.

24   1887. 'The Organisation of Industrial Education', *Industries*, 14 October.

25   1887. 'Technical Education', *The Engineer*, 11 November.

26   1887. 'The Technical Schools (Scotland) Act, 1887, and Some of its Relations to Elementary and Higher Education', lecture given at the Glasgow Philosophical Society. Carried in the society's newsletter, *Proceedings*, on 30 November (25 pages).

27   1888. 'University Extension and Technical Education', *Industries*, 27 January and other issues.

28   1888. *The Efficiency of Steamships from the Owner's Point of View*, lecture at Shipowners' Association, 12 March, published as a pamphlet by McCorquodale & Co.

29   1888. 'Reports on Engineering Sections of Glasgow International Exhibition.' Carried in serial form in *The Glasgow Herald*.

30   1888. 'Memoir of Mr. David Sandeman.' Carried in the newsletter of the Glasgow Philosophical Society, *Proceedings*.

31   1888. 'The First Century of the Marine Engine', lecture delivered at the Institution of Naval Architects, 25 July.

32   1888. 'The Glasgow and West of Scotland Technical College', *Nature*, 30 August. Reprinted in the 20 October issue of *The Educational News*.

33   1888. 'On the Horse Power of Marine Engines', lecture delivered at the Institution of Engineers in Scotland. Carried in the institution's newsletter, *Transactions*, on 23 October.

34   1888. *The Foundations of Social Politics*, lecture at the Ruskin Society of

Glasgow on 17 December. Published as a pamphlet by D. Bryce & Son in the following year (32 pages).

35 1889. 'The Steam Engine since the Days of Watt', lecture delivered at the Greenock Philosophical Society. Carried in the 18 January issue of the society's newsletter.

36 1889. 'Notes on Some Recent Steam Engine Trials', lecture delivered at the Institution of Engineers in Scotland on 22 January.

37 1889. 'The Training of Architects', lecture delivered at the Institution of Engineers in Scotland. Carried in the institution's newsletter, *Transactions*, on 4 February (21 pages).

38 1889. 'How to prepare for the Profession of Engineers.' Carried in the issues of March, April and May of *The Guide*.

39 1889. 'A Modern University, with Special Reference to the Requirements of Science', lecture delivered at the Glasgow University Club on 11 April. Carried in the issues of June and July of *The Scots Magazine*, and published as a pamphlet by S. Cowan & Co (25 pages).

40 1889. 'Reports on Engineering at the Paris Exhibition.' Carried in three issues of *The Glasgow Herald* in August.

41 1889. *On a University Faculty of Engineering*, lecture delivered at the Institution of Engineers in Scotland on 22 October. Published in book form by C. F. Hodgson & Son (40 pages).

42 1889. 'The Universities (Scotland) Act', *The Glasgow Herald*, 7/15 November.

43 1890. *Christianity and Social Problems*, lecture delivered at Bridgeton Free Church on 5 January. Published as a pamphlet by D. Bryce & Son (23 pages).

44 1890. 'Training for Trades and Crafts.' Carried in three issues from February to March of *Industries*.

45 1890. 'Missions and Missionaries'. Published as a pamphlet (11 pages) after appearing in the March issue of *The Scots Magazine*.

46 1890. 'The Requirements of Modern Education', lecture delivered at the Ruskin Society of Glasgow on 3 March.

47 1890. 'The Science Curriculum in the Universities'. Published as a pamphlet (7 pages) after appearing in the May issue of *The Scots Magazine*.

48 1890. 'The Future of University Extension in Scotland', *The University Extension Journal*, 1 August.

49 1890. 'Constitutional Government in Japan', *The Scots Magazine*, November/December.

50 1890. 'Memoir of Henry Muirhead, M. D., LL. D.', lecture delivered at the Glasgow Philosophical Society. Carried in the society's newsletter, *Proceedings*, on 5 November (9 pages).

51 1890. 'University Extension', lecture delivered at the Glasgow University Club on 17 November.

52 1891. 'The Needs of Young Men', *The Young Men's Christian Magazine*, February.

53 1891. 'The Aim of Missions', *The Scots Magazine*, March.

54 1891. 'An Educational Programme', a summary of lecture given on the occasion of the election for Glasgow School Board, March.

55 1891. *The Influence of Modern Industry on Social and Economic*

Conditions. Contributed to the Wholesale Co-operative Society in September and published as a pamphlet by the Manchester Co-operative Printing Society in the following year.

56   1892. 'The Race across the Atlantic', *Scottish Review*, January.

57   1892. *Science Teaching in Schools.* Originally lecture delivered at the Glasgow Branch of the Teachers' Guild on 5 February. Published by Blackie and Son in the following year, revised and enlarged as a book with 128 pages.

58   1892. 'The Possibilities of Machinery and Industry and Some of their Probable Results on Social and Economic Conditions.' Carried in the yearly report of the Wholesale Co-operative Society, *Annual*, in the following year.

59   1893. 'Technical Education in Glasgow and the West of Scotland, a Retrospect and a Prospect', lecture given at the Glasgow Philosophical Society, as a sequel to the one given in 1883. Carried in the society's newsletter, *Proceedings* (29 pages).

60   1893. 'The Life and Duties of the Citizen', the explanation of laws on evening continuation schools. Carried in several issues of *Young People's Magazine* after October.

61   1894. 'Education in Citizenship.' Carried in the yearly report of the Wholesale Co-operative Society, *Annual* (28 pages).

62   1894. 'Evening Continuation Schools', lecture delivered at the annual meeting of Educational Institute. Carried in *The Educational News* on 4 January.

63   1895. *The Evolution of Industry*, Macmillan & Co., London (285 pages). Reprinted in 1972 by Arno Press, New York. Translated into Japanese by Zenshiro Tsuboya and published in Japanese in 1896, under the title of *Kogyo Shinka Ron* (335 pages).

64   1895. 'The Recent Progress and Present Condition of Engineering Competition', *The Engineering Review*, October/November.

65   1896. 'The Future of Politics', *The Westminster Review*, January.

66   1896. 'The Liberal Education of Engineers and Manufactures', *Technical College Magazine*, December and other issues.

67   1897. 'Education in Relation to the Co-operative Movement', *The Progressive Review*, January.

68   1901. *Mechanical Engineering in Glasgow and the West of Scotland.* Originally included in *Handbook on Industries of Glasgow and the West of Scotland*, a handbook based on the meeting of British Association for the Advancement of Science held in Glasgow. Published in book form (59 pages).

69   1904. *Dai Nippon: the Britain of the East: a Study in National Evolution*, Blackie & Son, London (450 pages). Translated into Japanese by Isao Hirano and published in 1999 (545 pages).

70   1904. 'Education and National Efficiency in Japan', *Nature*, 15 December.

71   1905. *The Training and Work of Engineers in their Wider Aspects*, lecture delivered at the Scientific Society of the Glasgow and West of Scotland Technical College. Published by the college (23 pages).

72   1905. *The Continuation Classes of the School Board of Glasgow*, lecture delivered at the Exhibition of School Work in December. Published

as a pamphlet by McCorquodale & Co. in the following year (31 pages).

73 1906. 'Japanese Industries and Foreign Investments'. Originally carried in the February issue of *The Financial Review of Reviews*. Published in London as a part of Popular Financial Booklets (12 pages).

74 1906. 'The Commercial Morality of Japan', *The Financial Review of Reviews*, May.

75 1906. 'Legal Aspects of Foreign Investments in Japan', *The Financial Review of Reviews*, August.

76 1906. 'The Japanese Loan Conversion', *The Financial Review of Reviews*, September.

77 1906. *Education and Work*, lecture delivered at Dunfermline. Published as a pamphlet by A. Romanes & Son.

78 1907. 'University Reform: Scientific and Technical Studies', *The Glasgow Herald*, 12 April.

79 1908. 'Some Lessons from Japan.' Carried in the yearly report of the Wholesale Co-operative Society, *Annual* (21 pages).

80 1908. 'Engineering in Japan', *The Times* (Engineering Supplement), London, 18 March.

81 1908. *Continuation Classes in Glasgow and Neighbourhood*, lecture delivered on 20 November. Printed privately (31 pages).

82 1909. *Japan in World Politics: a Study in International Dynamics*, Blackie & Son, London(425 pages).

83 1909. 'Western Teaching for China', *Nature*, 25 March.

84 1910. 'Commercial Education in Japan', *The Glasgow Herald*, 26 November.

85 1911. 'The Far East, Engineering and Commerce', *The Glasgow Herald*, 29 December.

86 1912. *Education and National Life*, Blackie & Son, London (112 pages).

87 1913. *Education and Industrial Training of Boys and Girls*, Blackie & Son, London (118 pages).

88 1915. 'Supplementary Classes and their Place in the National Education.' The report for Scottish School Board Association, 8 December.

89 1916. 'Continuation Classes and their Place in the National Education.' The report for Scottish School Board Association, 6 December.

Dyer's Articles of Agreement

A rticles of Agreement, made & entered into this second day of April one thousand eight hundred & seventy three, between Henry Dyer presently of No. 449 Saint Vincent Street, Glasgow, Scotland, Esquire H. E. U. A. Bse, of the one part; and Hugh Mackay Matheson of No. 3 Lombard Street, London, Esquire, agent for the Minister of Public Works of His Majesty the Mikado of Japan, of the other part.

The said Henry Dyer engages himself in the service of the said Minister of Public Works and of his successors, for and during the space of five years, to commence from his arrival in Japan on the conditions following, that is to say,

1st. The said Henry Dyer shall proceed to Japan direct by the mail steamer leaving England on the 10th day of April current, & immediately upon his arrival, and thenceforth during the term aforesaid, shall faithfully and diligently & to the best of his knowledge and ability employ himself in the service of the said Minister of Public Works and his successors in office for the time being, as the Principal of the College of Civil Engineering at Yedo, and as the professor of Civil & Mechanical Engineering in the said College.

2nd. He shall devote his whole time and attention, with zeal and energy, to the due & faithful performance of the duties of his position as aforesaid, and shall use his utmost exertions to promote the establishment and successful maintenance of the said College, in all its branches, during the whole of the aforesaid period of five years, and shall not at any time absent himself from daily and due attendance at the said College, except on Sundays, or when unavoidably prevented by illness or during the regular annual holidays, or with the previous consent of the said Minister of Public Works for the time being.

3rd. He shall in all things be subservient to and obey the decisions & instructions of the said Minister of Public Works for the time being & shall not, during his continuance in the service, directly ore [sic] indirectly be engaged in any capacity whatsoever, other than in the service of the said Minister of Public Works as aforesaid, without the previous written authority and consent of the said Minister of Public Works, nor shall he engage in trading. And in consideration of the agreements hereinbefore contained on the part of the said Henry Dyer to be fulfilled, & of the diligent, faithful, & exclusive services to be rendered by him to the said

Minister of Public Works for the time being, the said Hugh Mackay Matheson, as such agent as aforesaid, both hereby promise and agree with the said Henry Dyer in manner following, that is to say,

4th. That the said Minister of Public Works shall pay the said Henry Dyer the sum of two hundred and fifty pounds stg for defraying the expenses of his outfit and passage to Japan and also during the aforesaid term of five years, a salary or sum in Dollars equal at the exchange of four shillings and six pence per Dollar to one thousand five hundred pounds sterling per annum, payable monthly, to commence from the date of his arrival in Japan; and on completion and fulfillment of the service hereby agreed to be rendered by the said Henry Dyer the said Minister of Public Works for the time being will defray his expenses home to England, and if, in the course of his engagement, he should be permanently disable [*sic*] by sickness, regularly certified by two approved medical men as not arising from his own intemperance or misconduct, then the said Minister of Public Works for the time being will defray his expenses home to England, and further, during the period of his engagement the said Minister of Public Works for the time being will provide the said Henry Dyer with a suitable unfurnished house as a place of residence.

5th. That if the said Henry Dyer shall at any time neglect or refuse, or from any cause whatsoever (other than unavoidable sickness as aforesaid), become or be unable to perform or comply with all or any of the articles of this Agreement or any of the duties required by him, or all of the decisions or instructions of Public Works for the time shall in any manner misconduct himself, or shall enter into trading, or employ himself in any capacity whatsoever otherwise than in the sole employ and interest of the said College, without the previous written authority or consent of the said Minister of Public Works for the time being, it shall be lawful for the said Minister to declare the employment of the said Henry Dyer at an end, & immediately thereupon the salary and every other payment which the said Henry Dyer may then or might thereafter be entitled to receive, and all benefit and advantage whatsoever to be derived by him under or by virtue of this agreement, shall cease.

6th. That in case the said Minister of Public Works for the time being shall at the expiration of the said term of five years be desirous of continuing the services of the said Henry Dyer for a further period not exceeding five years, and shall give notice to the said Henry Dyer of his desire, at least six months before the expiry of the said term of five years, and specify the extended term for which he desires such services to continue, and if the said Henry Dyer shall consent to continue in the service of the said Minister of Public Works during such extended period, all the stipulations and provisions of the present Agreement shall continue in force and be binding on the said Minister of Public Works for the time being and on his successors in office and the said Henry Dyer until the expiration of such extended term, not exceeding Ten years from the date of his arrival in Japan.

7th. The said Henry Dyer hereby binds himself under penalty of one thousand pounds stg to the said Minister of Public Works and his successors in office for the time being diligently and faithfully to keep & perform the various stipulations, agreements, matters, & things contained in this agreement until the end and expiration thereof, whether by effluxion of time or otherwise howsoever.

Declaring always, as it is hereby specially declared and agreed to, that it shall be always free to His said Majesty the Mikado of Japan, and his successors at any time to transfer the control of the said College from the said Minister of Public Works for the time being to any other Department or Minister now existing, or that at any time hereafter during the continuance of this engagement may be created for the better administration of his Government, and in such case all the various stipulations, agreements, matters & things contained in this Agreement shall hold good, and be binding upon the Minister or Administrators of such department to which the control of the said College may be transfered [*sic*], and his or their successors in office, and also upon the said Henry Dyer.

In witness whereof the said parties to these presents have hereunto set their hands and seats the day and year first above, written.

(Sgd) by Henry Dyer
(Sgd) by H. M. Matheson

Index